STORY BY
REINA SORATANI
ART BY
HARU HARUKAWA

# I Swear I Won't Bother You AGAIN!

3

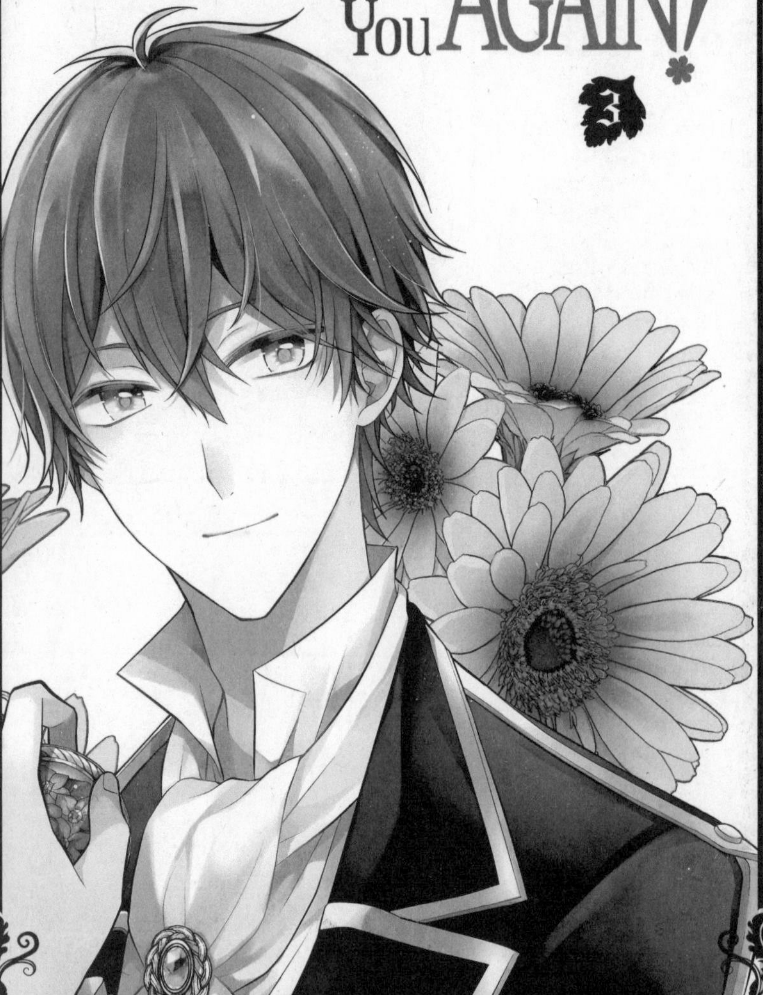

# ⚜ Characters ⚜

## Violette Rem Vahan

Duke Vahan's elder daughter and a second-year student at the Royal Tanzanite Academy. Violette was imprisoned for attempting to murder her half sister Maryjune—then she found herself one year in the past.

## Marin

Violette's maid.

## Maryjune Vahan

Duke Vahan's younger daughter; and a first-year student at the Royal Tanzanite Academy. Violette's half sister.

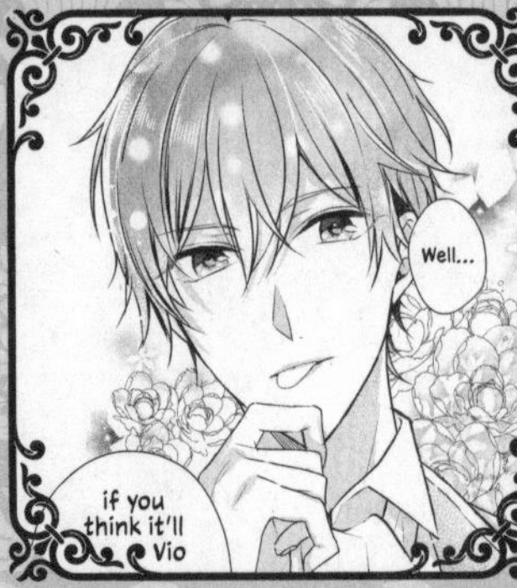
Well...
if you think it'll Vio

## Yulan Cugurs

Violette's childhood friend and a first-year student at the Royal Tanzanite Academy. Yulan's parents are royalty, and his father is Duralia's prime minister.

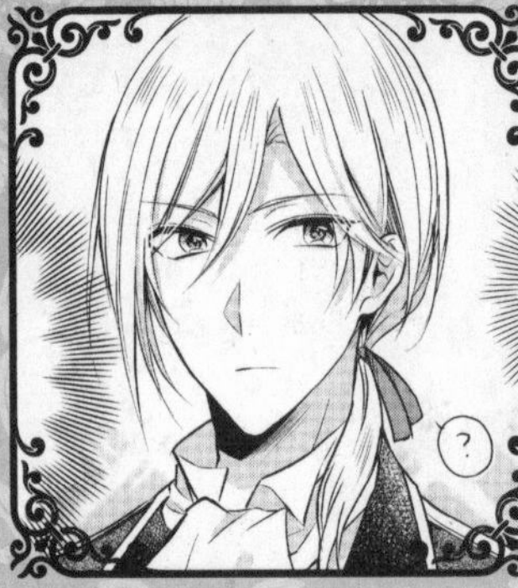
?

## Claudia Acrucis

Duralia's crown prince.
A third-year student and student council president at the Royal Tanzanite Academy. Next in line for the throne.

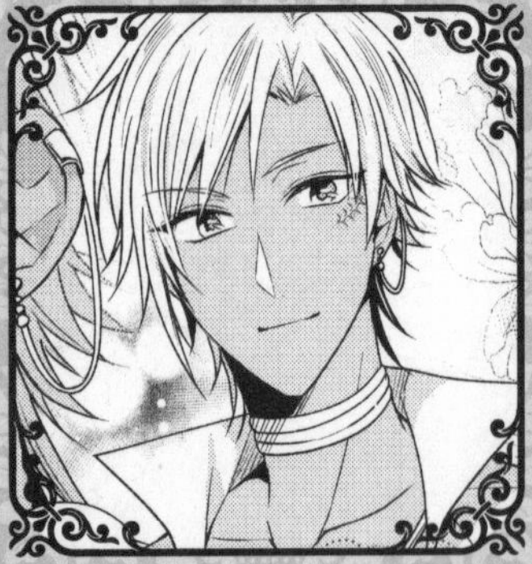

## Gia Forte

The prince of Sina. Yulan's classmate since middle school.

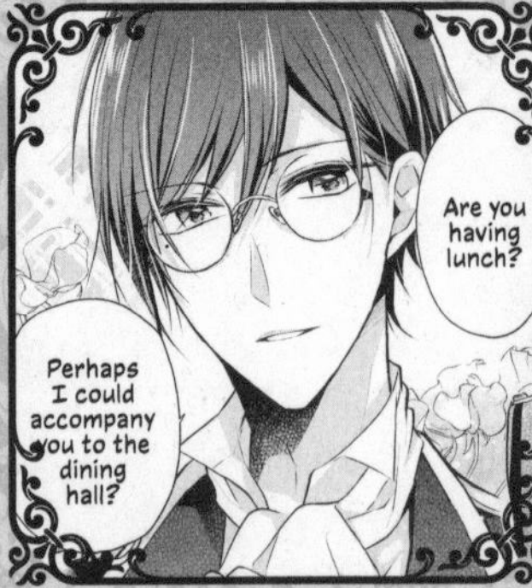
Are you having lunch?
Perhaps I could accompany you to the dining hall?

## Milania Dior

A third-year student and student council vice president at the Royal Tanzanite Academy. Close friends with Prince Claudia.

## Story

Driven by jealousy, Violette committed a terrible crime and was imprisoned. Behind bars, she wished she'd walked a different path. To her shock, she awakened one year in the past! Violette swore she wouldn't bother anyone again, vowing to make the right choices this time. She planned to join a convent, lie low, and live a quiet, modest life—but things keep going awry. Violette did her utmost to help Maryjune shine at the school arts festival, but then she had to step in when Prince Claudia ripped his cloak just before going onstage. Later, as she and Yulan studied quietly together, Maryjune, Milania, and Claudia popped up—turning the tutoring session into a boisterous study group!

# Contents

# CHAPTER 12

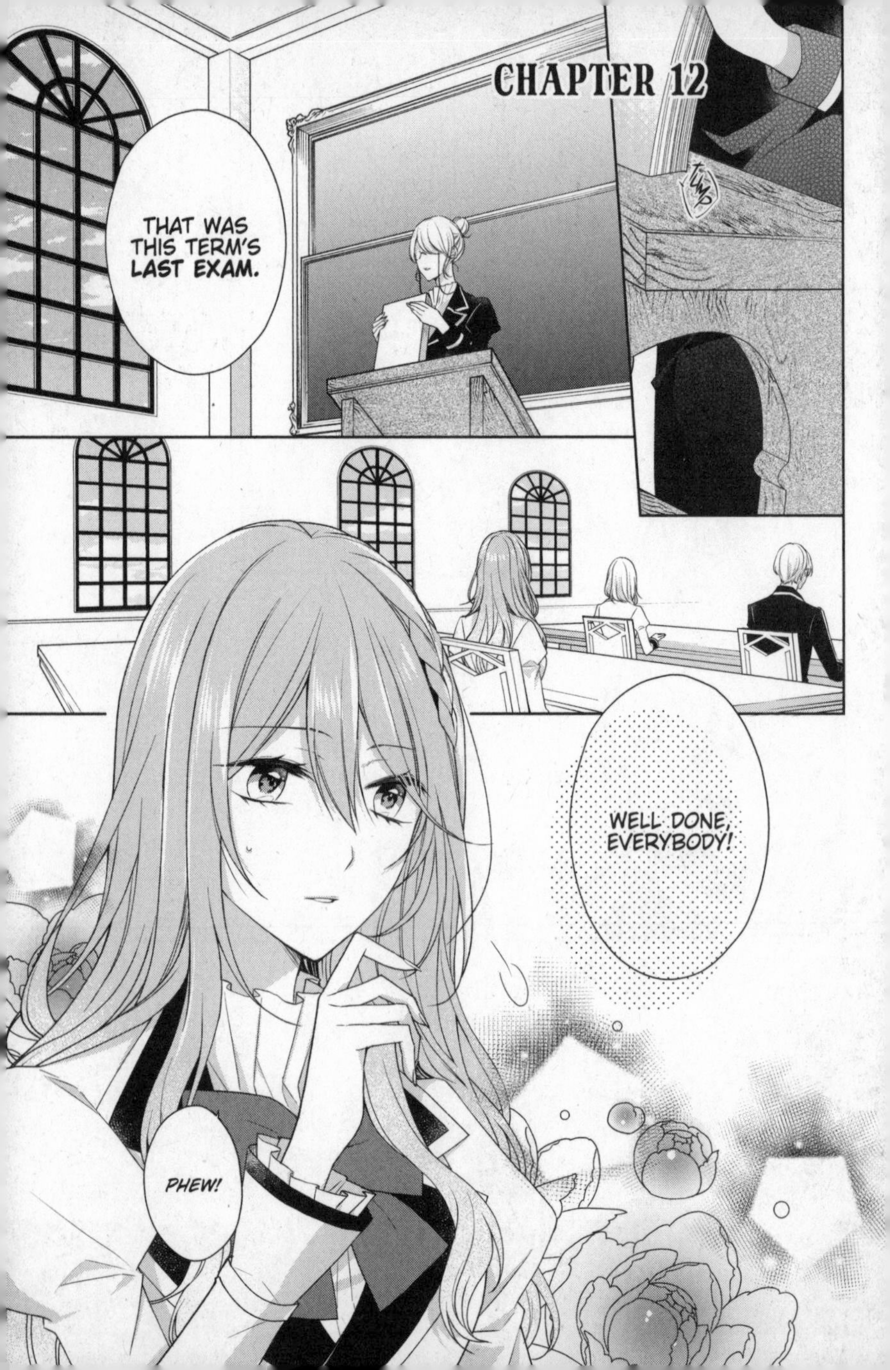
TUMP
THAT WAS THIS TERM'S LAST EXAM.
WELL DONE, EVERYBODY!
PHEW!

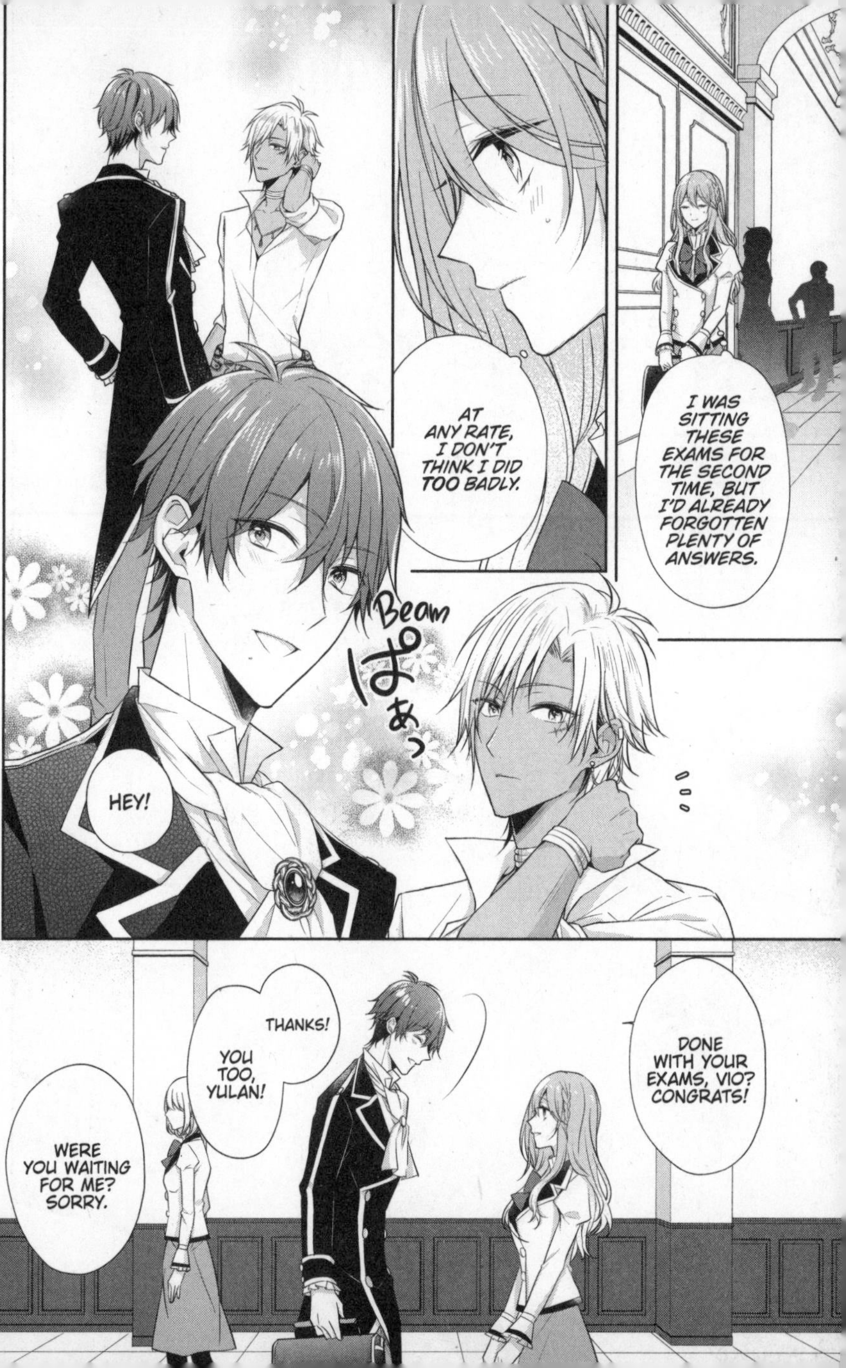
I WAS SITTING THESE EXAMS FOR THE SECOND TIME, BUT I'D ALREADY FORGOTTEN PLENTY OF ANSWERS.
AT ANY RATE, I DON'T THINK I DID TOO BADLY.
HEY!
Beam
ぱあっ
...
DONE WITH YOUR EXAMS, VIO? CONGRATS!
THANKS!
YOU TOO, YULAN!
WERE YOU WAITING FOR ME? SORRY.

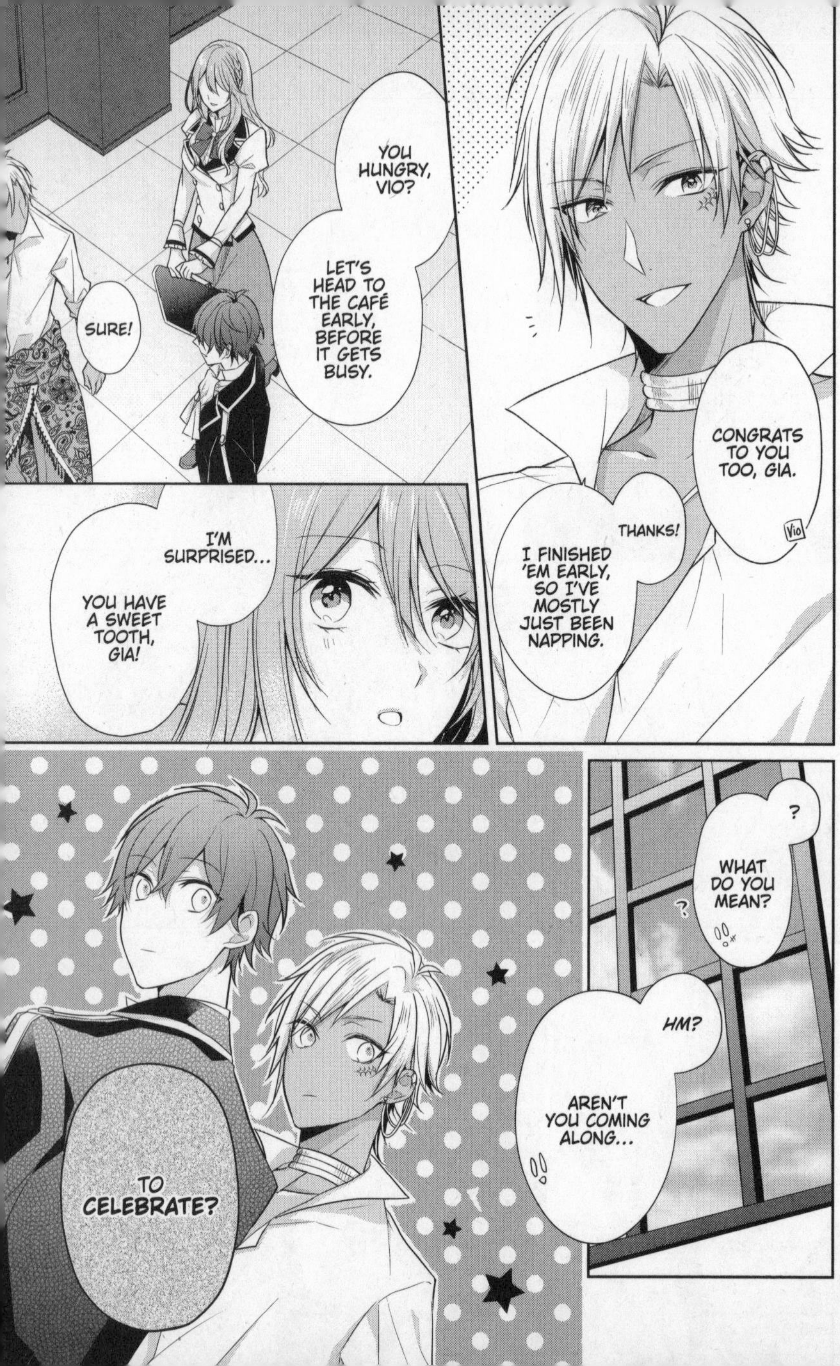

CONGRATS TO YOU TOO, GIA.
Vio
THANKS!
I FINISHED 'EM EARLY, SO I'VE MOSTLY JUST BEEN NAPPING.
YOU HUNGRY, VIO?
LET'S HEAD TO THE CAFÉ EARLY, BEFORE IT GETS BUSY.
SURE!
I'M SURPRISED...
YOU HAVE A SWEET TOOTH, GIA!
?
WHAT DO YOU MEAN?
HM?
AREN'T YOU COMING ALONG...
TO CELEBRATE?

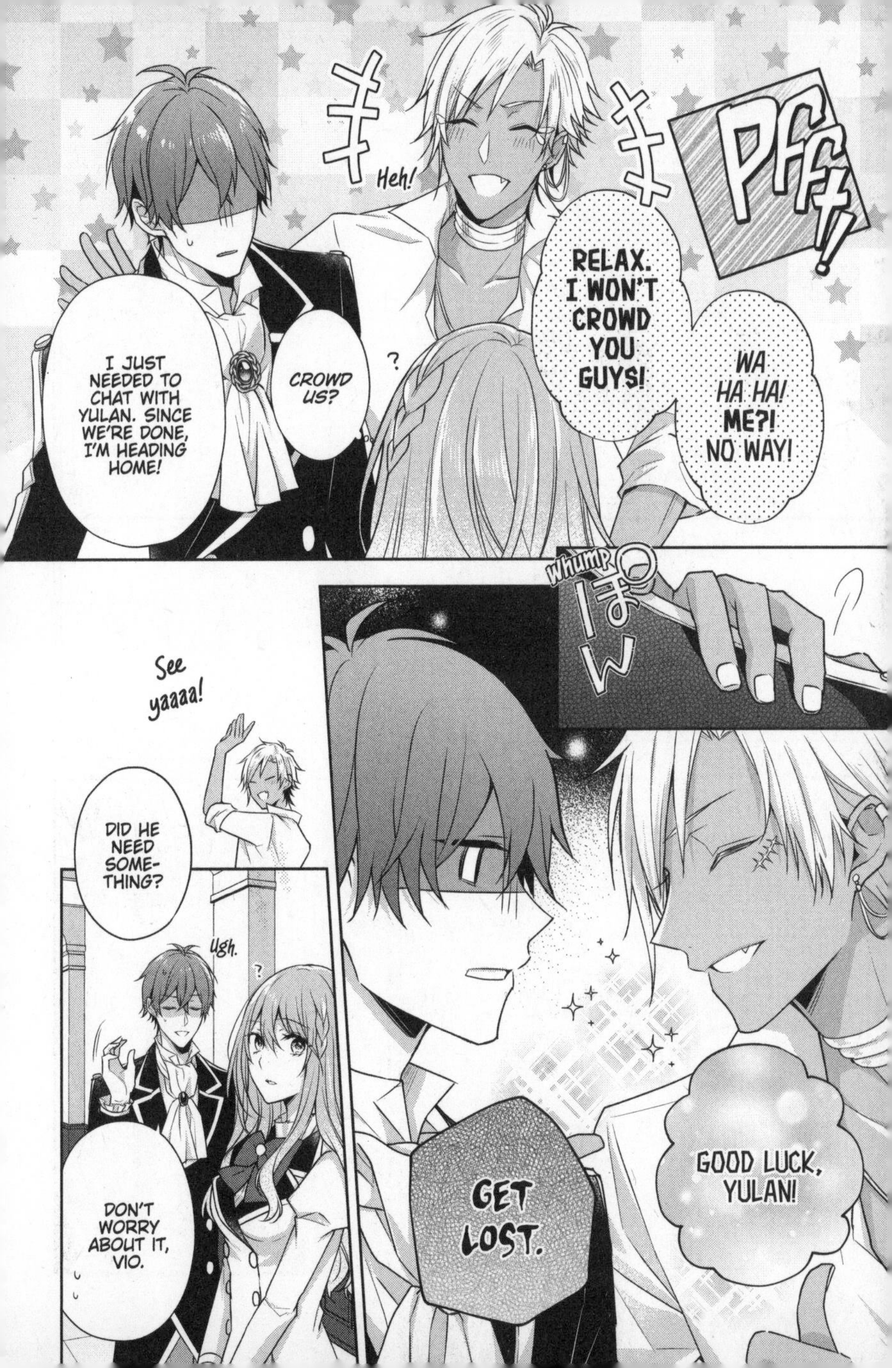
Pfff!
Heh!
RELAX. I WON'T CROWD YOU GUYS!
?
CROWD US?
WA HA HA! ME?! NO WAY!
I JUST NEEDED TO CHAT WITH YULAN. SINCE WE'RE DONE, I'M HEADING HOME!
whump
ぽん
GOOD LUCK, YULAN!
GET LOST.
See yaaaa!
DID HE NEED SOMETHING?
Ugh.
?
DON'T WORRY ABOUT IT, VIO.

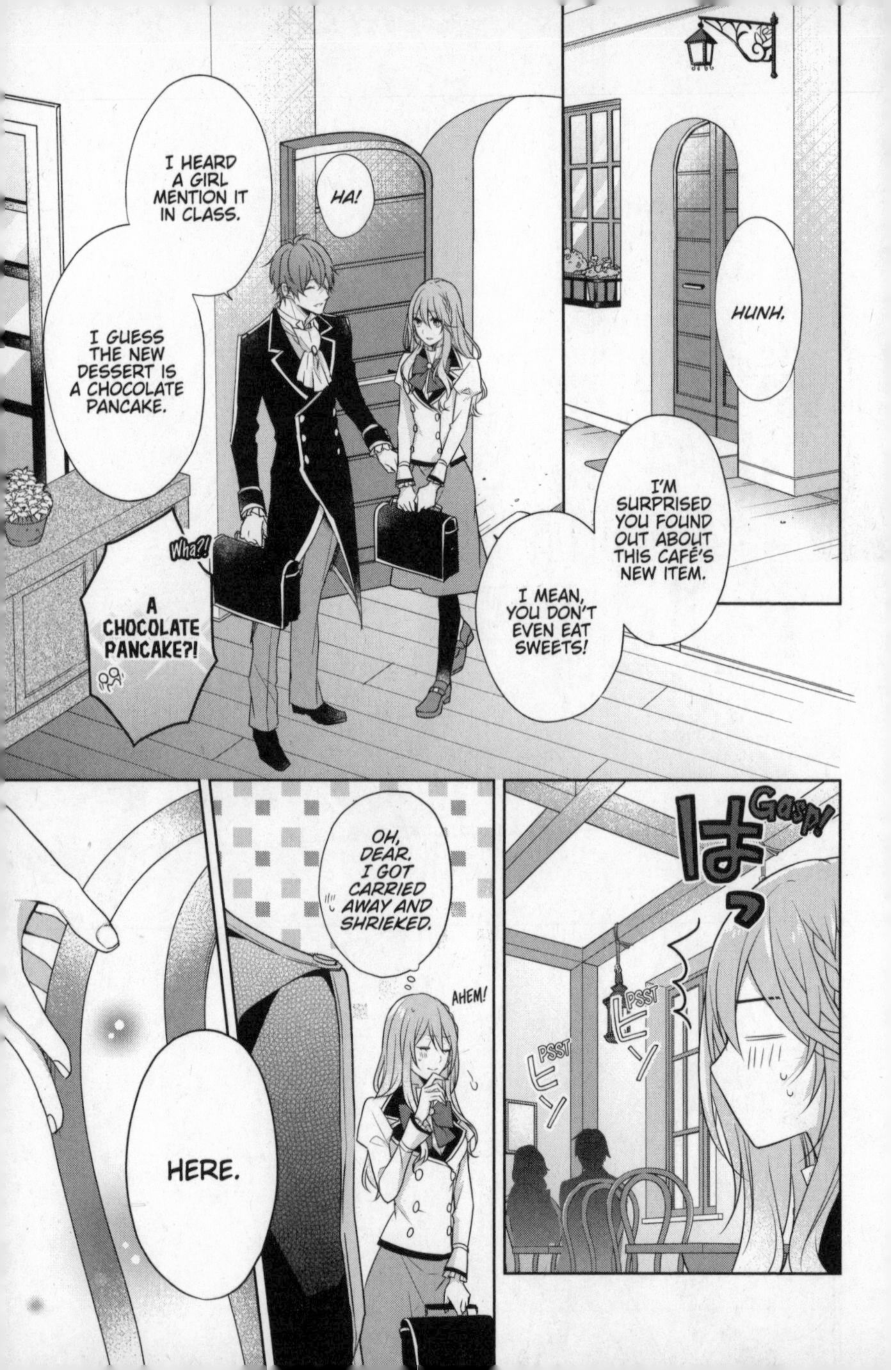
HUNH.
I'M SURPRISED YOU FOUND OUT ABOUT THIS CAFÉ'S NEW ITEM.
I MEAN, YOU DON'T EVEN EAT SWEETS!
HA!
I HEARD A GIRL MENTION IT IN CLASS.
I GUESS THE NEW DESSERT IS A CHOCOLATE PANCAKE.
Wha?!
A CHOCOLATE PANCAKE?!
はっ
Gasp!
PSST
ヒソ
PSST
ヒソ
OH, DEAR. I GOT CARRIED AWAY AND SHRIEKED.
AHEM!
HERE.

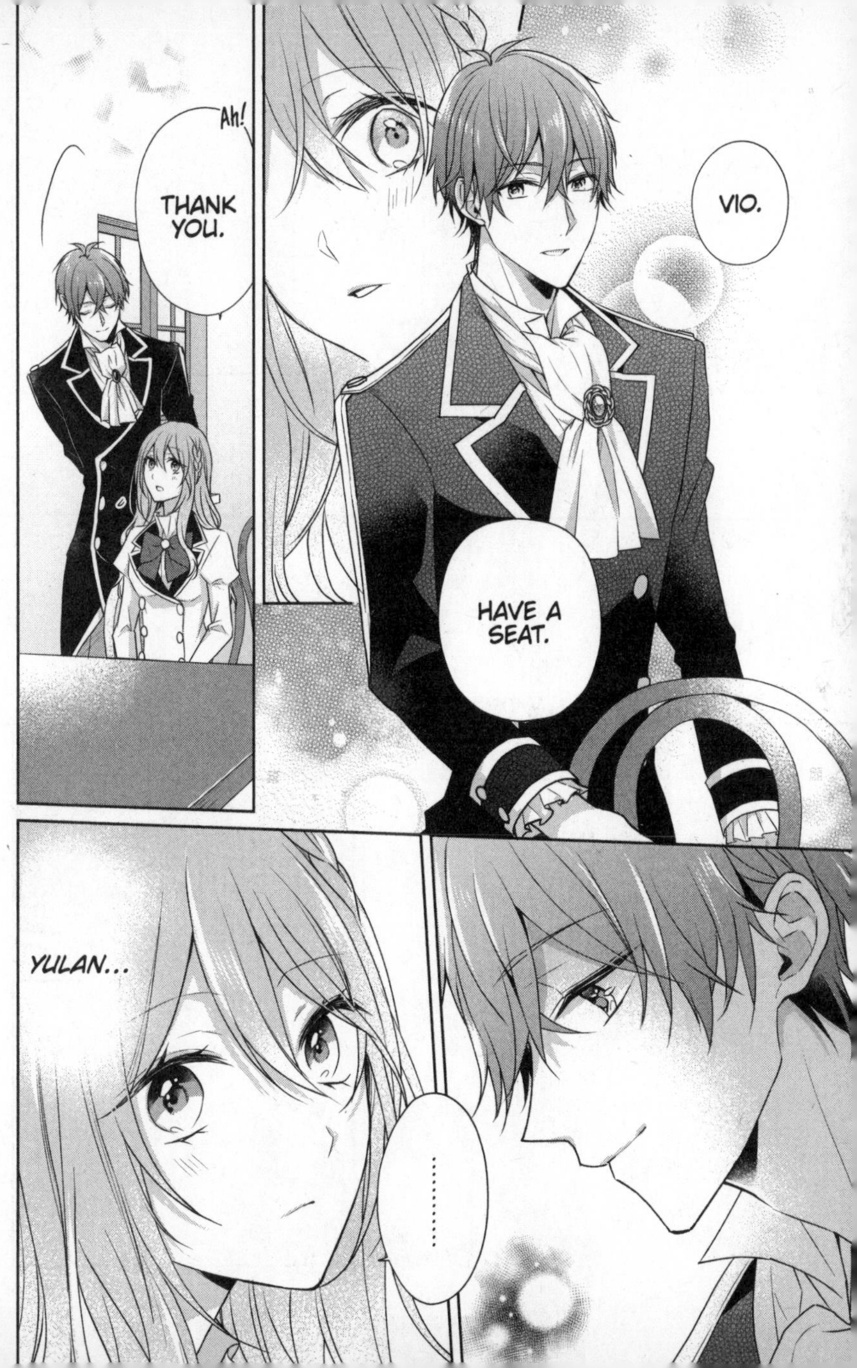
VIO.
HAVE A SEAT.
Ah!
THANK YOU.
......
YULAN...

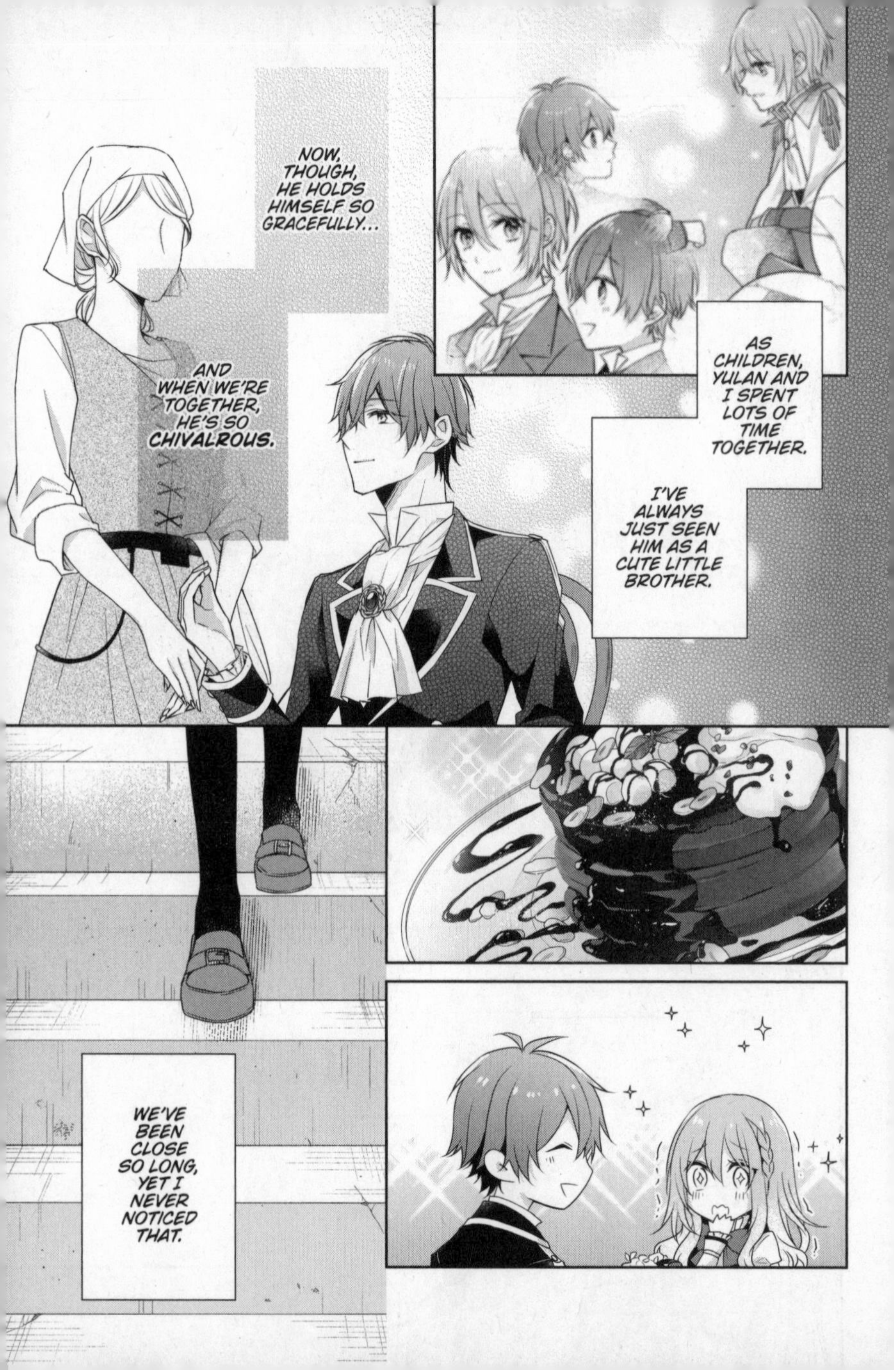
AS CHILDREN, YULAN AND I SPENT LOTS OF TIME TOGETHER.
I'VE ALWAYS JUST SEEN HIM AS A CUTE LITTLE BROTHER.
NOW, THOUGH, HE HOLDS HIMSELF SO GRACEFULLY...
AND WHEN WE'RE TOGETHER, HE'S SO CHIVALROUS.
WE'VE BEEN CLOSE SO LONG, YET I NEVER NOTICED THAT.

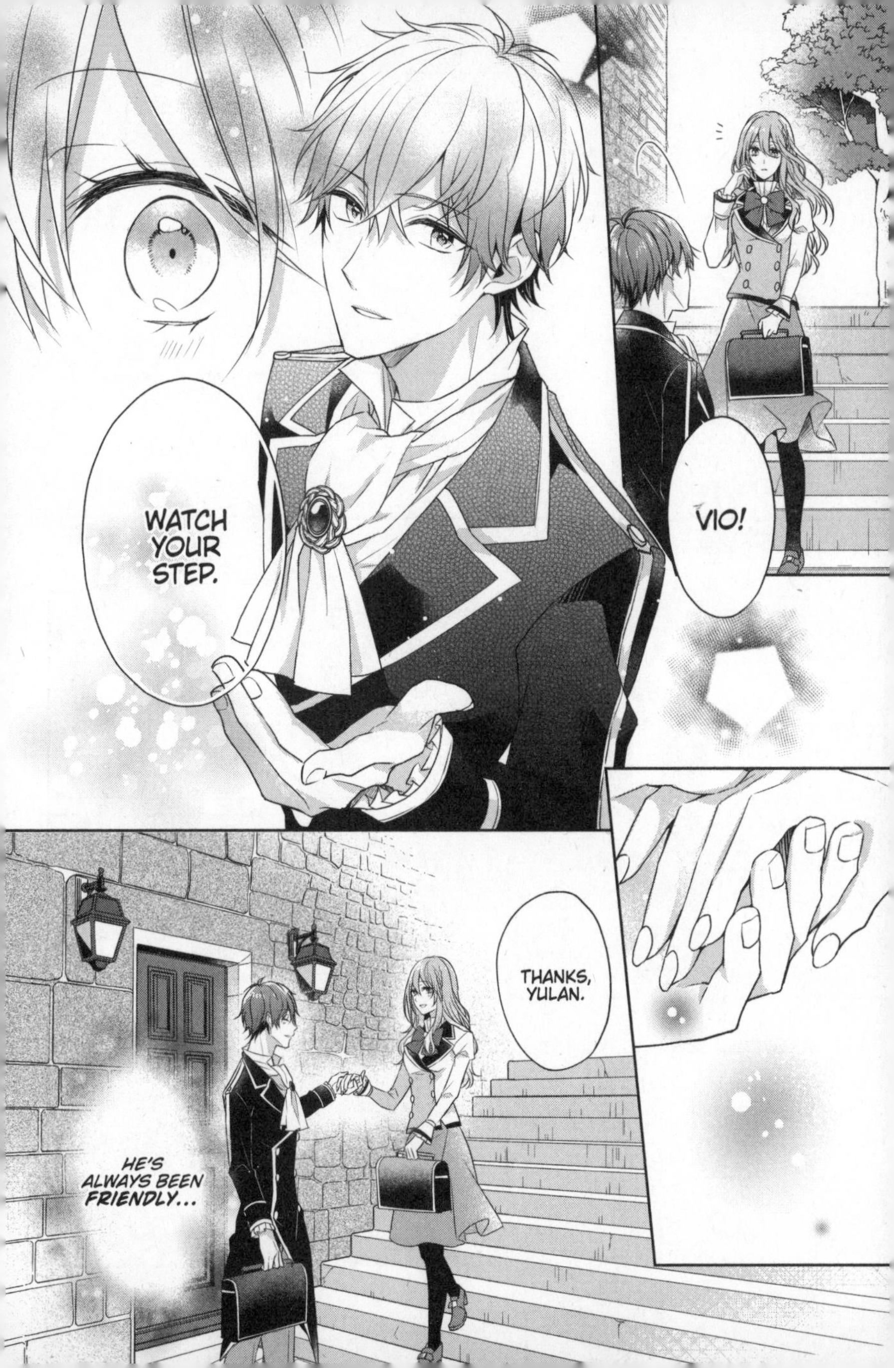
VIO!
WATCH YOUR STEP.
THANKS, YULAN.
HE'S ALWAYS BEEN FRIENDLY...

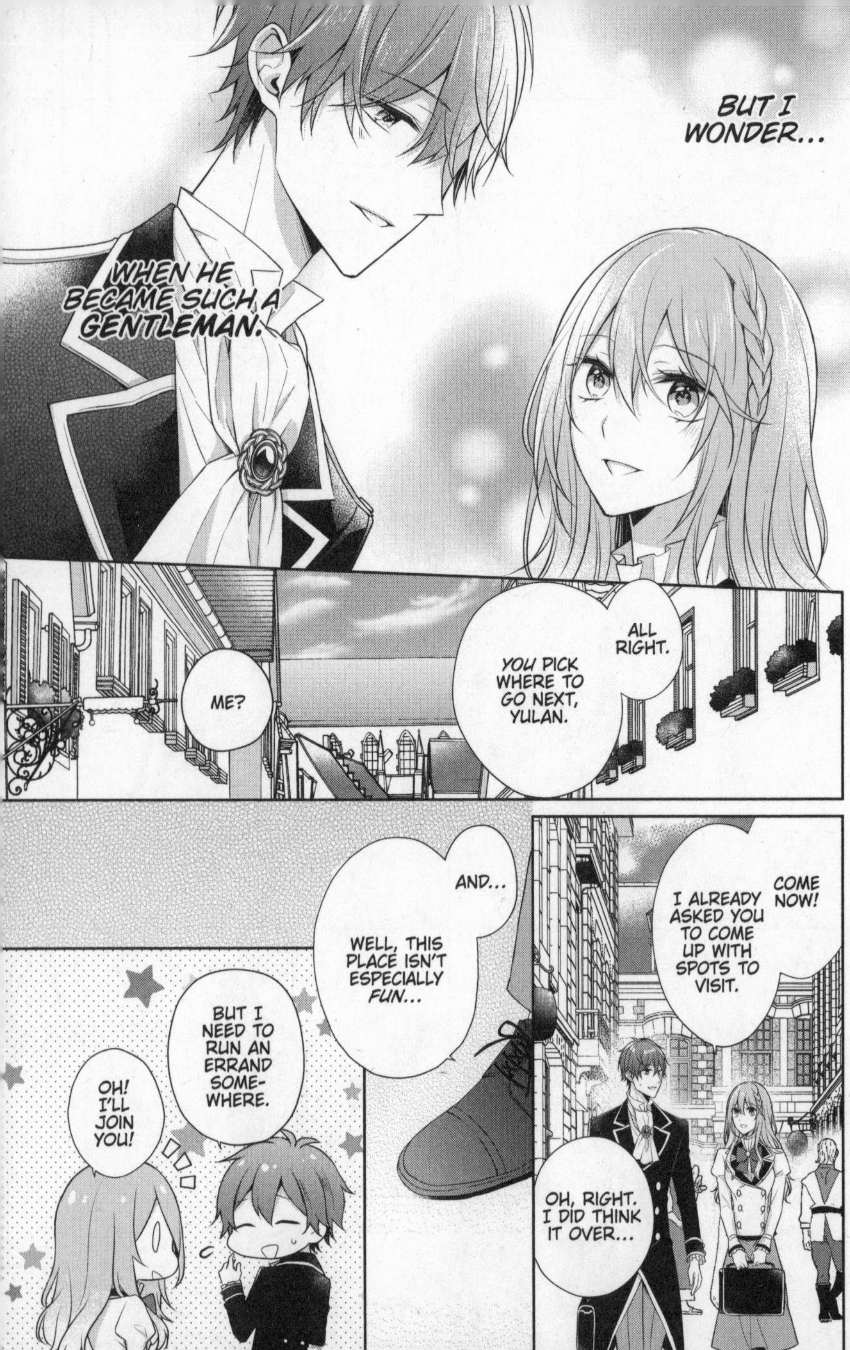
BUT I WONDER...
WHEN HE BECAME SUCH A GENTLEMAN.
ALL RIGHT.
YOU PICK WHERE TO GO NEXT, YULAN.
ME?
COME NOW!
I ALREADY ASKED YOU TO COME UP WITH SPOTS TO VISIT.
OH, RIGHT. I DID THINK IT OVER...
AND...
WELL, THIS PLACE ISN'T ESPECIALLY FUN...
BUT I NEED TO RUN AN ERRAND SOME-WHERE.
OH! I'LL JOIN YOU!

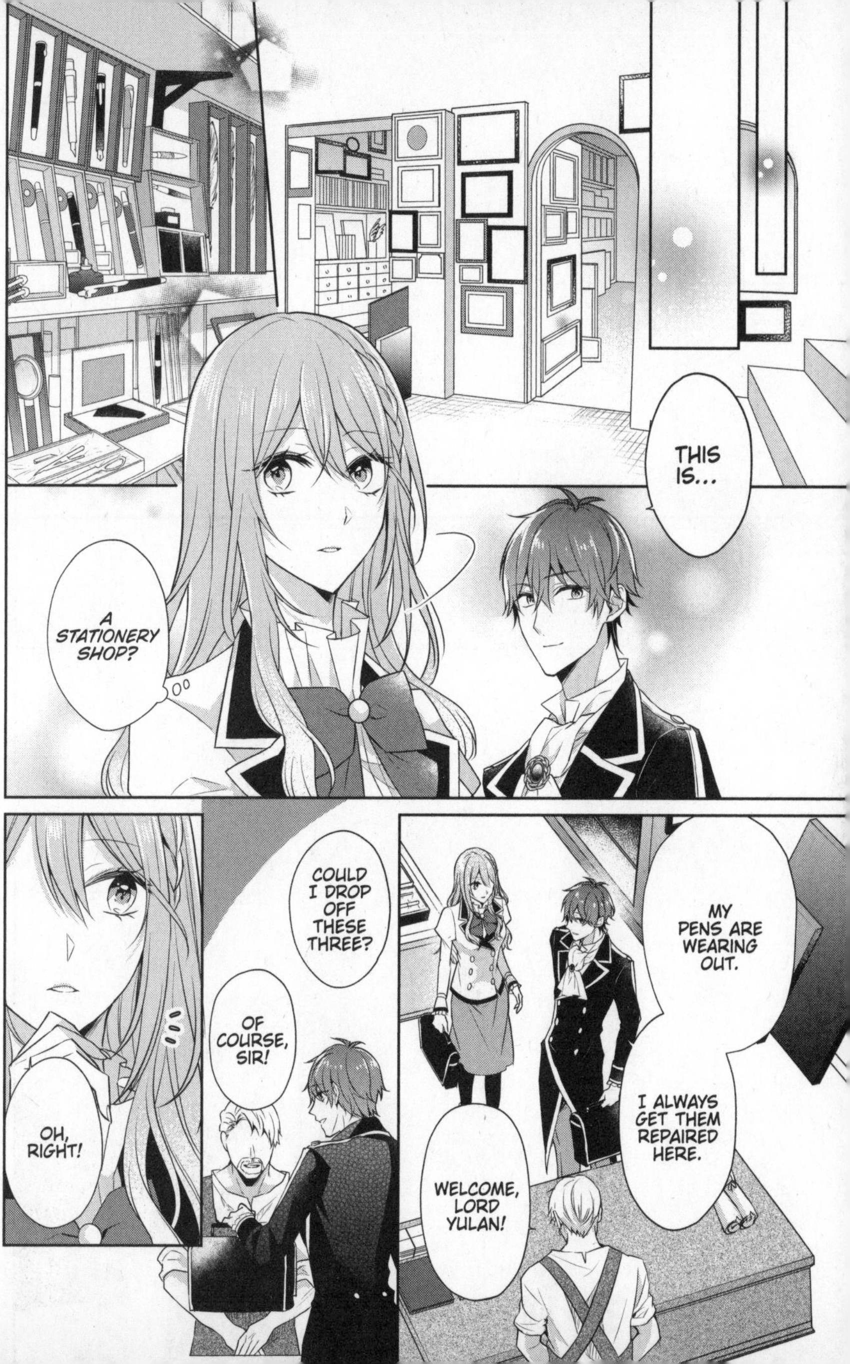
THIS IS...
A STATIONERY SHOP?
MY PENS ARE WEARING OUT.
I ALWAYS GET THEM REPAIRED HERE.
WELCOME, LORD YULAN!
COULD I DROP OFF THESE THREE?
OF COURSE, SIR!
OH, RIGHT!

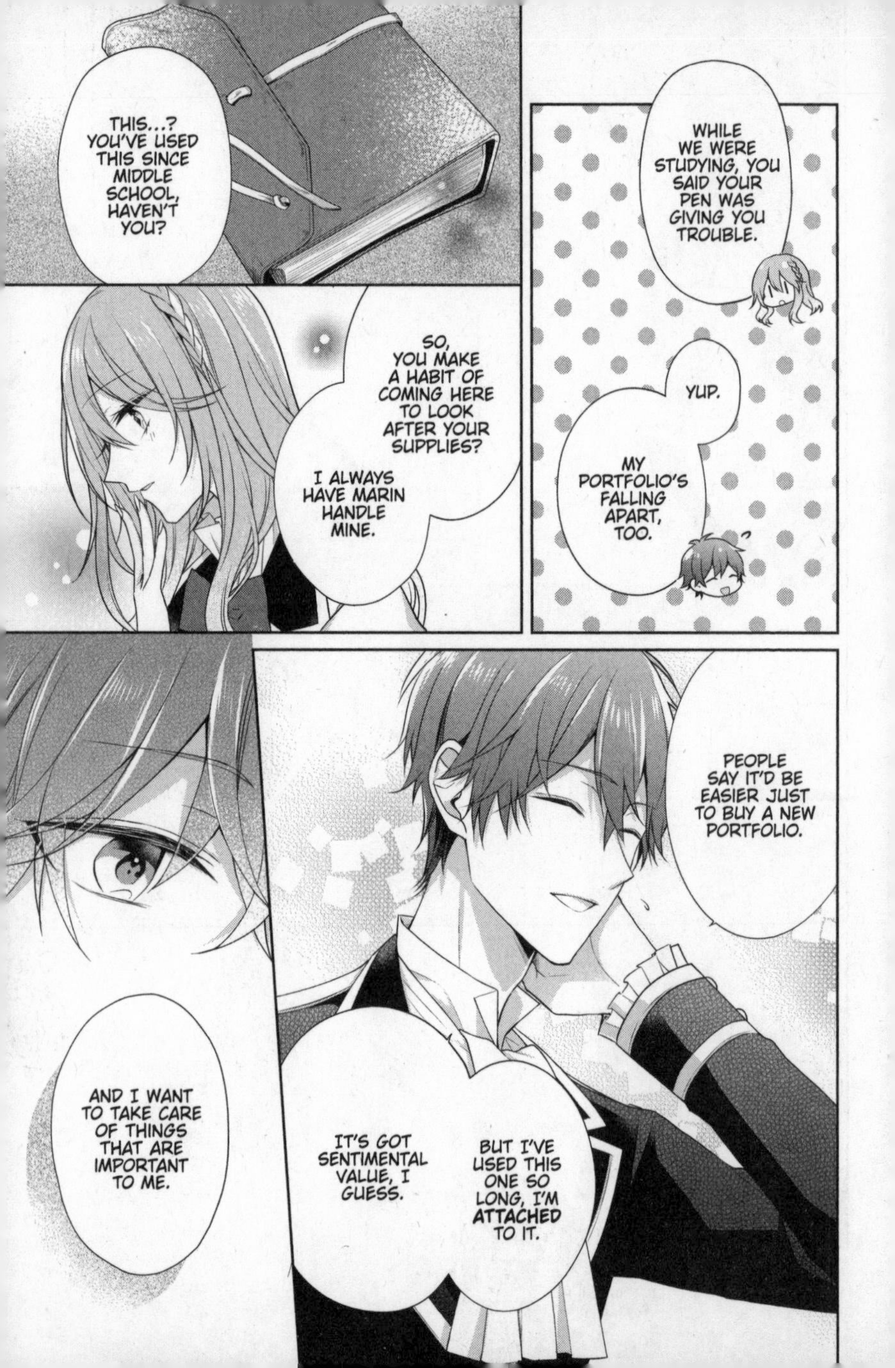
WHILE WE WERE STUDYING, YOU SAID YOUR PEN WAS GIVING YOU TROUBLE.
YUP.
MY PORTFOLIO'S FALLING APART, TOO.
THIS...? YOU'VE USED THIS SINCE MIDDLE SCHOOL, HAVEN'T YOU?
SO, YOU MAKE A HABIT OF COMING HERE TO LOOK AFTER YOUR SUPPLIES?
I ALWAYS HAVE MARIN HANDLE MINE.
PEOPLE SAY IT'D BE EASIER JUST TO BUY A NEW PORTFOLIO.
BUT I'VE USED THIS ONE SO LONG, I'M ATTACHED TO IT.
IT'S GOT SENTIMENTAL VALUE, I GUESS.
AND I WANT TO TAKE CARE OF THINGS THAT ARE IMPORTANT TO ME.

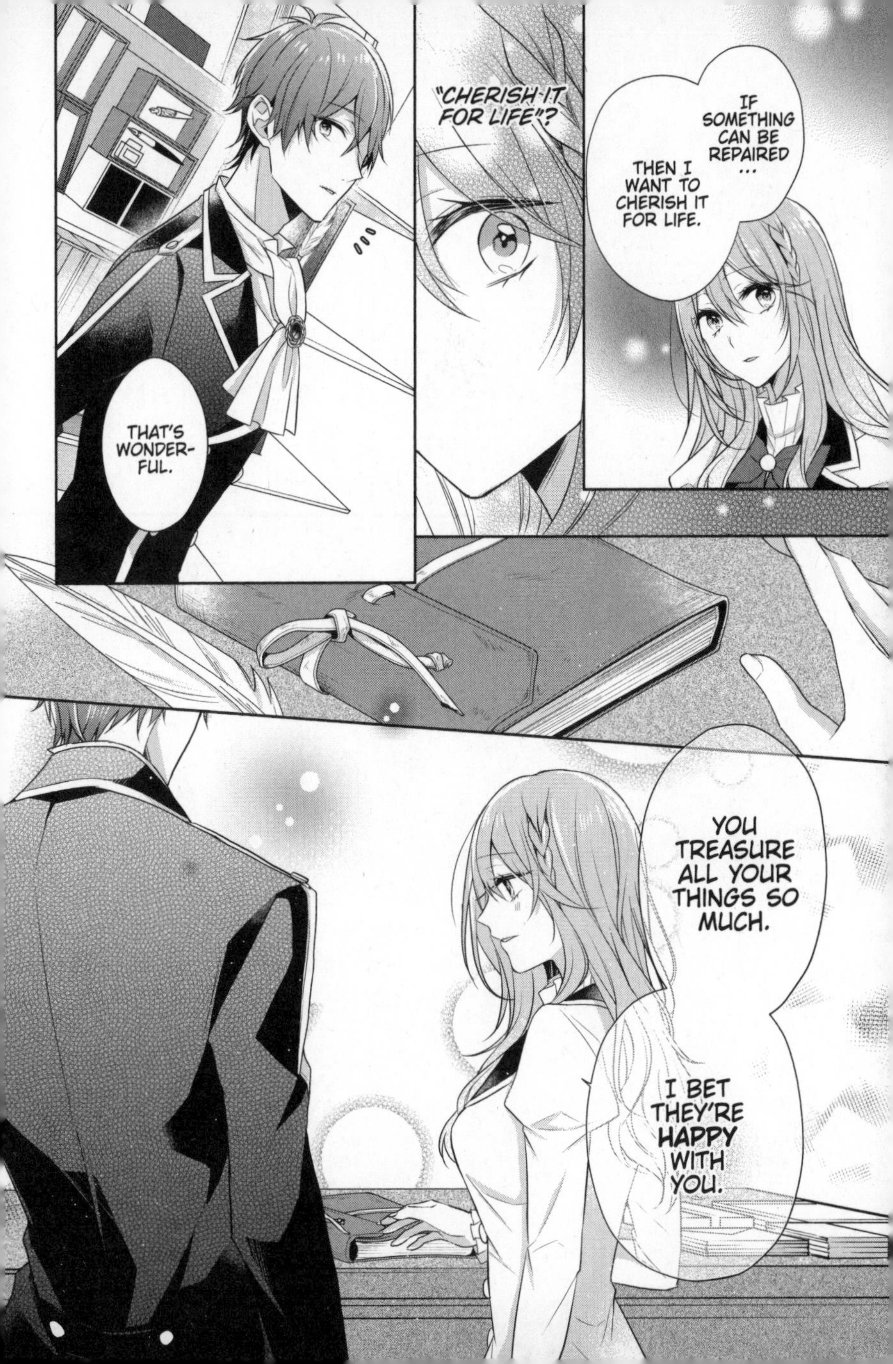
IF SOMETHING CAN BE REPAIRED ...
THEN I WANT TO CHERISH IT FOR LIFE.
"CHERISH IT FOR LIFE"?
...
THAT'S WONDER-FUL.
YOU TREASURE ALL YOUR THINGS SO MUCH.
I BET THEY'RE **HAPPY** WITH YOU.

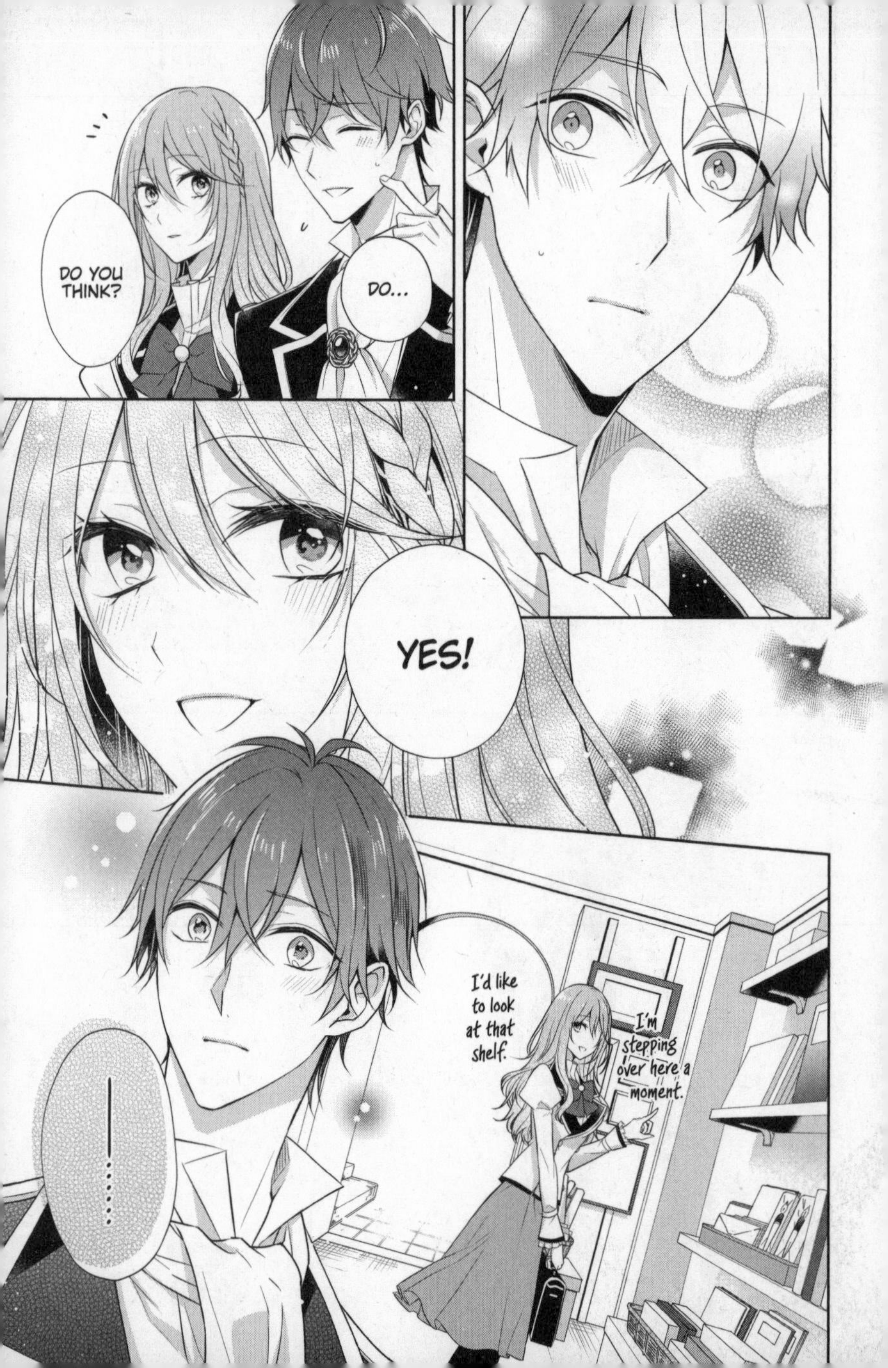
DO...
DO YOU THINK?
YES!
I'd like to look at that shelf.
I'm stepping over here a moment.
......

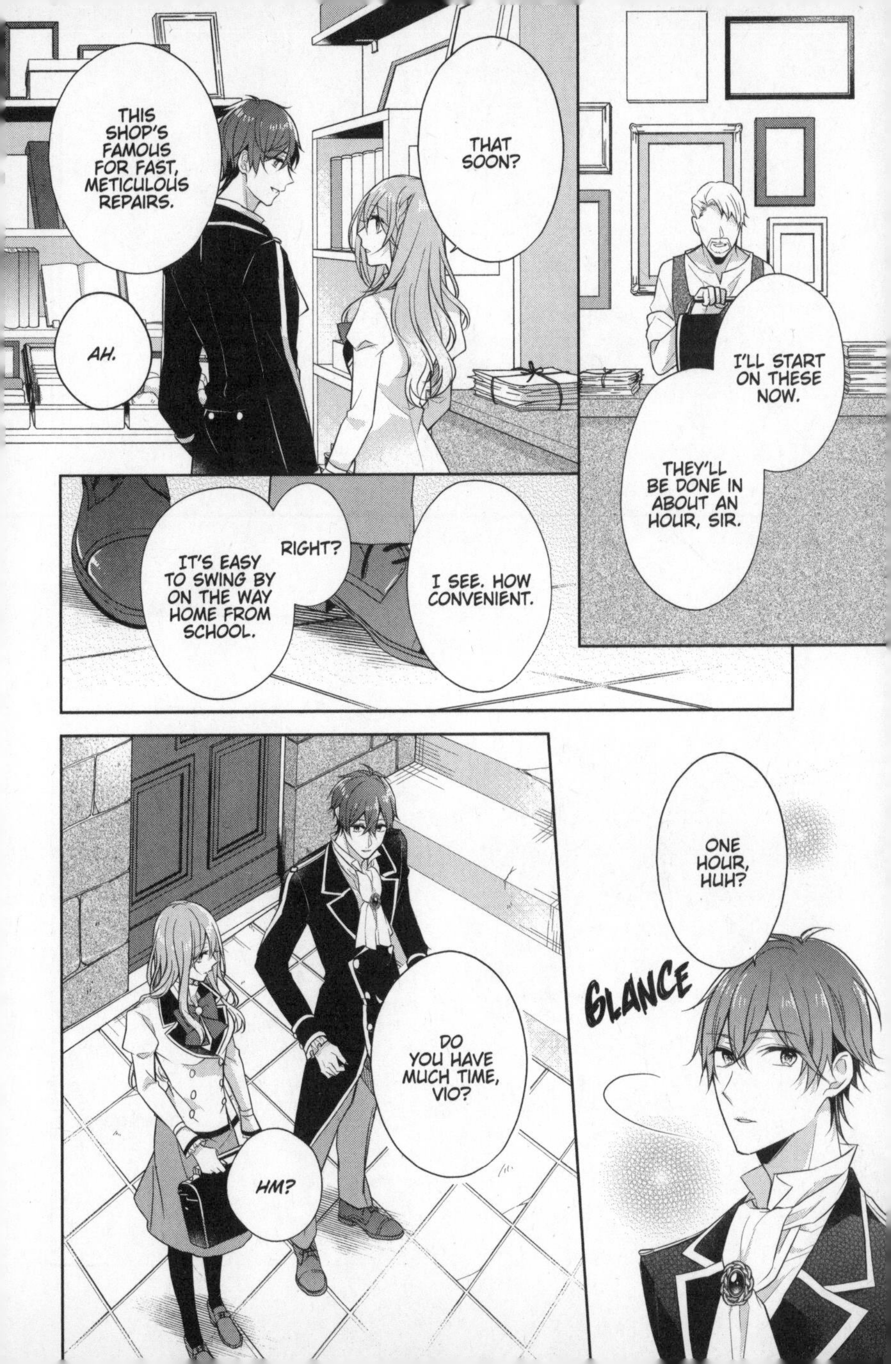
I'LL START ON THESE NOW.
THEY'LL BE DONE IN ABOUT AN HOUR, SIR.
THAT SOON?
THIS SHOP'S FAMOUS FOR FAST, METICULOUS REPAIRS.
AH.
I SEE. HOW CONVENIENT.
RIGHT?
IT'S EASY TO SWING BY ON THE WAY HOME FROM SCHOOL.
ONE HOUR, HUH?
GLANCE
DO YOU HAVE MUCH TIME, VIO?
HM?

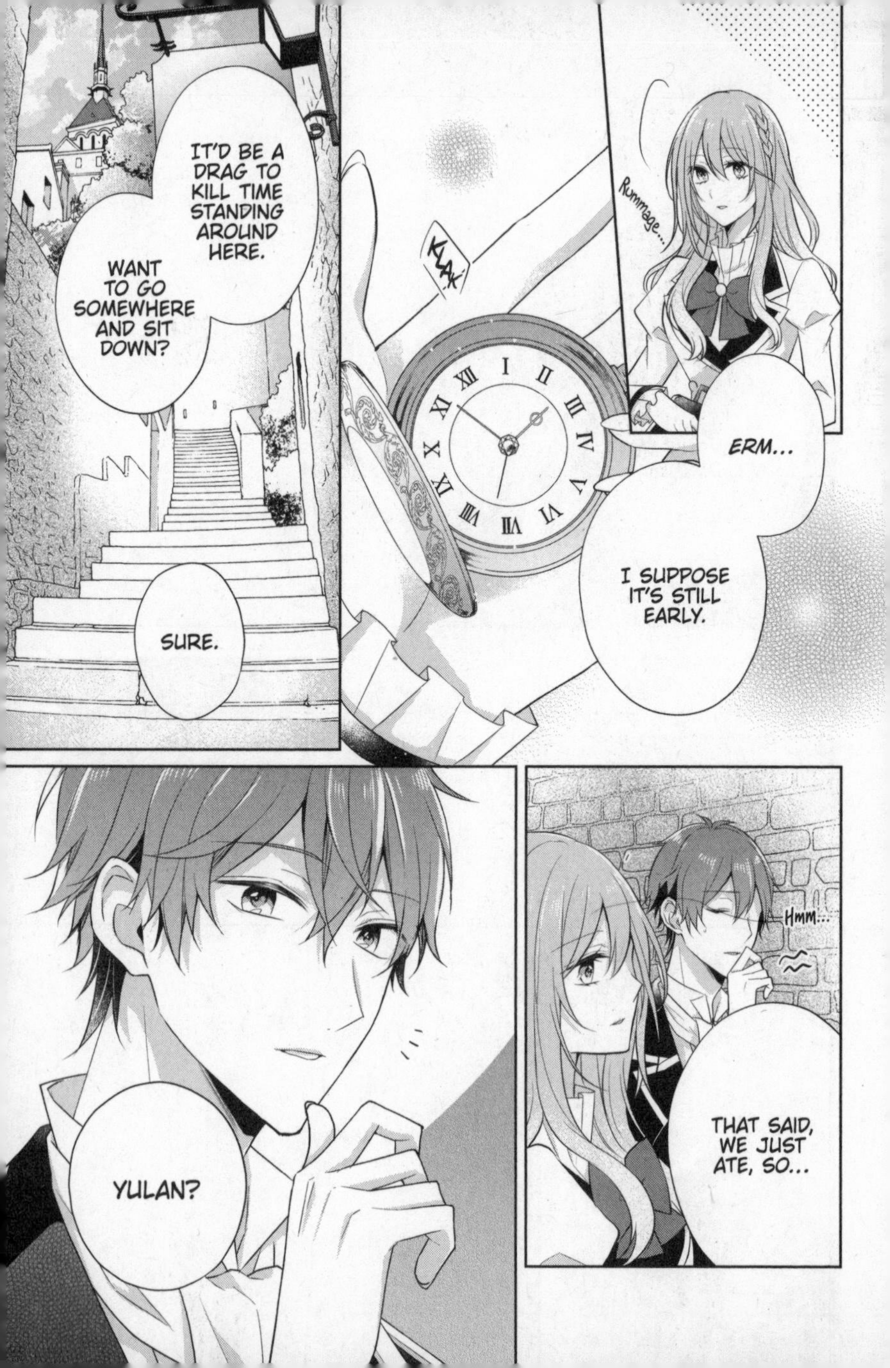
Rummage...
KLAK
ERM...
I SUPPOSE IT'S STILL EARLY.
IT'D BE A DRAG TO KILL TIME STANDING AROUND HERE.
WANT TO GO SOMEWHERE AND SIT DOWN?
SURE.
Hmm...
THAT SAID, WE JUST ATE, SO...
YULAN?

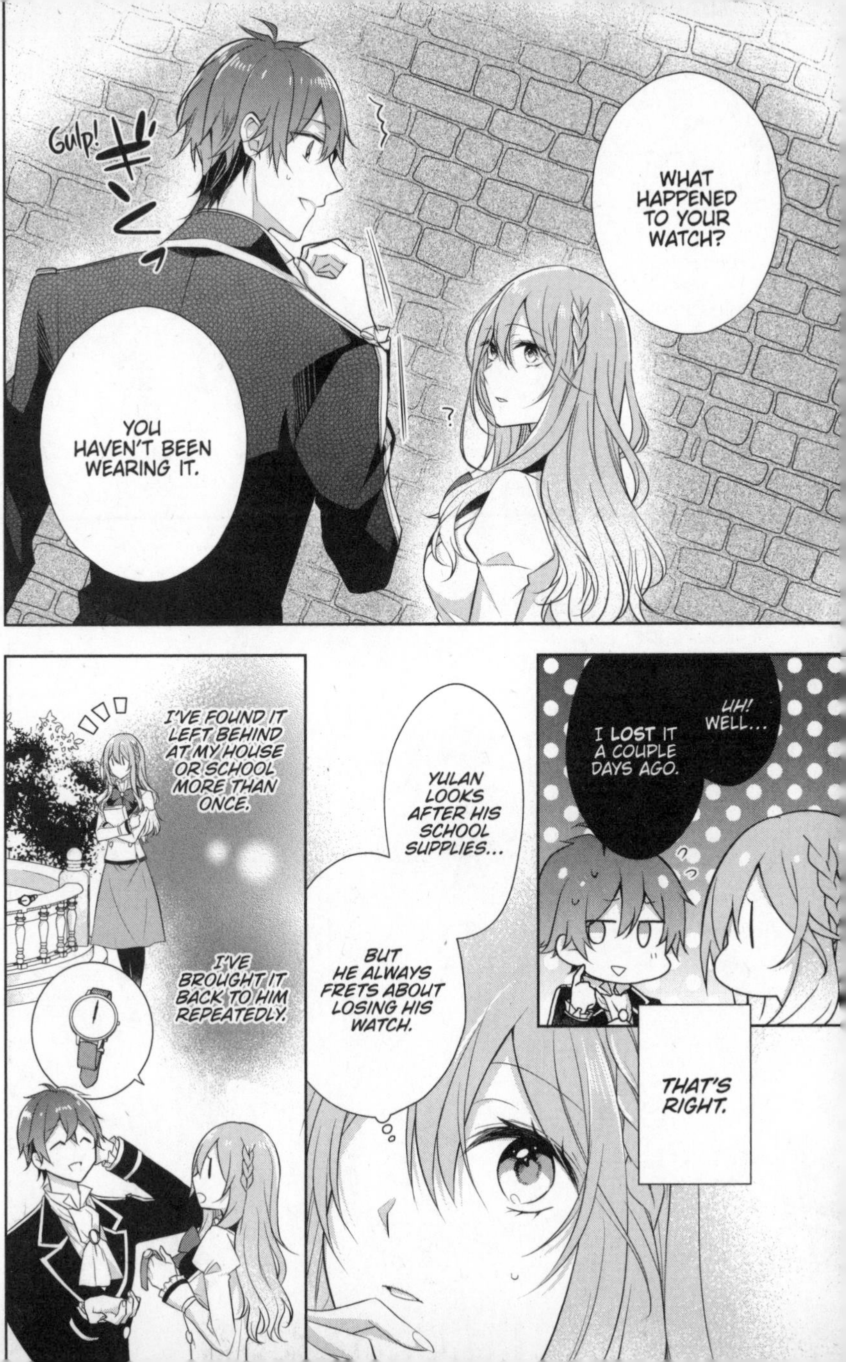
WHAT HAPPENED TO YOUR WATCH?
Gulp!
YOU HAVEN'T BEEN WEARING IT.
UH! WELL...
I LOST IT A COUPLE DAYS AGO.
YULAN LOOKS AFTER HIS SCHOOL SUPPLIES...
BUT HE ALWAYS FRETS ABOUT LOSING HIS WATCH.
THAT'S RIGHT.
I'VE FOUND IT LEFT BEHIND AT MY HOUSE OR SCHOOL MORE THAN ONCE.
I'VE BROUGHT IT BACK TO HIM REPEATEDLY.

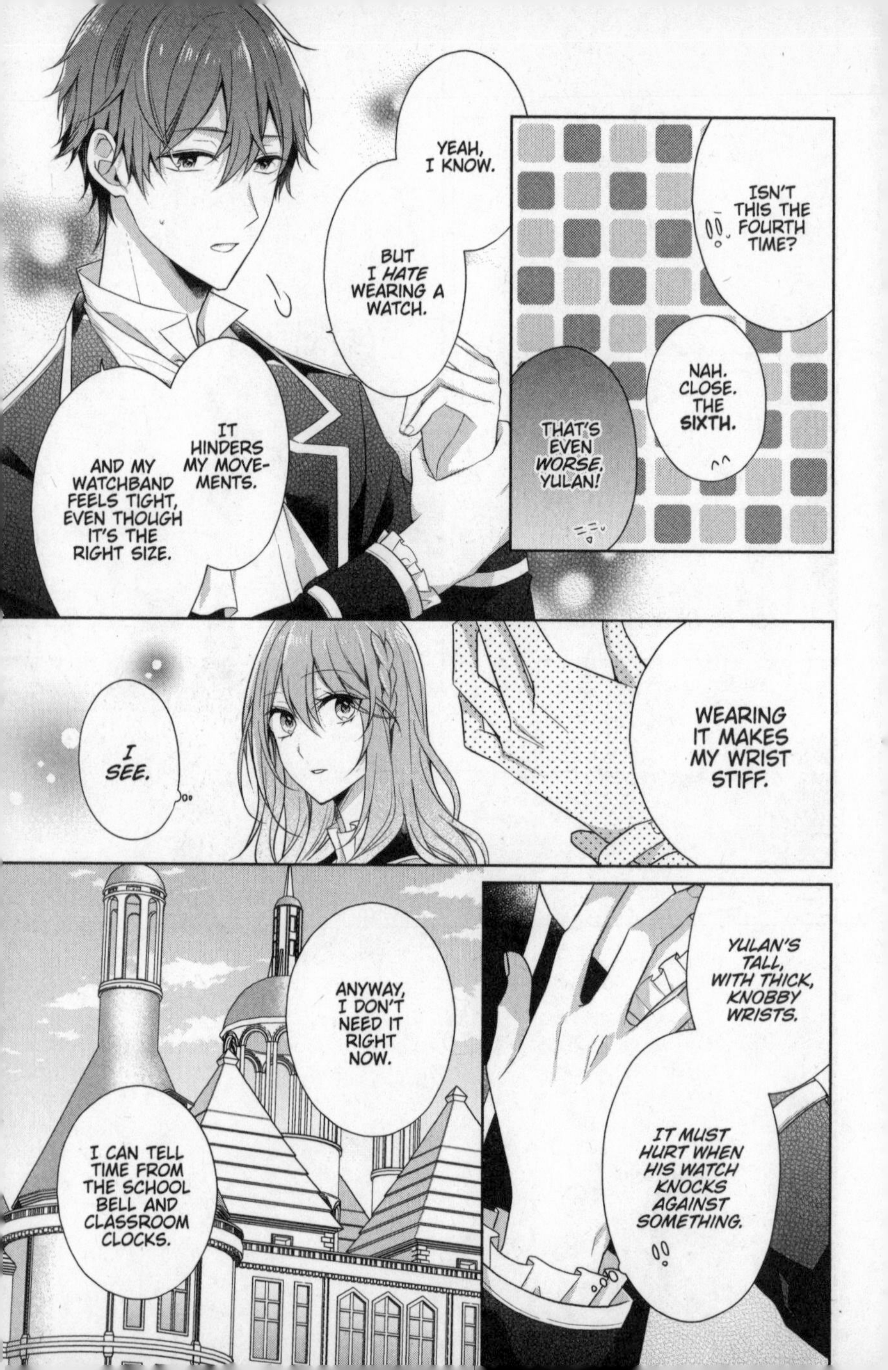
ISN'T THIS THE FOURTH TIME?
NAH. CLOSE. THE SIXTH.
THAT'S EVEN WORSE, YULAN!
YEAH, I KNOW.
BUT I HATE WEARING A WATCH.
IT HINDERS MY MOVEMENTS.
AND MY WATCHBAND FEELS TIGHT, EVEN THOUGH IT'S THE RIGHT SIZE.
WEARING IT MAKES MY WRIST STIFF.
I SEE.
YULAN'S TALL, WITH THICK, KNOBBY WRISTS.
IT MUST HURT WHEN HIS WATCH KNOCKS AGAINST SOMETHING.
ANYWAY, I DON'T NEED IT RIGHT NOW.
I CAN TELL TIME FROM THE SCHOOL BELL AND CLASSROOM CLOCKS.

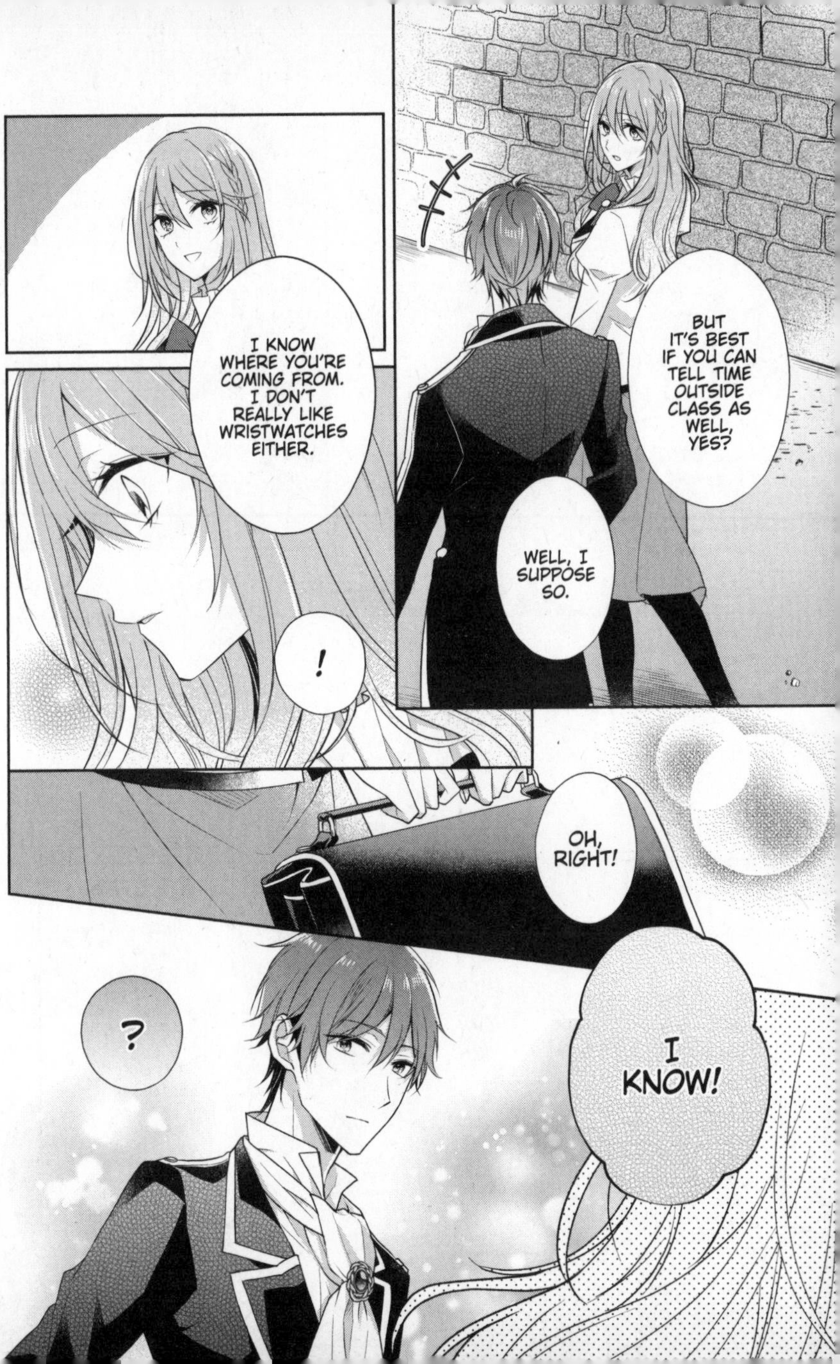
BUT IT'S BEST IF YOU CAN TELL TIME OUTSIDE CLASS AS WELL, YES?
WELL, I SUPPOSE SO.
I KNOW WHERE YOU'RE COMING FROM. I DON'T REALLY LIKE WRISTWATCHES EITHER.
!
OH, RIGHT!
I KNOW!
?

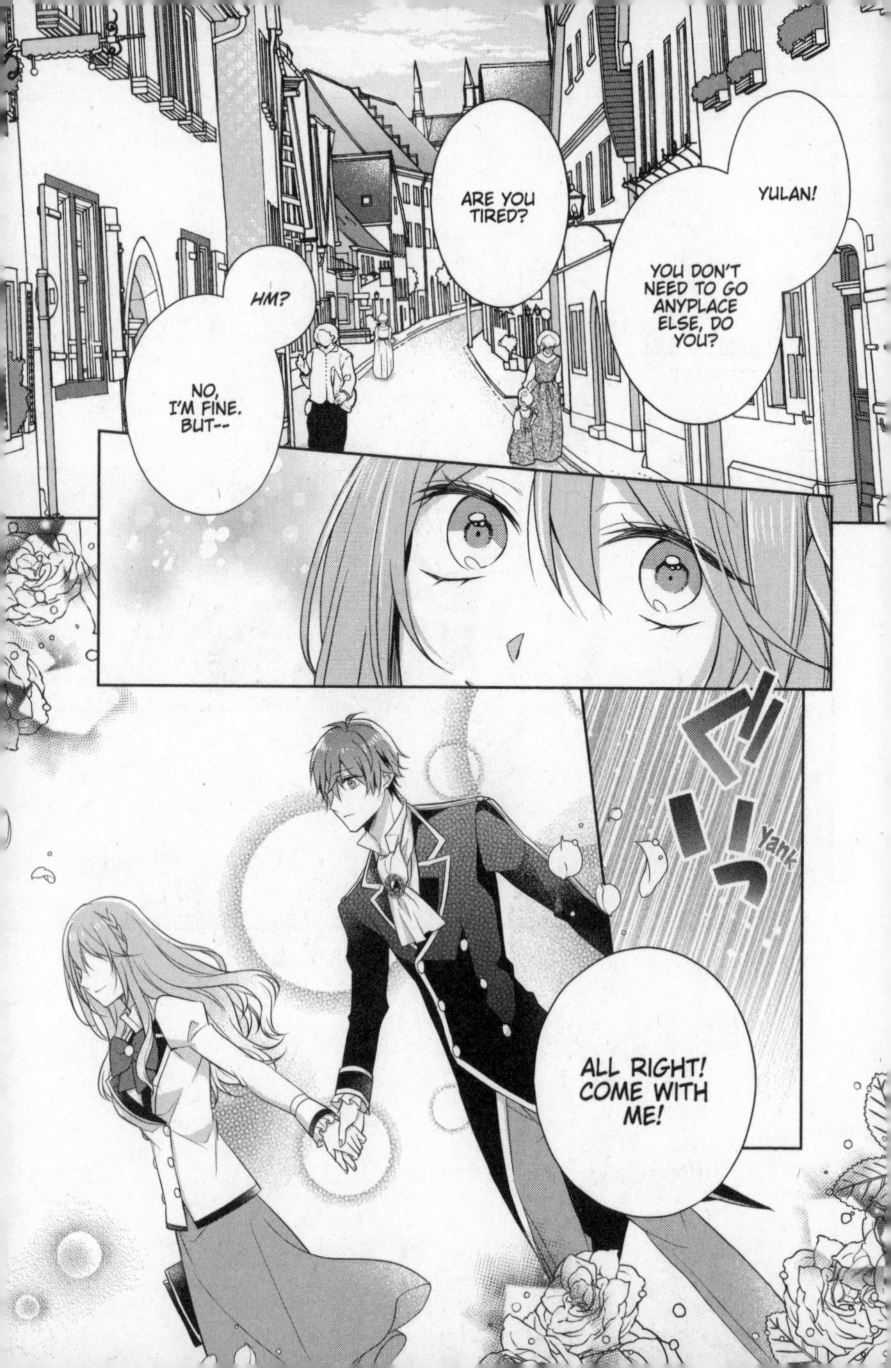
YULAN!
YOU DON'T NEED TO GO ANYPLACE ELSE, DO YOU?
ARE YOU TIRED?
HM?
NO, I'M FINE. BUT--
Yank
ALL RIGHT! COME WITH ME!

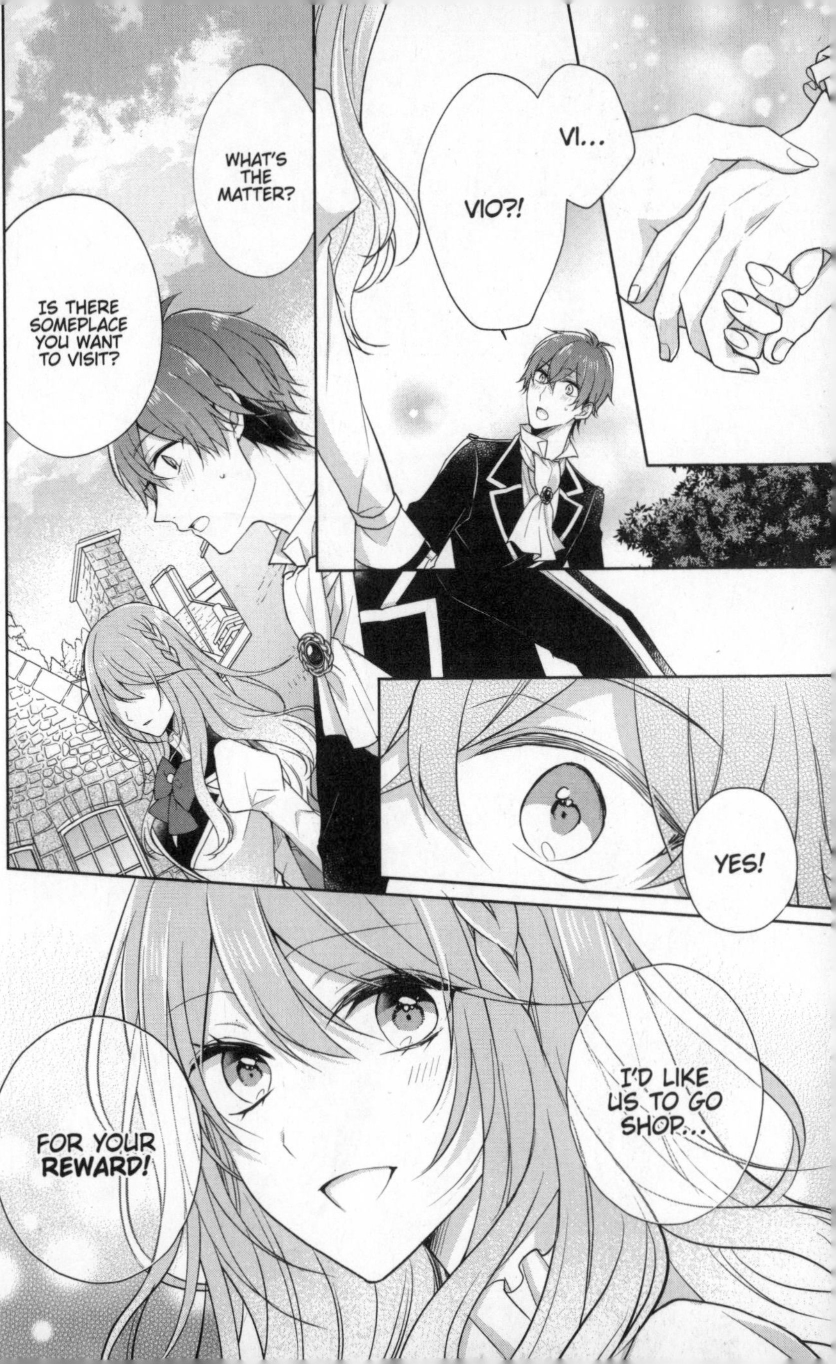
VI...
VIO?!
WHAT'S THE MATTER?
IS THERE SOMEPLACE YOU WANT TO VISIT?
YES!
I'D LIKE US TO GO SHOP...
FOR YOUR REWARD!

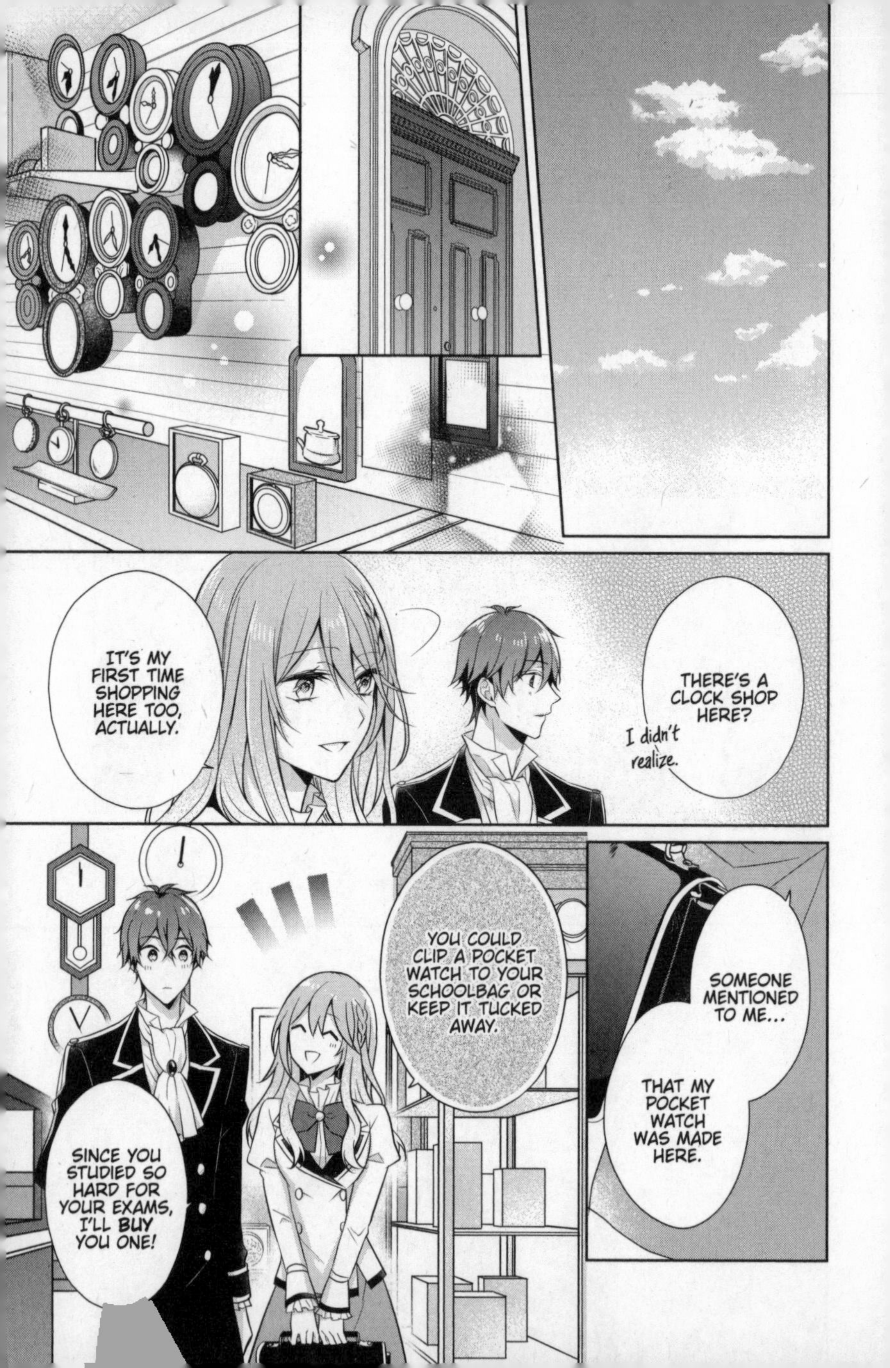
THERE'S A CLOCK SHOP HERE?
I didn't realize.
IT'S MY FIRST TIME SHOPPING HERE TOO, ACTUALLY.
SOMEONE MENTIONED TO ME...
THAT MY POCKET WATCH WAS MADE HERE.
YOU COULD CLIP A POCKET WATCH TO YOUR SCHOOLBAG OR KEEP IT TUCKED AWAY.
SINCE YOU STUDIED SO HARD FOR YOUR EXAMS, I'LL **BUY** YOU ONE!

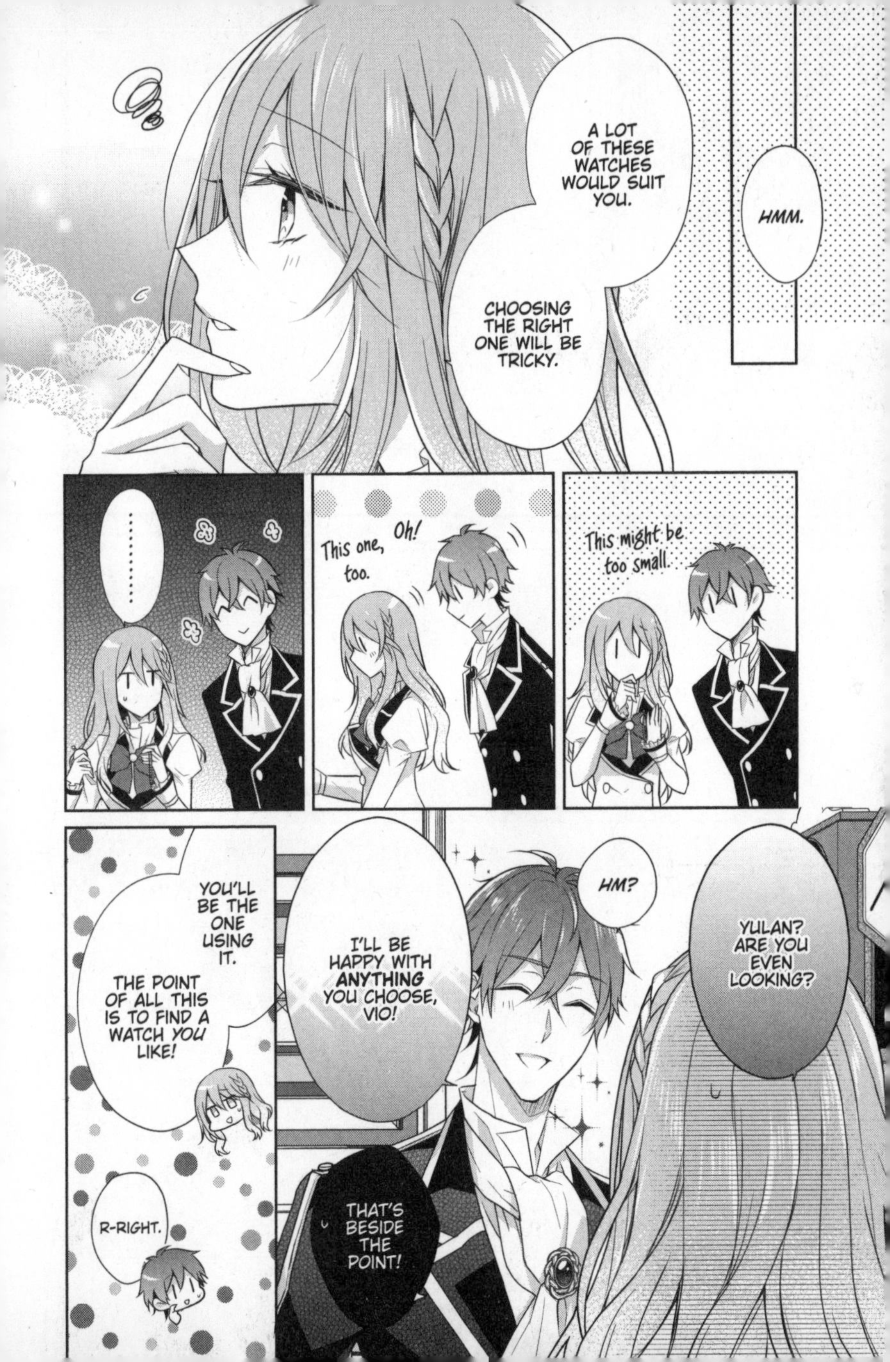
HMM.
A LOT OF THESE WATCHES WOULD SUIT YOU.
CHOOSING THE RIGHT ONE WILL BE TRICKY.
This might be too small.
Oh!
This one, too.
……
YULAN? ARE YOU EVEN LOOKING?
HM?
I'LL BE HAPPY WITH ANYTHING YOU CHOOSE, VIO!
THAT'S BESIDE THE POINT!
YOU'LL BE THE ONE USING IT.
THE POINT OF ALL THIS IS TO FIND A WATCH YOU LIKE!
R-RIGHT.

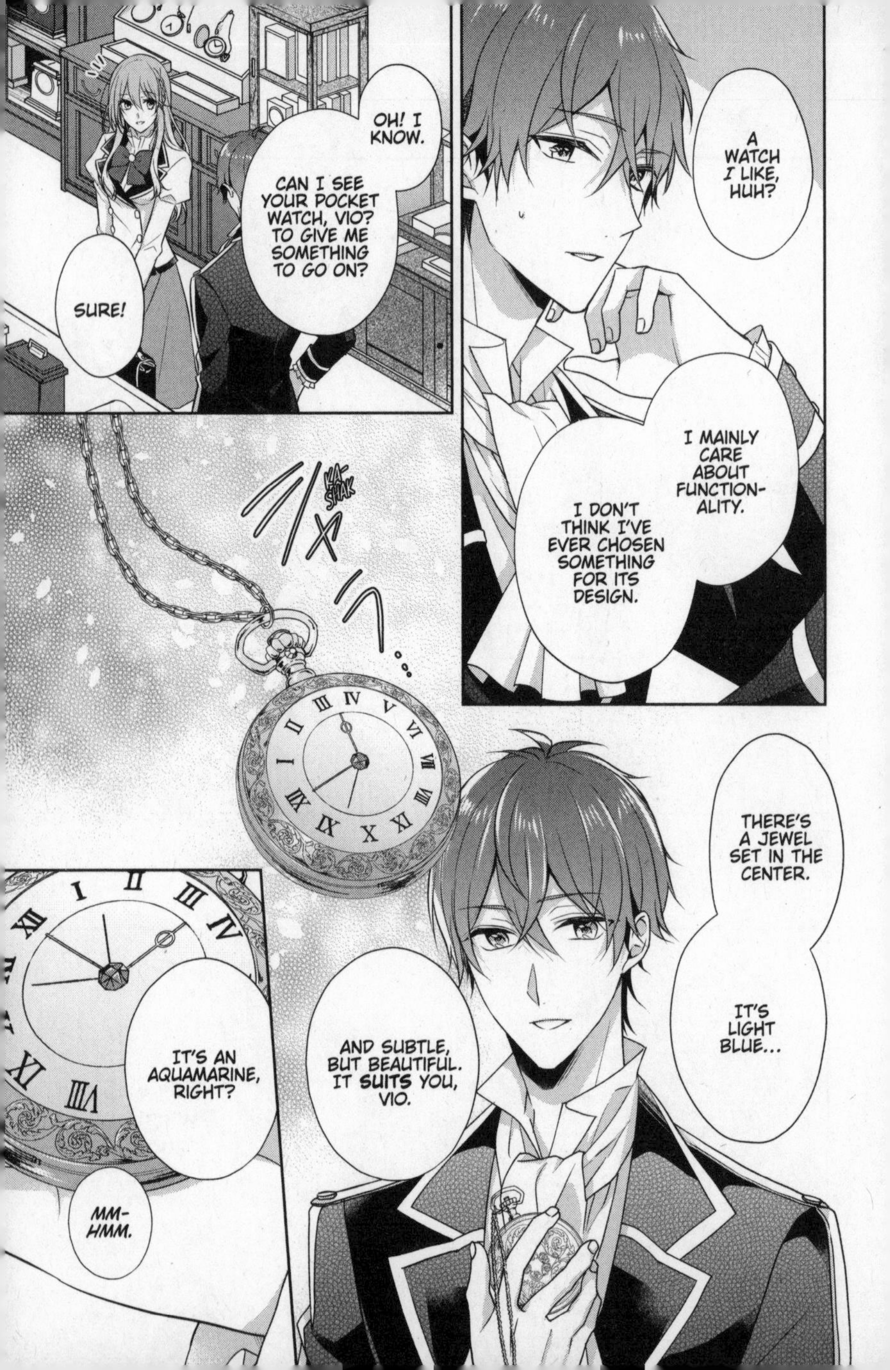
A WATCH I LIKE, HUH?
I MAINLY CARE ABOUT FUNCTION-ALITY.
I DON'T THINK I'VE EVER CHOSEN SOMETHING FOR ITS DESIGN.
OH! I KNOW.
CAN I SEE YOUR POCKET WATCH, VIO? TO GIVE ME SOMETHING TO GO ON?
SURE!
KA-SHAK
...
THERE'S A JEWEL SET IN THE CENTER.
IT'S LIGHT BLUE...
AND SUBTLE, BUT BEAUTIFUL. IT SUITS YOU, VIO.
IT'S AN AQUAMARINE, RIGHT?
MM-HMM.

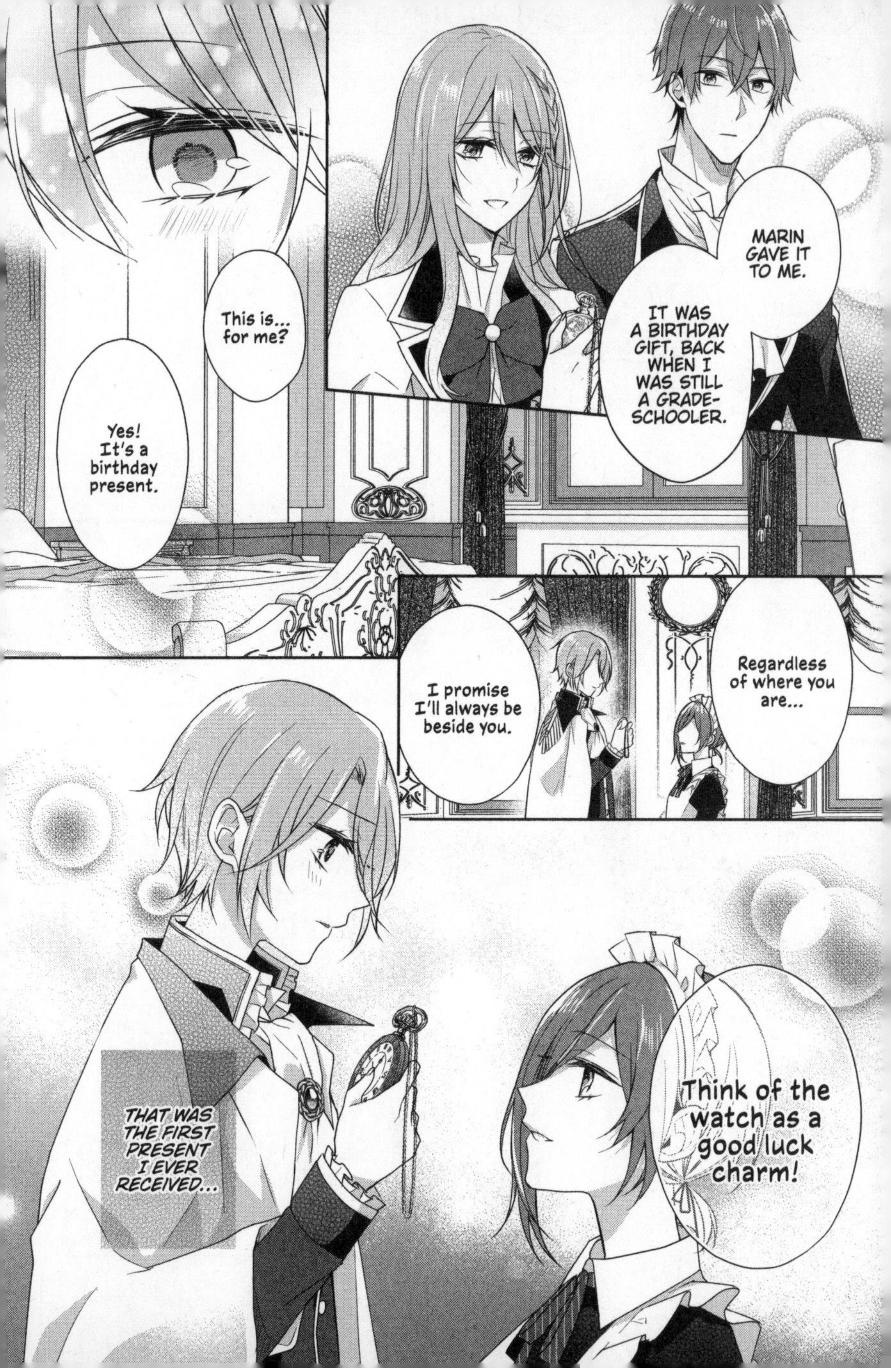
MARIN GAVE IT TO ME.
IT WAS A BIRTHDAY GIFT, BACK WHEN I WAS STILL A GRADE-SCHOOLER.
This is... for me?
Yes! It's a birthday present.
Regardless of where you are...
I promise I'll always be beside you.
Think of the watch as a good luck charm!
THAT WAS THE FIRST PRESENT I EVER RECEIVED...

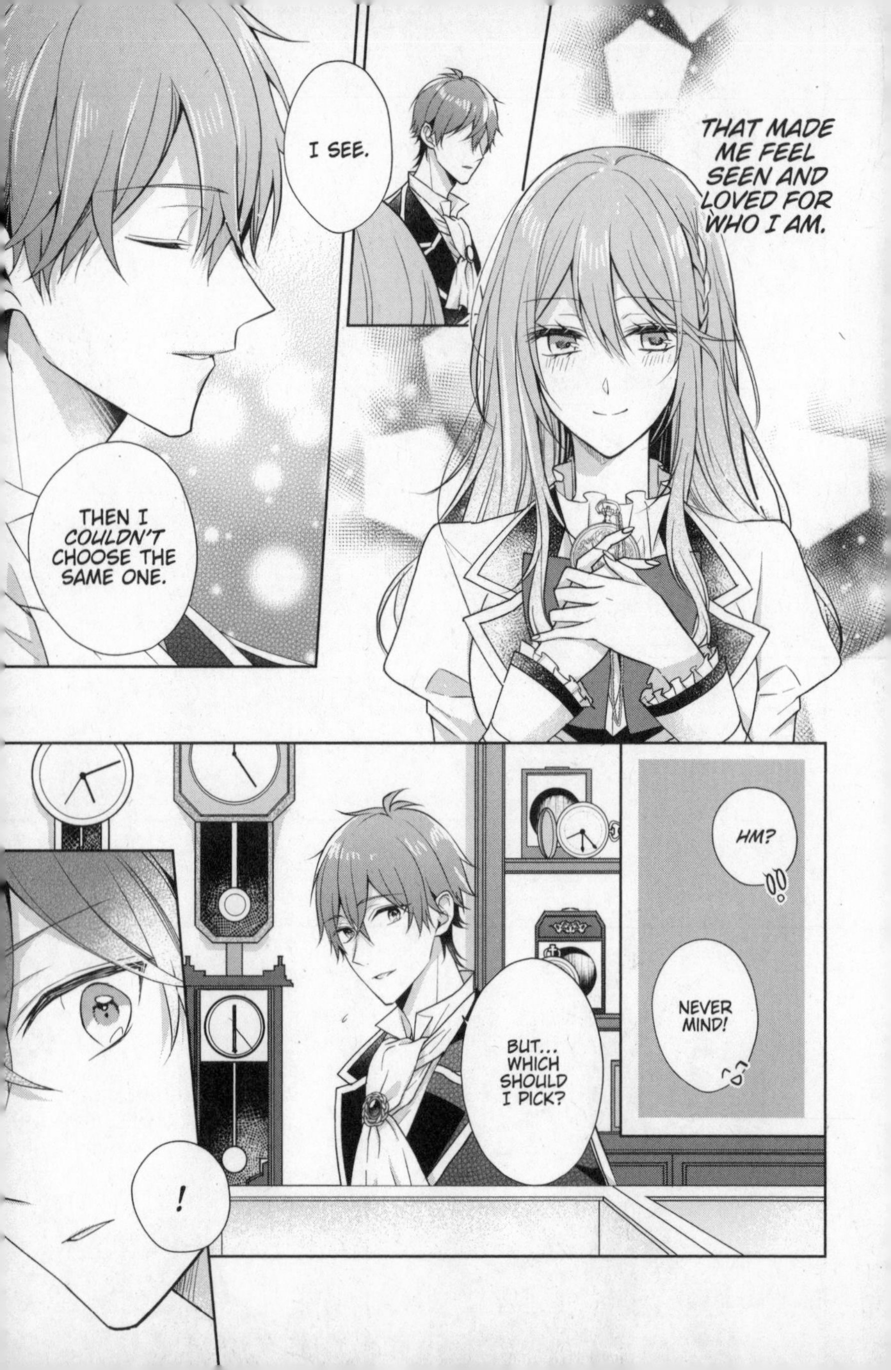
THAT MADE ME FEEL SEEN AND LOVED FOR WHO I AM.
I SEE.
THEN I COULDN'T CHOOSE THE SAME ONE.
HM?
NEVER MIND!
BUT... WHICH SHOULD I PICK?
!

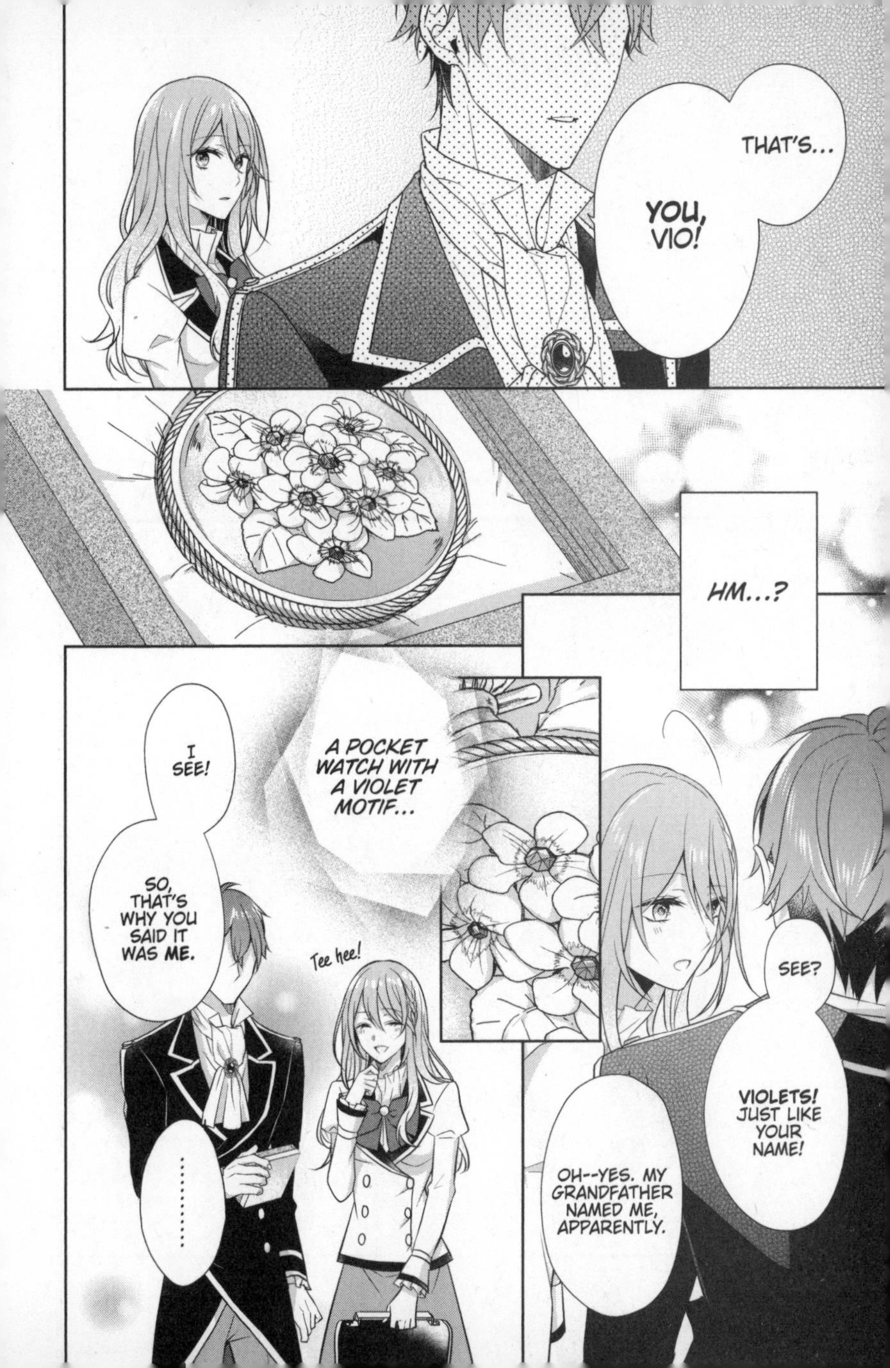
THAT'S...
YOU, VIO!
HM...?
SEE?
VIOLETS! JUST LIKE YOUR NAME!
OH--YES. MY GRANDFATHER NAMED ME, APPARENTLY.
A POCKET WATCH WITH A VIOLET MOTIF...
I SEE!
SO, THAT'S WHY YOU SAID IT WAS ME.
Tee hee!
......

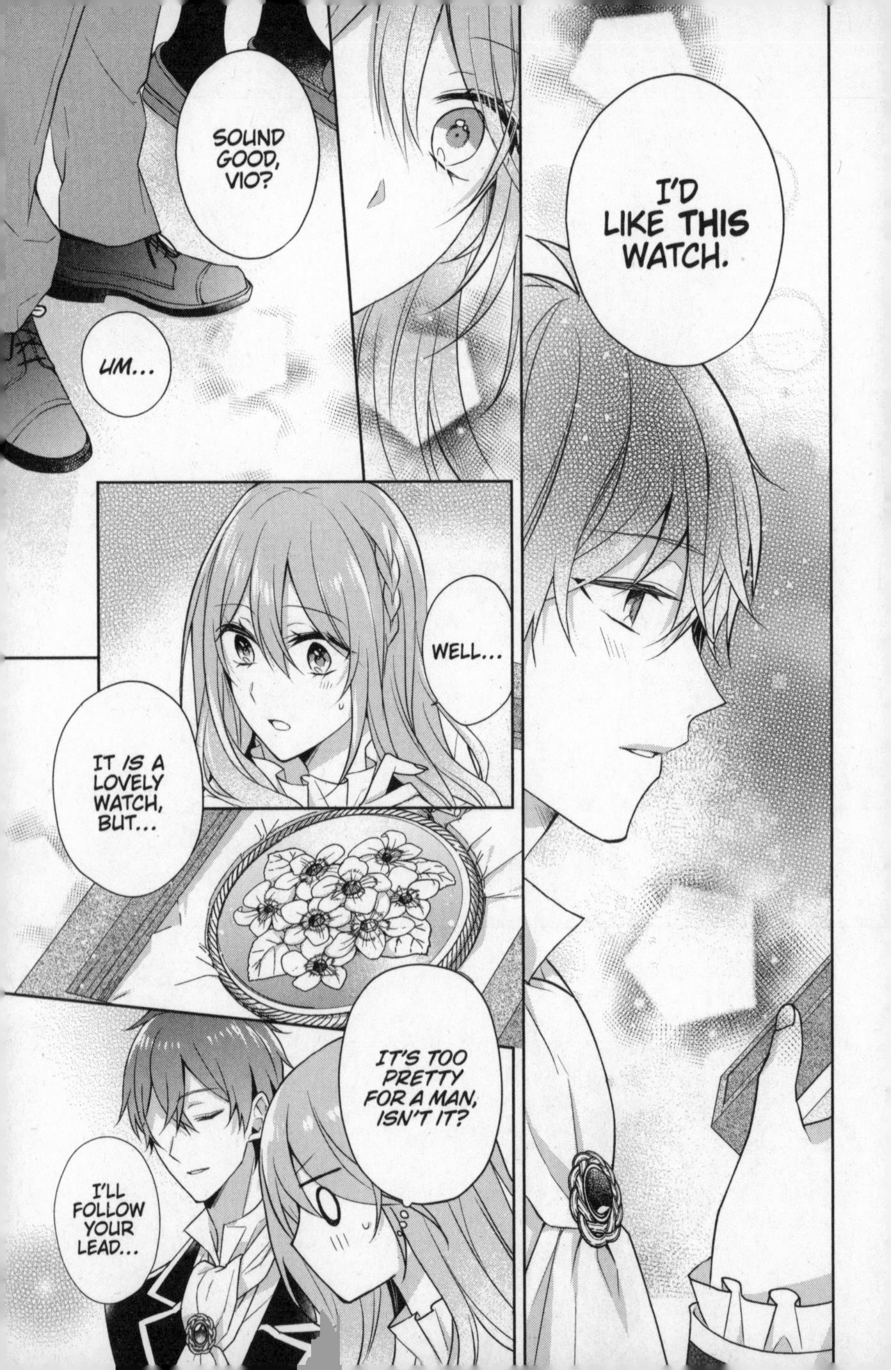
I'D LIKE THIS WATCH.
SOUND GOOD, VIO?
UM...
WELL...
IT IS A LOVELY WATCH, BUT...
IT'S TOO PRETTY FOR A MAN, ISN'T IT?
I'LL FOLLOW YOUR LEAD...

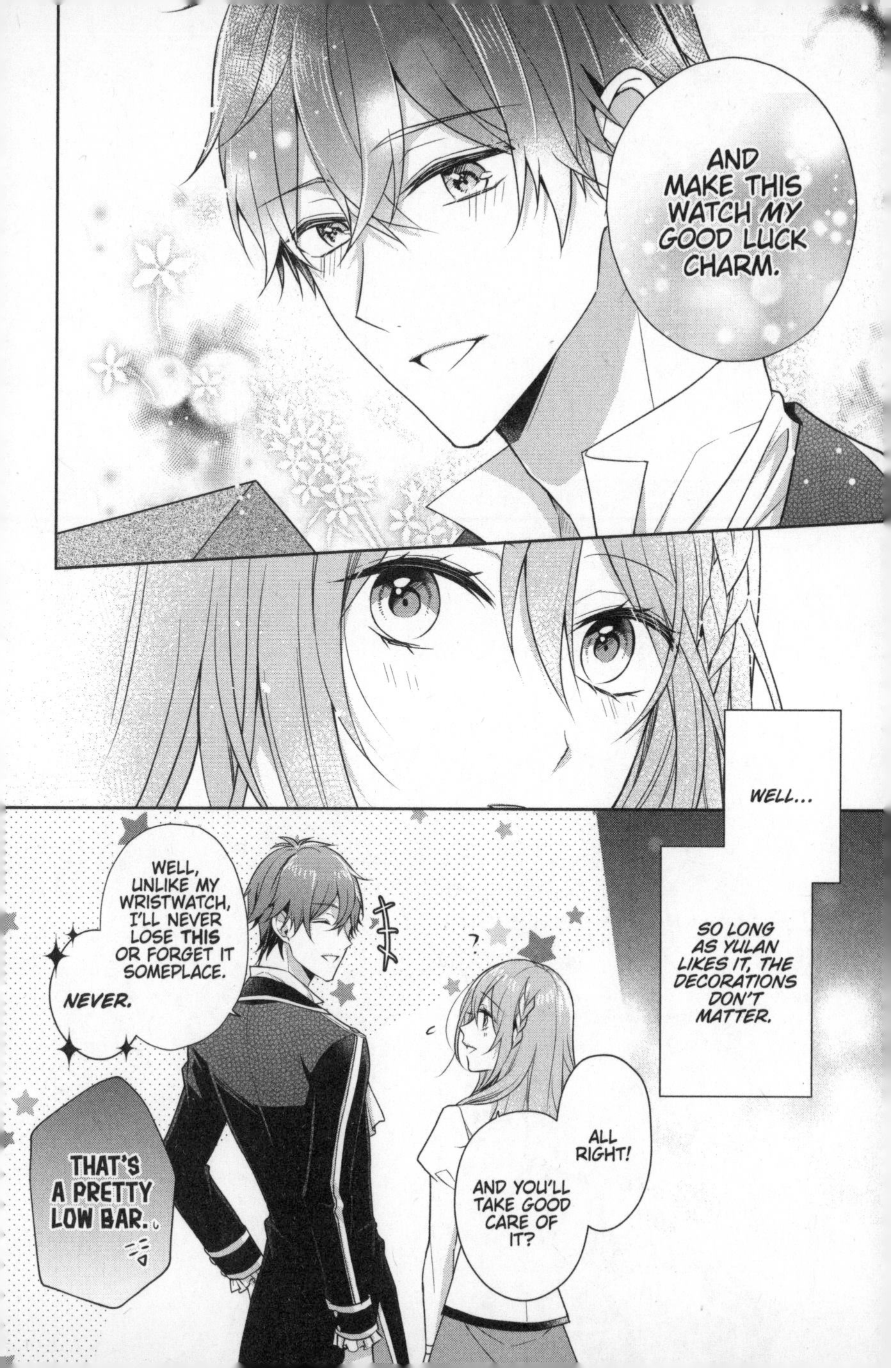
AND MAKE THIS WATCH MY GOOD LUCK CHARM.
WELL...
SO LONG AS YULAN LIKES IT, THE DECORATIONS DON'T MATTER.
ALL RIGHT!
AND YOU'LL TAKE GOOD CARE OF IT?
WELL, UNLIKE MY WRISTWATCH, I'LL NEVER LOSE THIS OR FORGET IT SOMEPLACE.
NEVER.
THAT'S A PRETTY LOW BAR.

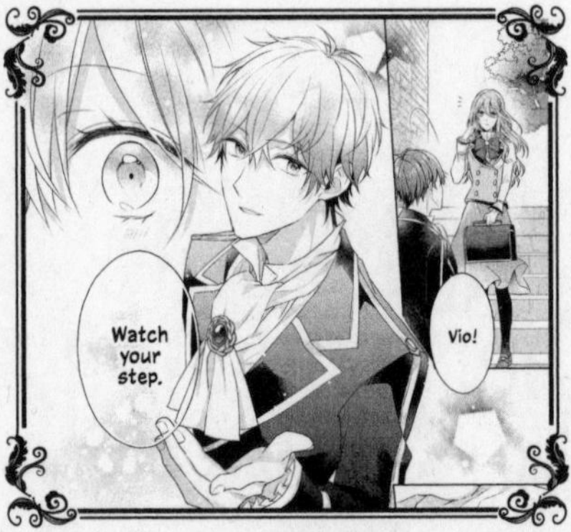
Vio!
Watch your step.

I Swear I Won't
Bother You AGAIN!

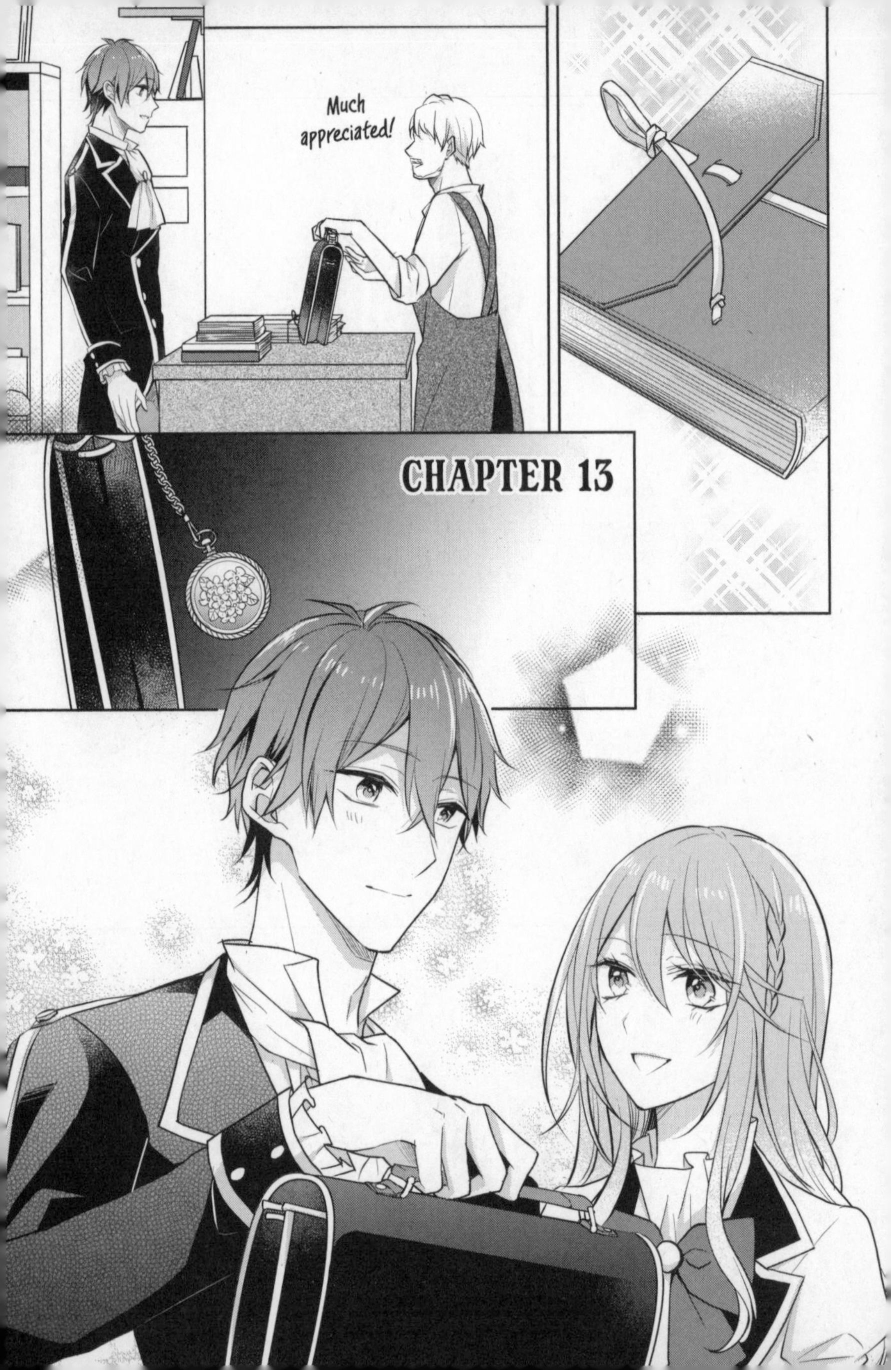
Much appreciated!
CHAPTER 13

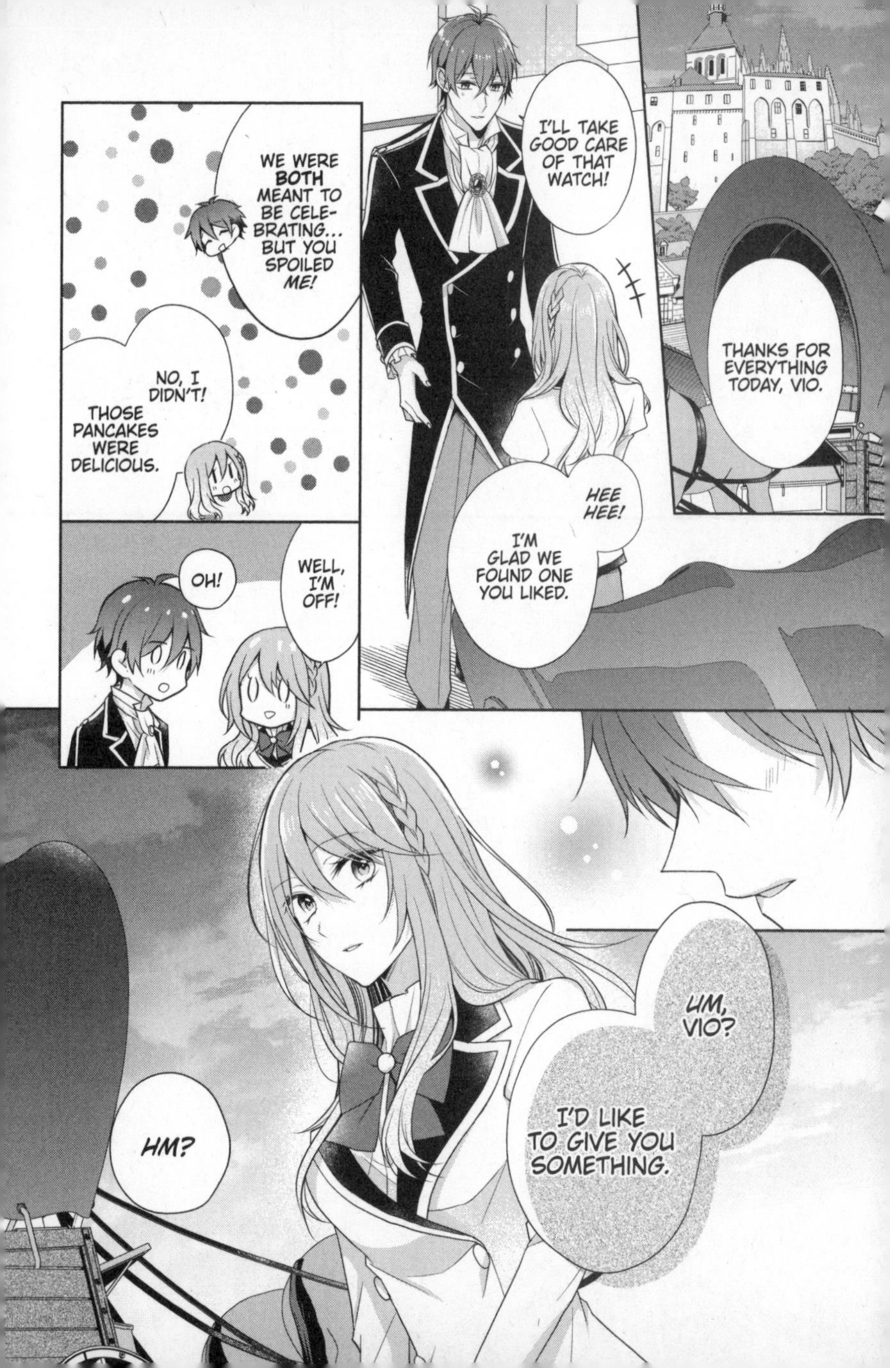
THANKS FOR EVERYTHING TODAY, VIO.
I'LL TAKE GOOD CARE OF THAT WATCH!
HEE HEE!
I'M GLAD WE FOUND ONE YOU LIKED.
WE WERE BOTH MEANT TO BE CELEBRATING... BUT YOU SPOILED ME!
NO, I DIDN'T!
THOSE PANCAKES WERE DELICIOUS.
WELL, I'M OFF!
OH!
UM, VIO?
I'D LIKE TO GIVE YOU SOMETHING.
HM?

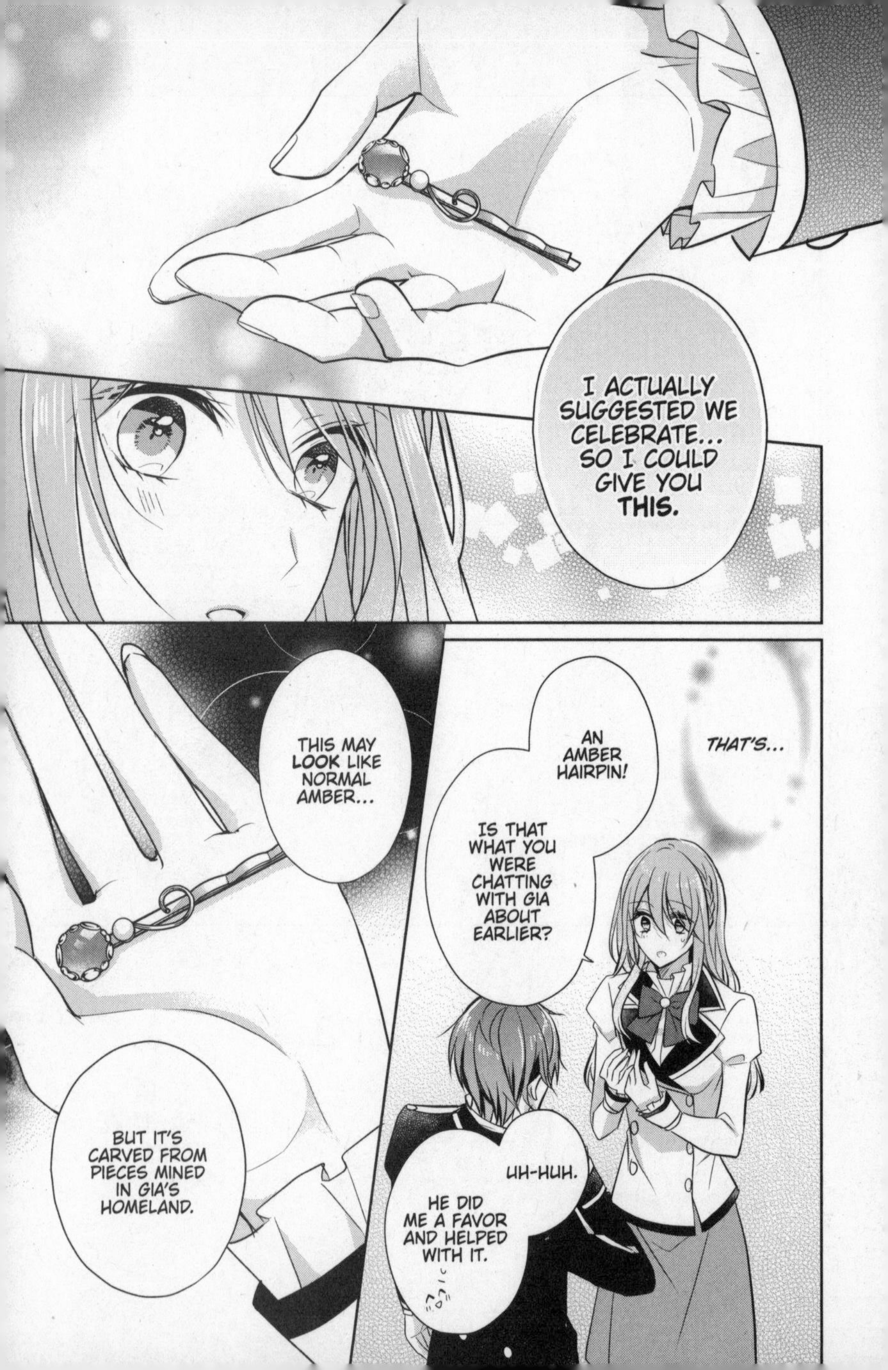
I ACTUALLY SUGGESTED WE CELEBRATE... SO I COULD GIVE YOU **THIS.**
*THAT'S...*
AN AMBER HAIRPIN!
IS THAT WHAT YOU WERE CHATTING WITH GIA ABOUT EARLIER?
UH-HUH.
HE DID ME A FAVOR AND HELPED WITH IT.
THIS MAY **LOOK** LIKE NORMAL AMBER...
BUT IT'S CARVED FROM PIECES MINED IN GIA'S HOMELAND.

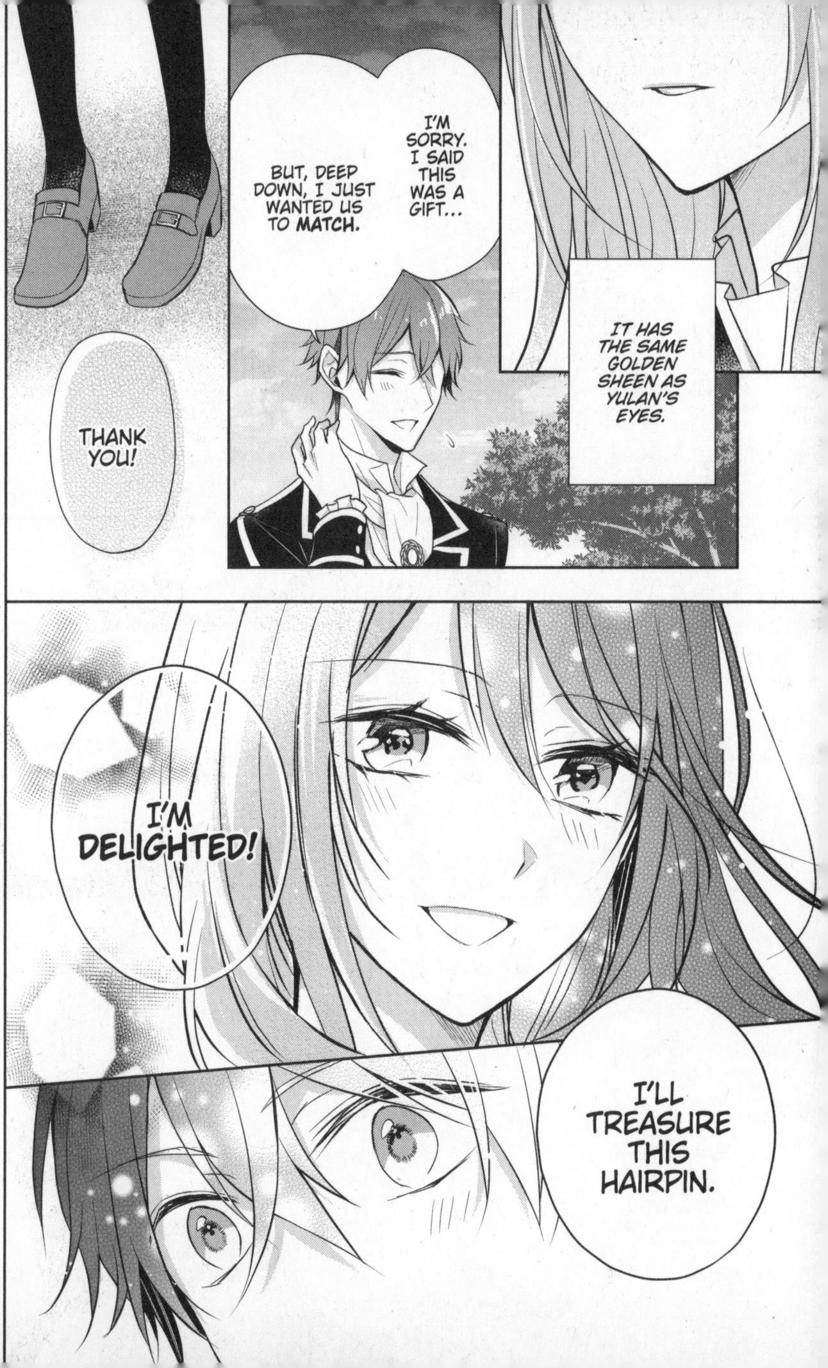
IT HAS THE SAME GOLDEN SHEEN AS YULAN'S EYES.
I'M SORRY. I SAID THIS WAS A GIFT...
BUT, DEEP DOWN, I JUST WANTED US TO MATCH.
THANK YOU!
I'M DELIGHTED!
I'LL TREASURE THIS HAIRPIN.

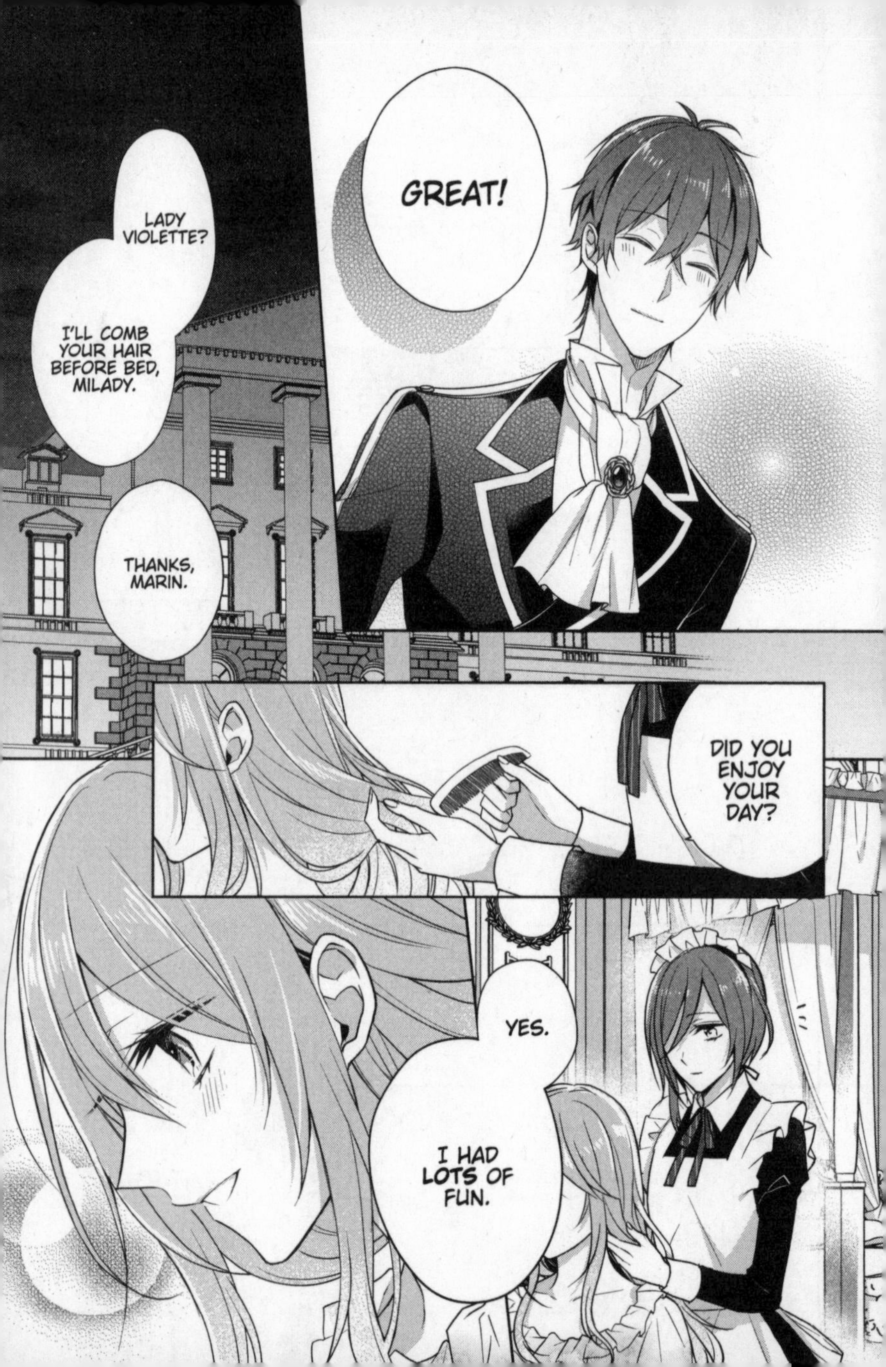
GREAT!
LADY VIOLETTE?
I'LL COMB YOUR HAIR BEFORE BED, MILADY.
THANKS, MARIN.
DID YOU ENJOY YOUR DAY?
YES.
I HAD LOTS OF FUN.

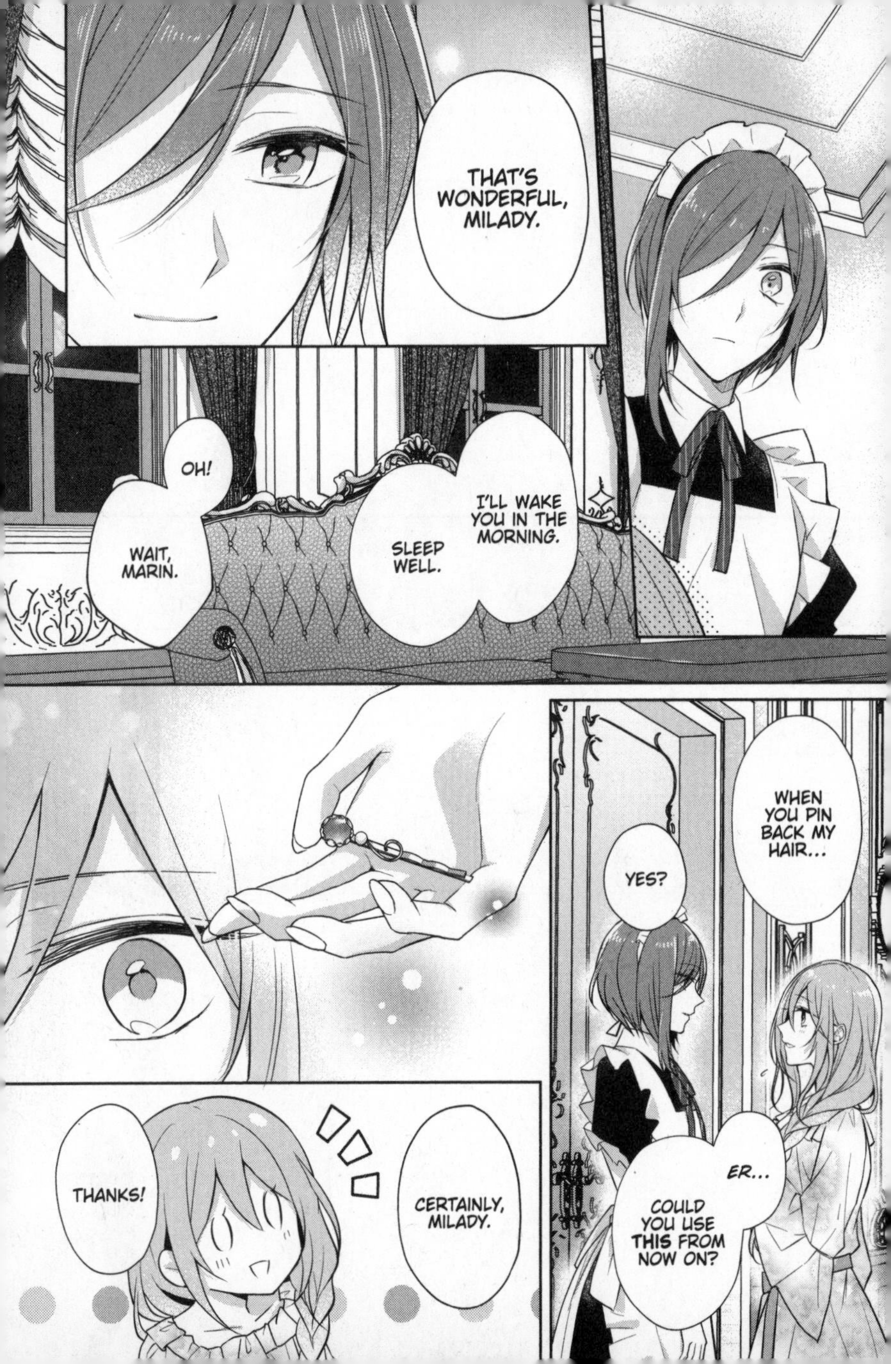
THAT'S WONDERFUL, MILADY.
I'LL WAKE YOU IN THE MORNING.
SLEEP WELL.
OH!
WAIT, MARIN.
WHEN YOU PIN BACK MY HAIR...
YES?
ER...
COULD YOU USE THIS FROM NOW ON?
CERTAINLY, MILADY.
THANKS!

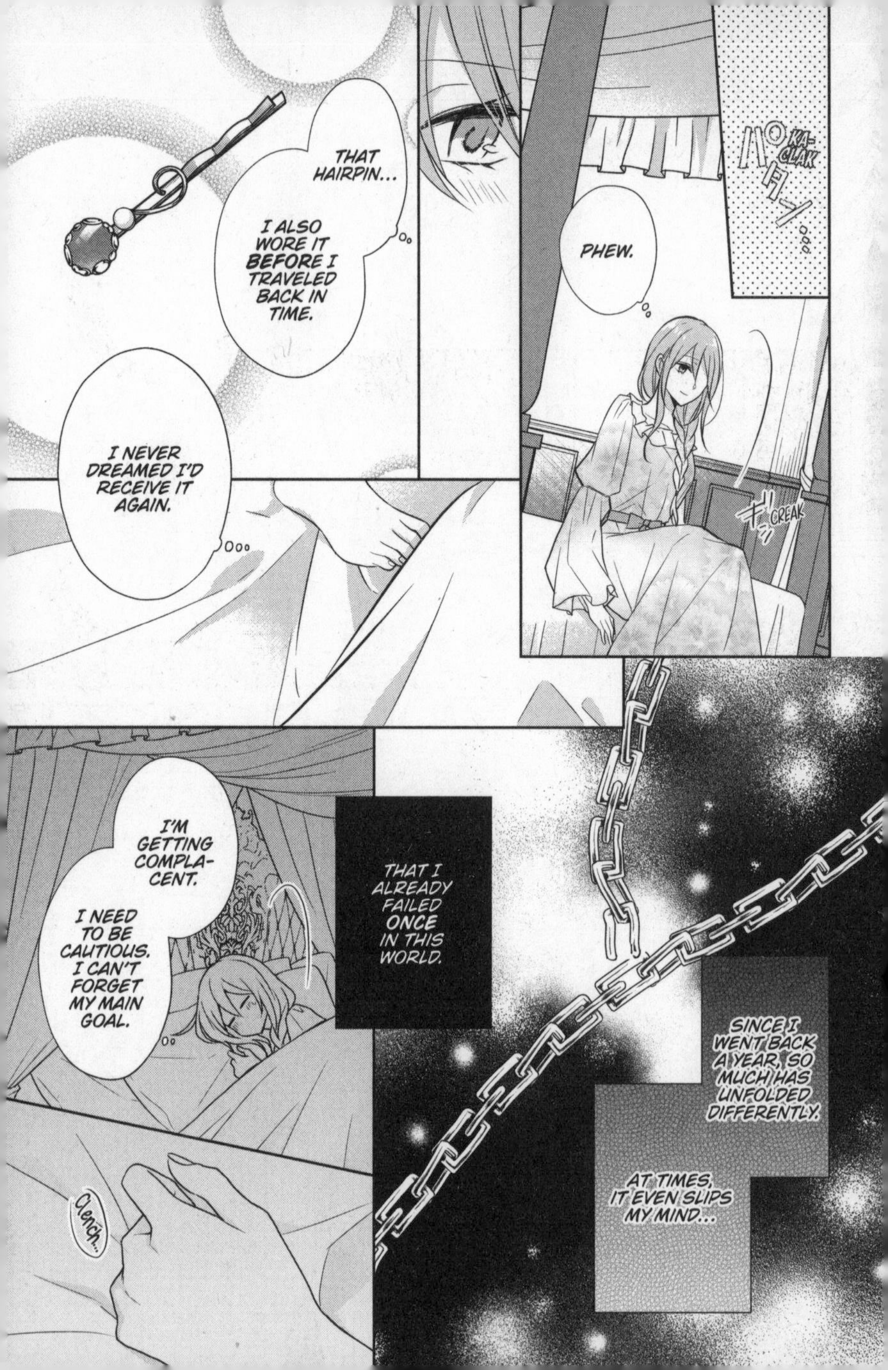
KA-CLAK
PHEW.
CREAK
THAT HAIRPIN...
I ALSO WORE IT BEFORE I TRAVELED BACK IN TIME.
I NEVER DREAMED I'D RECEIVE IT AGAIN.
SINCE I WENT BACK A YEAR, SO MUCH HAS UNFOLDED DIFFERENTLY.
AT TIMES, IT EVEN SLIPS MY MIND...
THAT I ALREADY FAILED ONCE IN THIS WORLD.
I'M GETTING COMPLACENT.
I NEED TO BE CAUTIOUS. I CAN'T FORGET MY MAIN GOAL.
Clench...

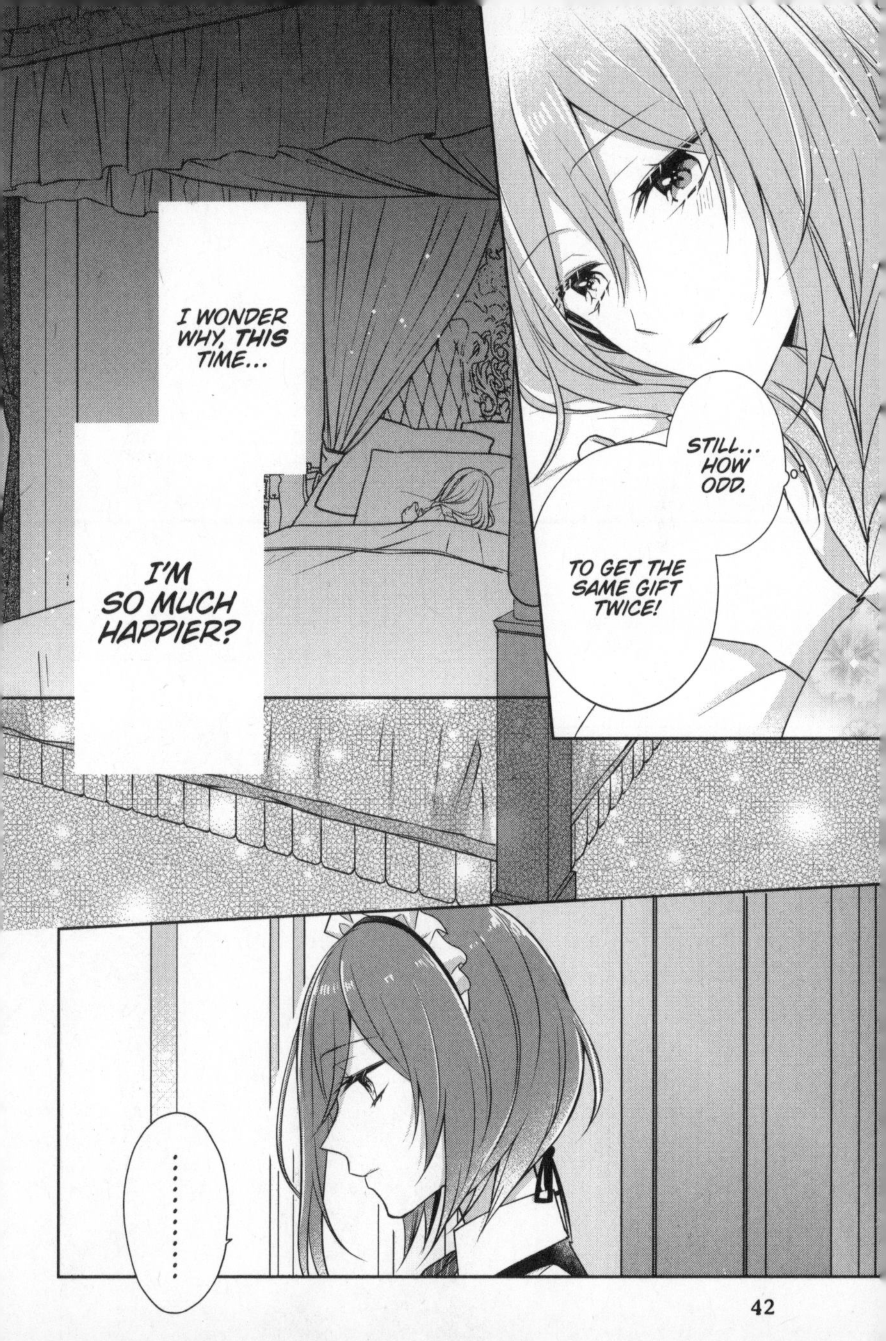
STILL... HOW ODD.
TO GET THE SAME GIFT TWICE!
I WONDER WHY, THIS TIME...
I'M SO MUCH HAPPIER?
........

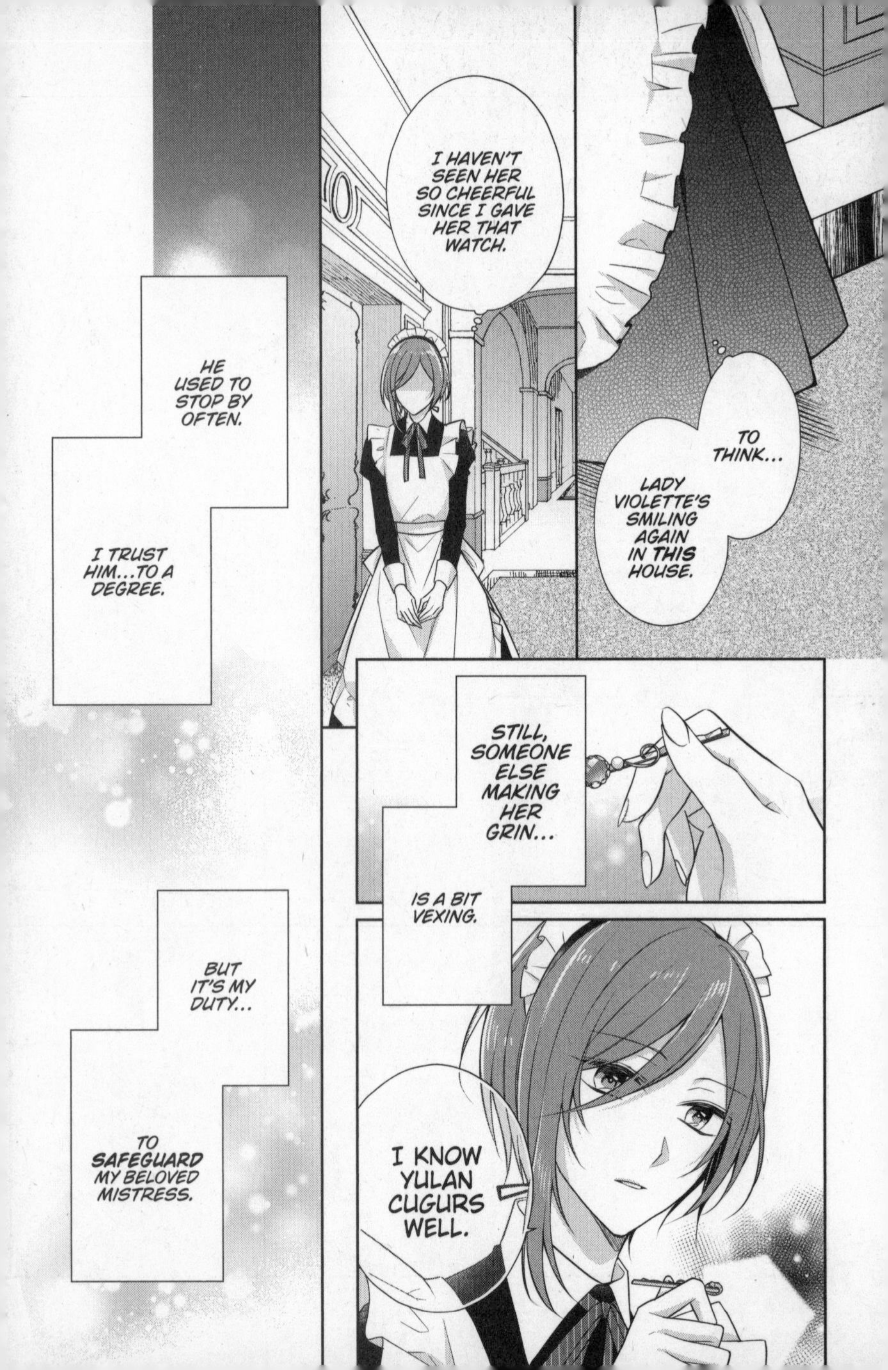
TO THINK...
LADY VIOLETTE'S SMILING AGAIN IN THIS HOUSE.
I HAVEN'T SEEN HER SO CHEERFUL SINCE I GAVE HER THAT WATCH.
STILL, SOMEONE ELSE MAKING HER GRIN...
IS A BIT VEXING.
I KNOW YULAN CUGURS WELL.
HE USED TO STOP BY OFTEN.
I TRUST HIM...TO A DEGREE.
BUT IT'S MY DUTY...
TO SAFEGUARD MY BELOVED MISTRESS.

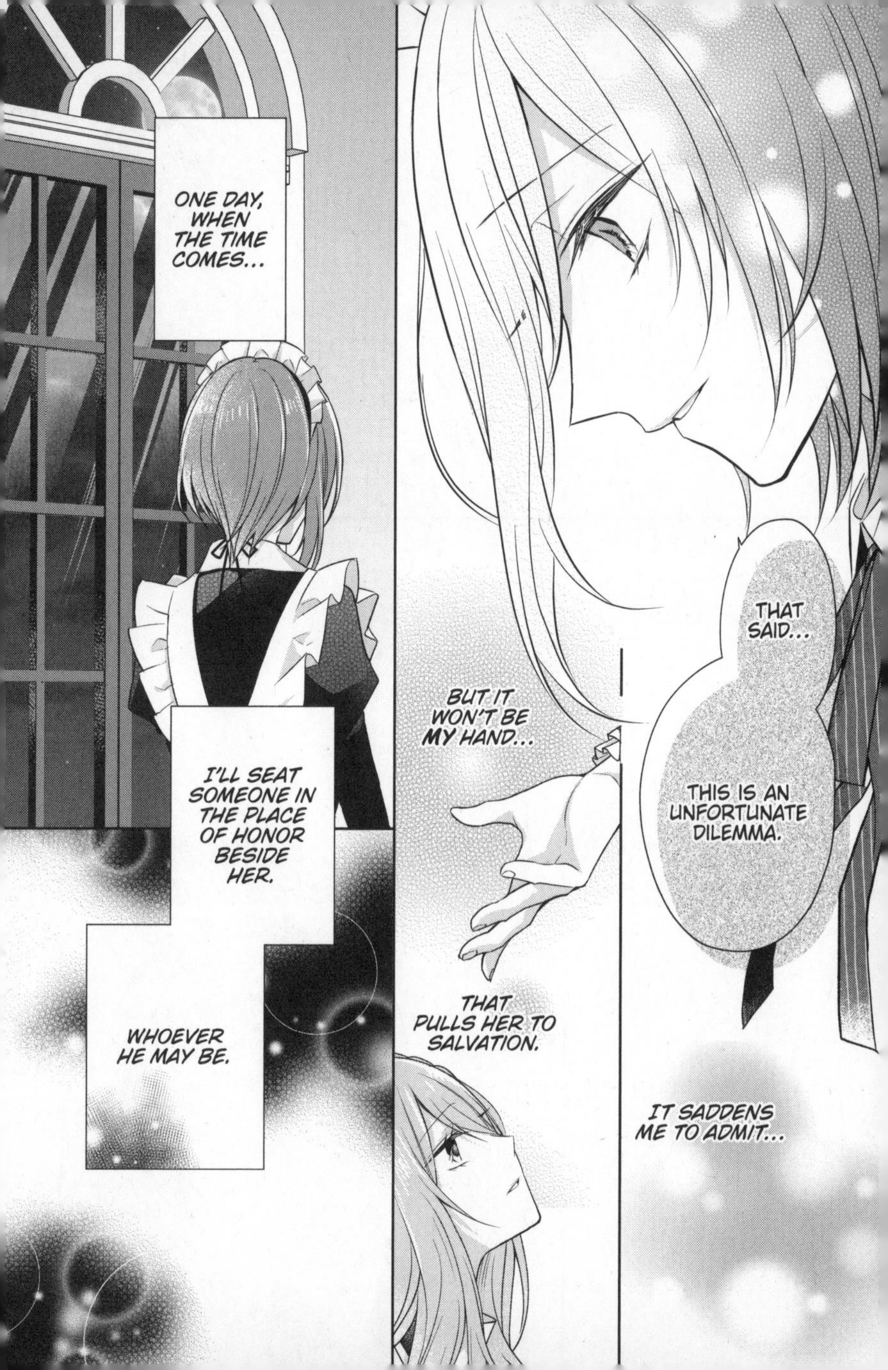
THAT SAID...
THIS IS AN UNFORTUNATE DILEMMA.
IT SADDENS ME TO ADMIT...
BUT IT WON'T BE MY HAND...
THAT PULLS HER TO SALVATION.
ONE DAY, WHEN THE TIME COMES...
I'LL SEAT SOMEONE IN THE PLACE OF HONOR BESIDE HER.
WHOEVER HE MAY BE.

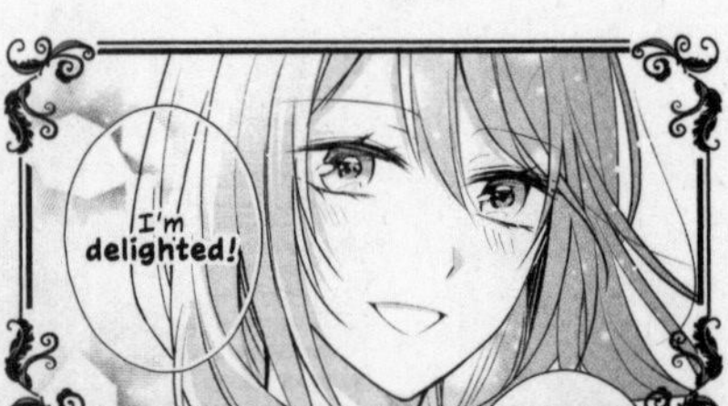
I'm delighted!

# CHAPTER 13.5

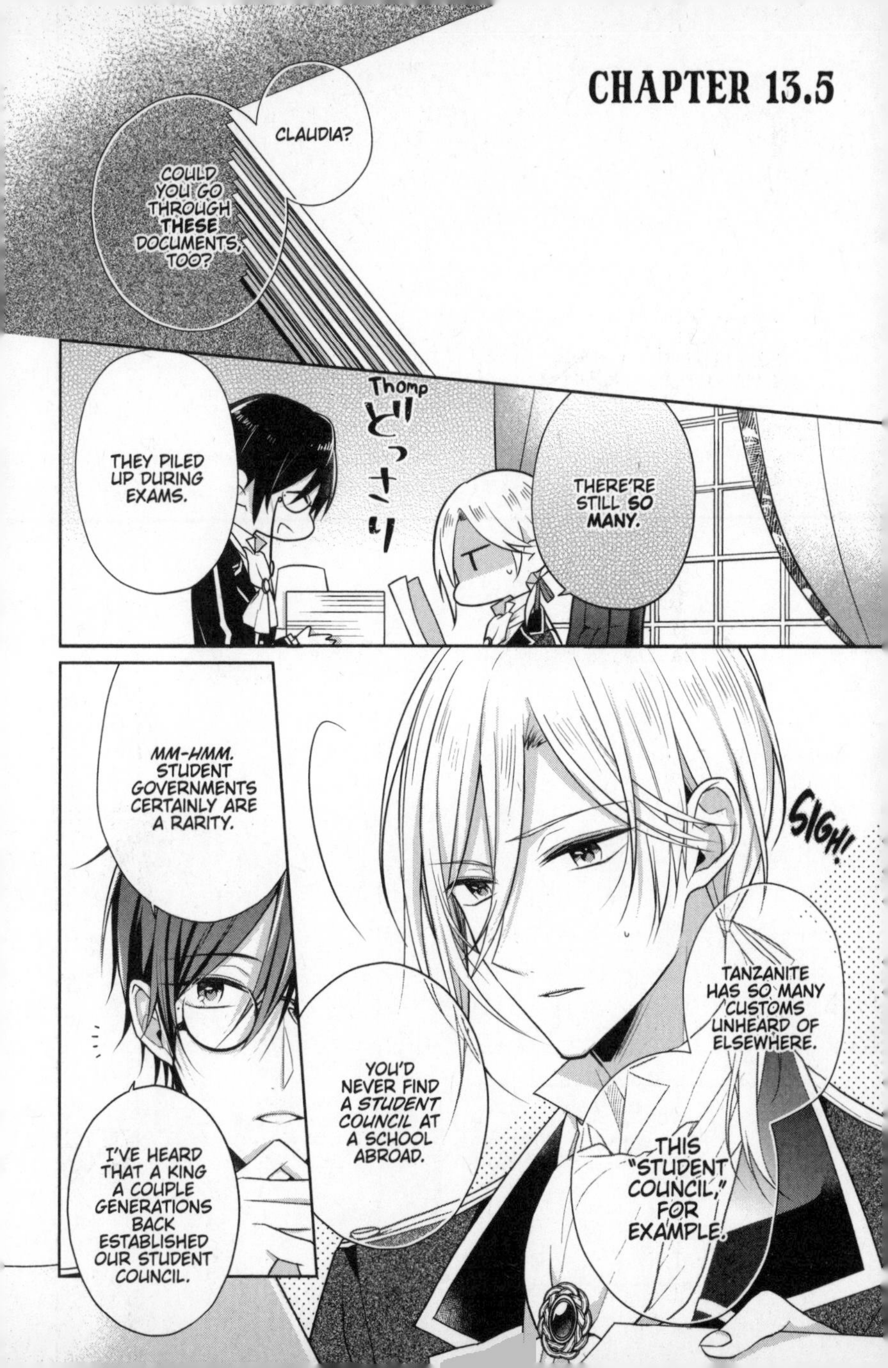
CLAUDIA?
COULD YOU GO THROUGH THESE DOCUMENTS, TOO?
THERE'RE STILL SO MANY.
Thomp
どっさり
THEY PILED UP DURING EXAMS.
SIGH!
TANZANITE HAS SO MANY CUSTOMS UNHEARD OF ELSEWHERE.
THIS "STUDENT COUNCIL," FOR EXAMPLE.
MM-HMM. STUDENT GOVERNMENTS CERTAINLY ARE A RARITY.
YOU'D NEVER FIND A STUDENT COUNCIL AT A SCHOOL ABROAD.
I'VE HEARD THAT A KING A COUPLE GENERATIONS BACK ESTABLISHED OUR STUDENT COUNCIL.

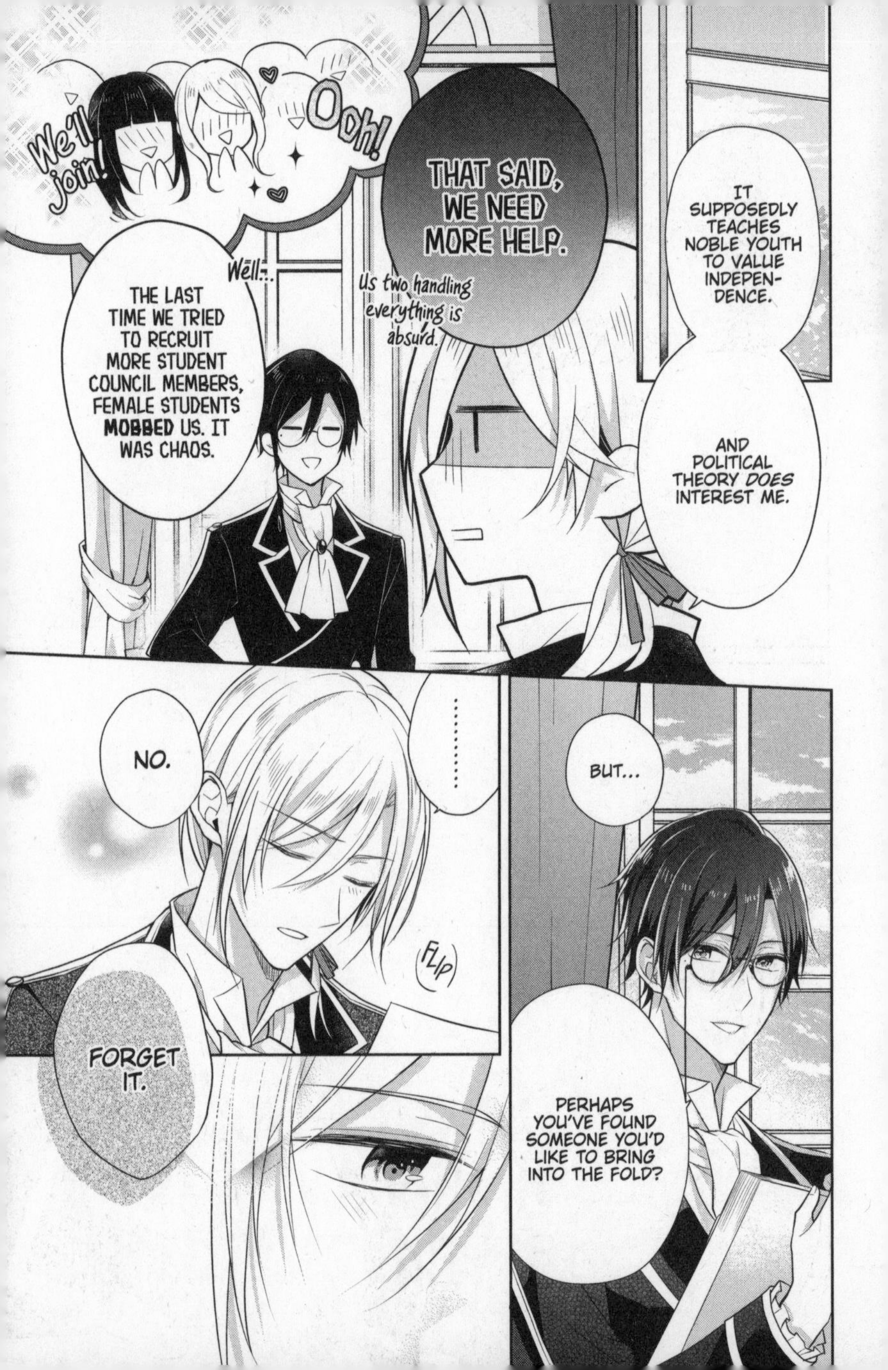
IT SUPPOSEDLY TEACHES NOBLE YOUTH TO VALUE INDEPENDENCE.
AND POLITICAL THEORY *DOES* INTEREST ME.
THAT SAID, WE NEED MORE HELP.
Us two handling everything is absurd.
Well...
THE LAST TIME WE TRIED TO RECRUIT MORE STUDENT COUNCIL MEMBERS, FEMALE STUDENTS **MOBBED** US. IT WAS CHAOS.
Ooh!
We'll join!
BUT...
PERHAPS YOU'VE FOUND SOMEONE YOU'D LIKE TO BRING INTO THE FOLD?
......
NO.
FLIP
FORGET IT.

# I Swear I Won't Bother You AGAIN!

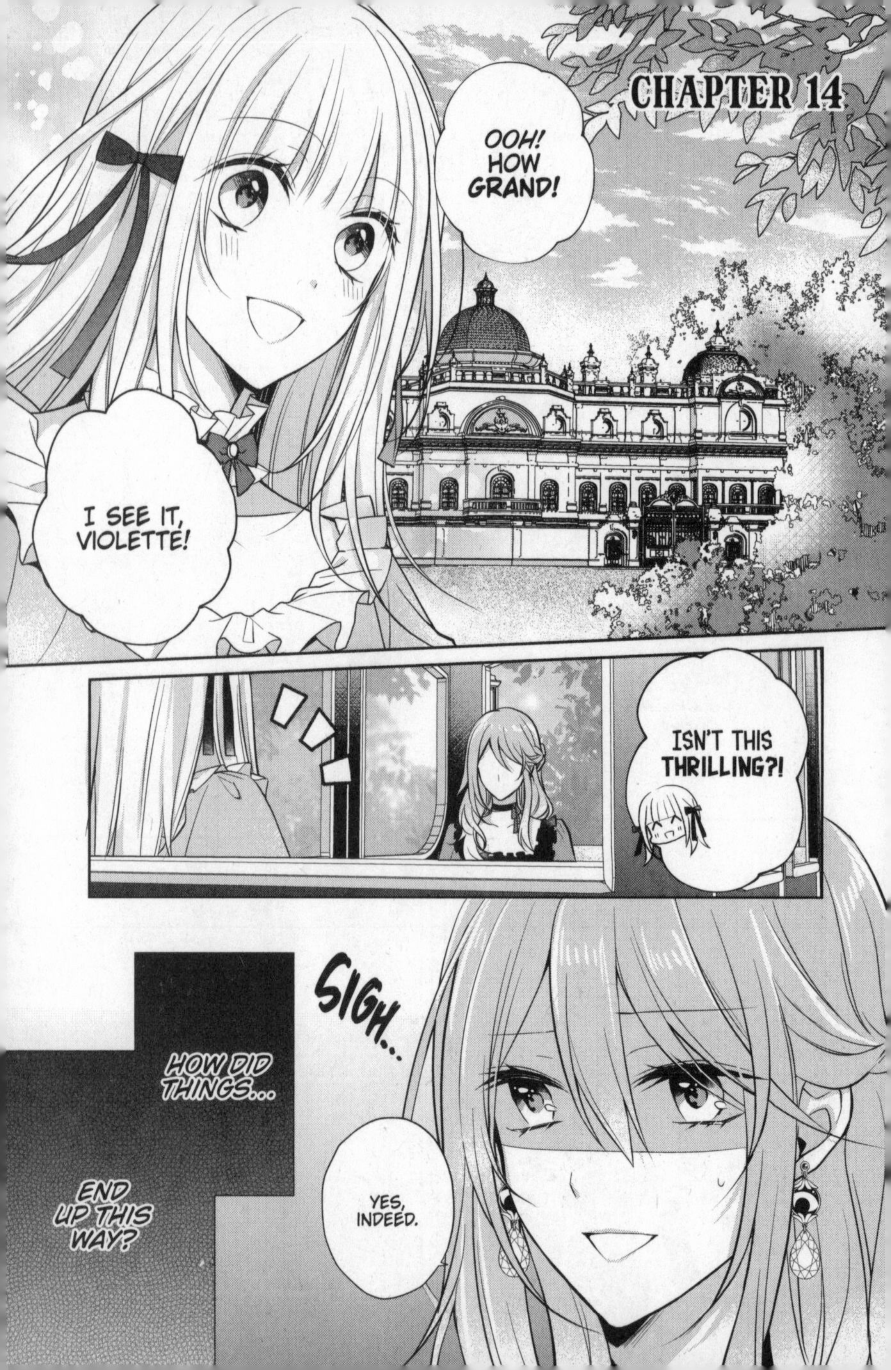
CHAPTER 14
OOH! HOW GRAND!
I SEE IT, VIOLETTE!
ISN'T THIS THRILLING?!
SIGH...
YES, INDEED.
HOW DID THINGS...
END UP THIS WAY?

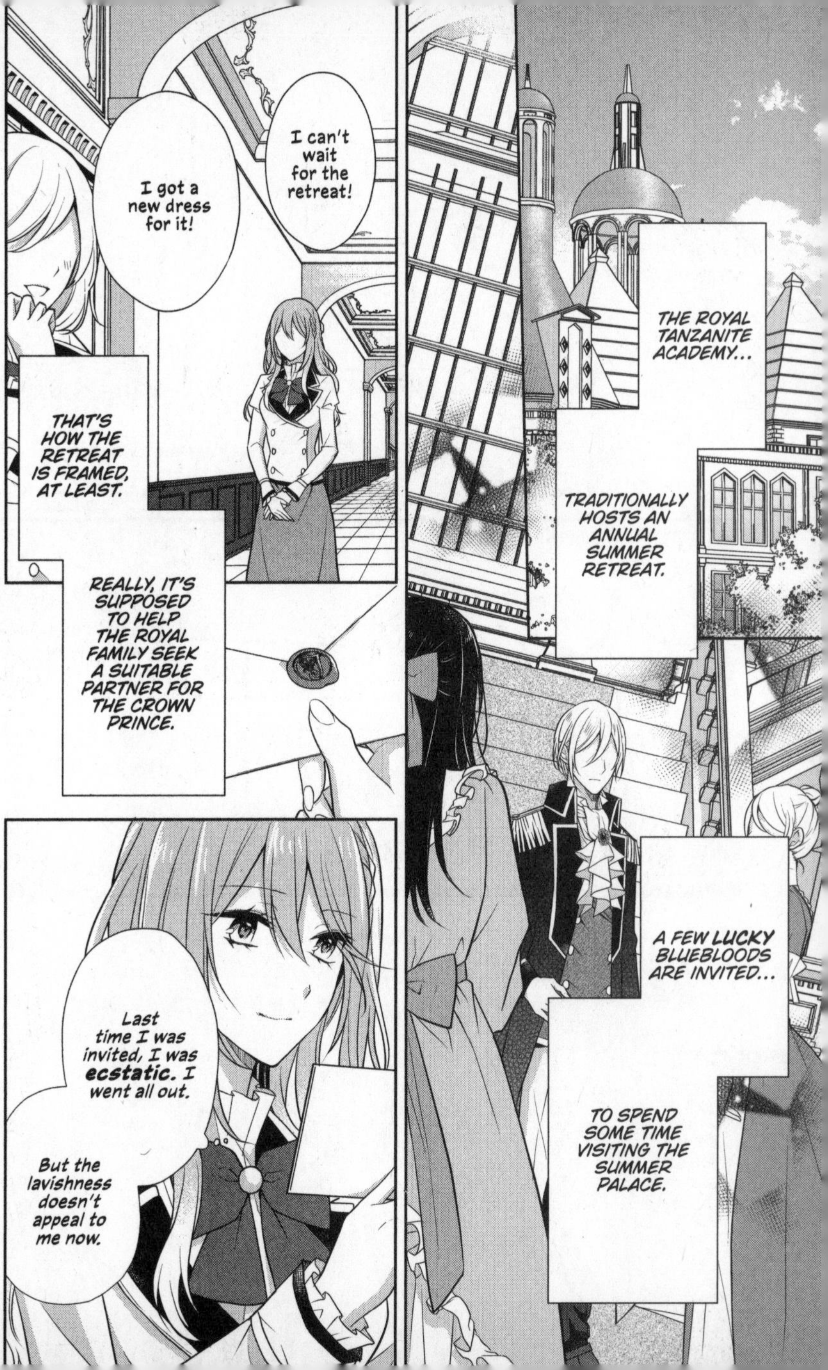

THE ROYAL TANZANITE ACADEMY...
TRADITIONALLY HOSTS AN ANNUAL SUMMER RETREAT.
A FEW LUCKY BLUEBLOODS ARE INVITED...
TO SPEND SOME TIME VISITING THE SUMMER PALACE.
I can't wait for the retreat!
I got a new dress for it!
THAT'S HOW THE RETREAT IS FRAMED, AT LEAST.
REALLY, IT'S SUPPOSED TO HELP THE ROYAL FAMILY SEEK A SUITABLE PARTNER FOR THE CROWN PRINCE.
Last time I was invited, I was ecstatic. I went all out.
But the lavishness doesn't appeal to me now.

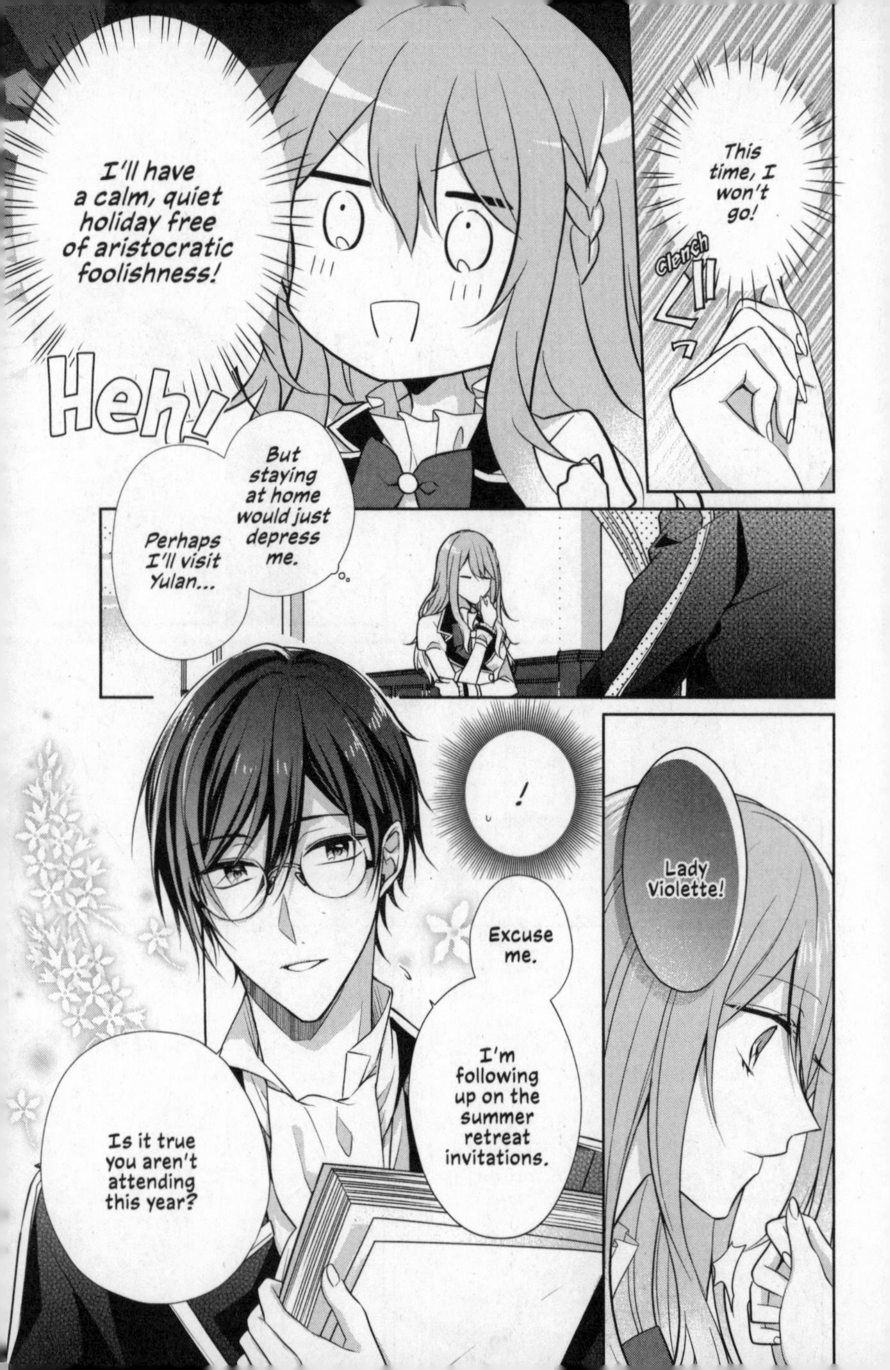
This time, I won't go!
Clench
I'll have a calm, quiet holiday free of aristocratic foolishness!
Heh!
But staying at home would just depress me.
Perhaps I'll visit Yulan...
Lady Violette!
!
Excuse me.
I'm following up on the summer retreat invitations.
Is it true you aren't attending this year?

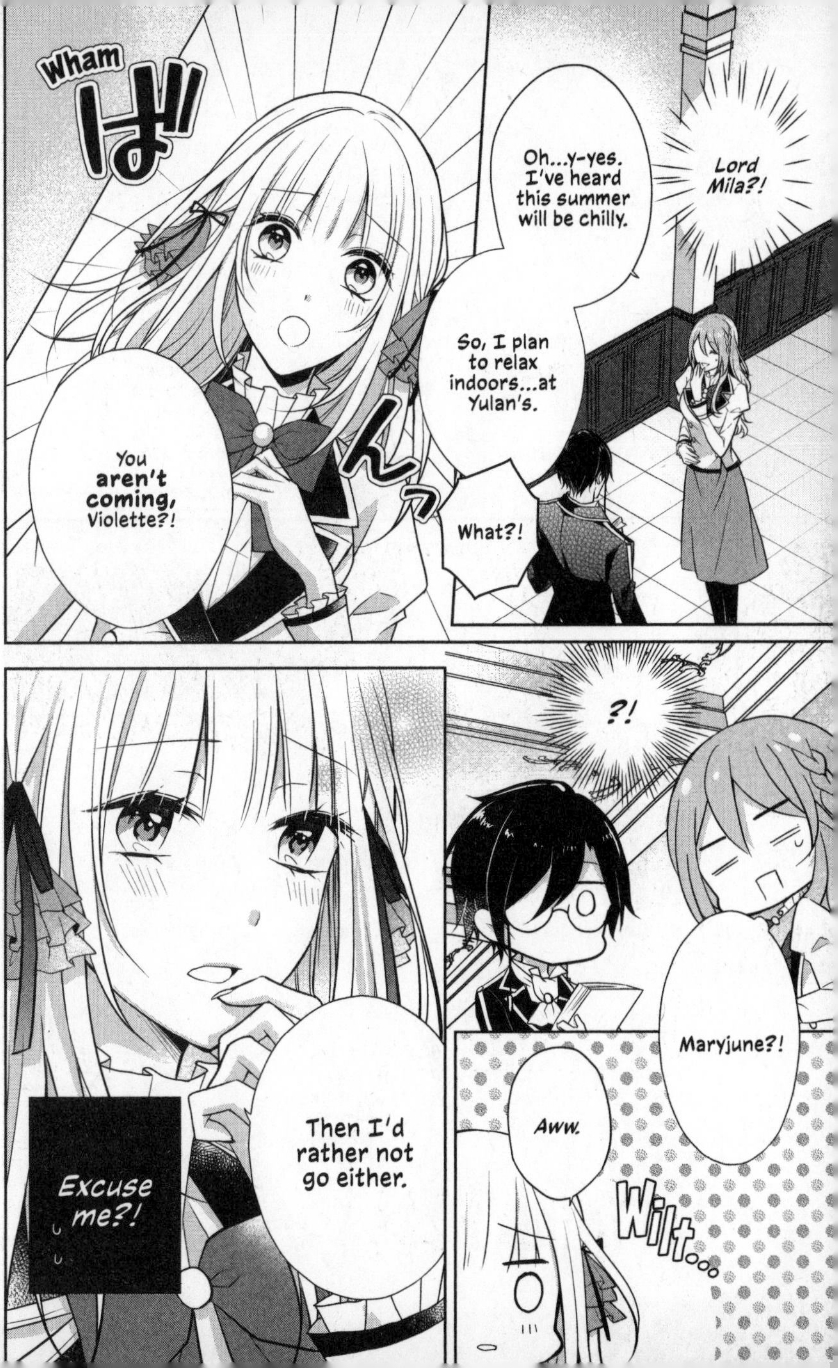

Lord Mila?!
Oh...y-yes. I've heard this summer will be chilly.
So, I plan to relax indoors...at Yulan's.
What?!
Wham
ばっ
You aren't coming, Violette?!
んっ
?!
Maryjune?!
Aww.
Wilt...
Then I'd rather not go either.
Excuse me?!

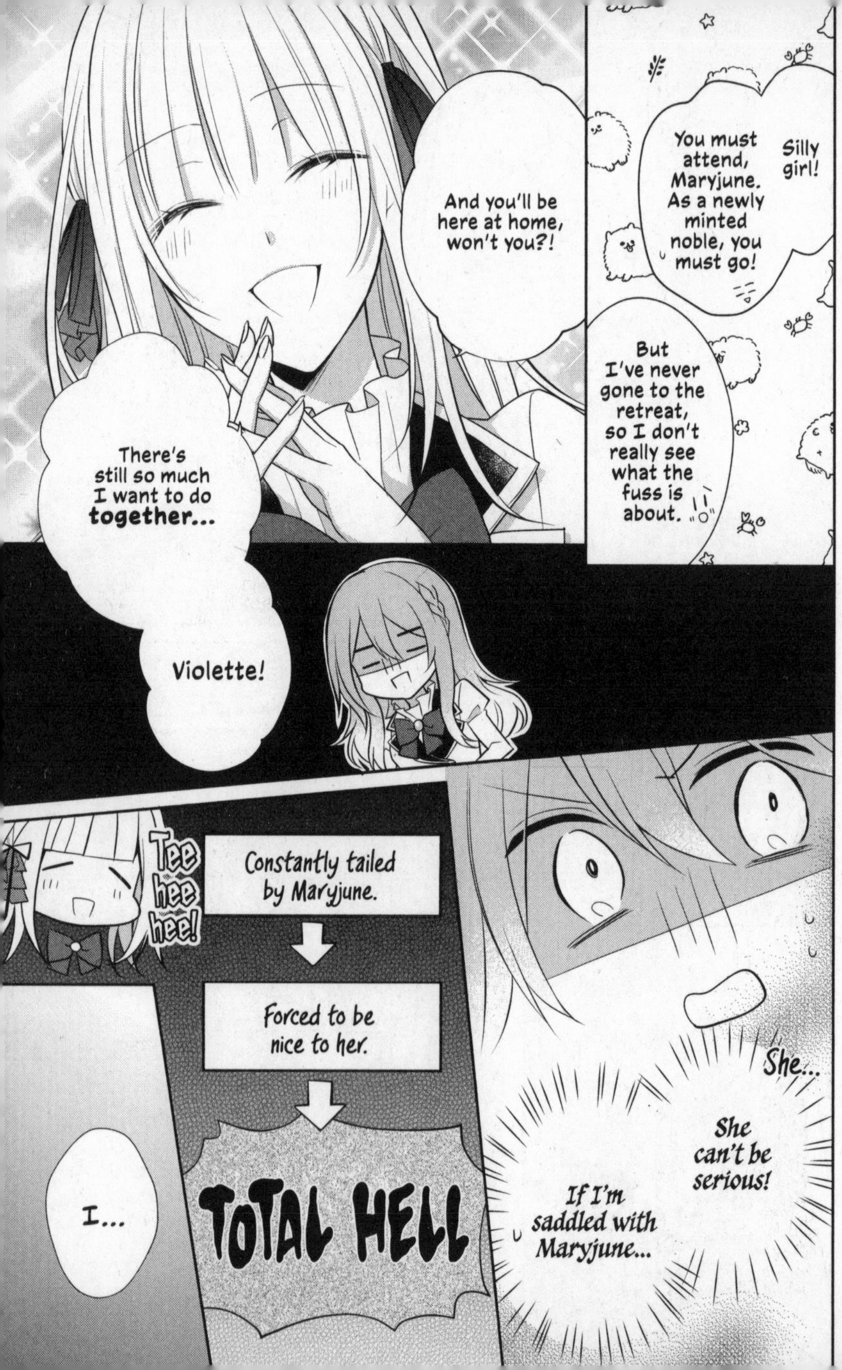

Silly girl!
You must attend, Maryjune. As a newly minted noble, you must go!
But I've never gone to the retreat, so I don't really see what the fuss is about.
And you'll be here at home, won't you?!
There's still so much I want to do **together...**
Violette!
She...
She can't be serious!
If I'm saddled with Maryjune...
Tee hee hee!
Constantly tailed by Maryjune.
Forced to be nice to her.
TOTAL HELL
I...

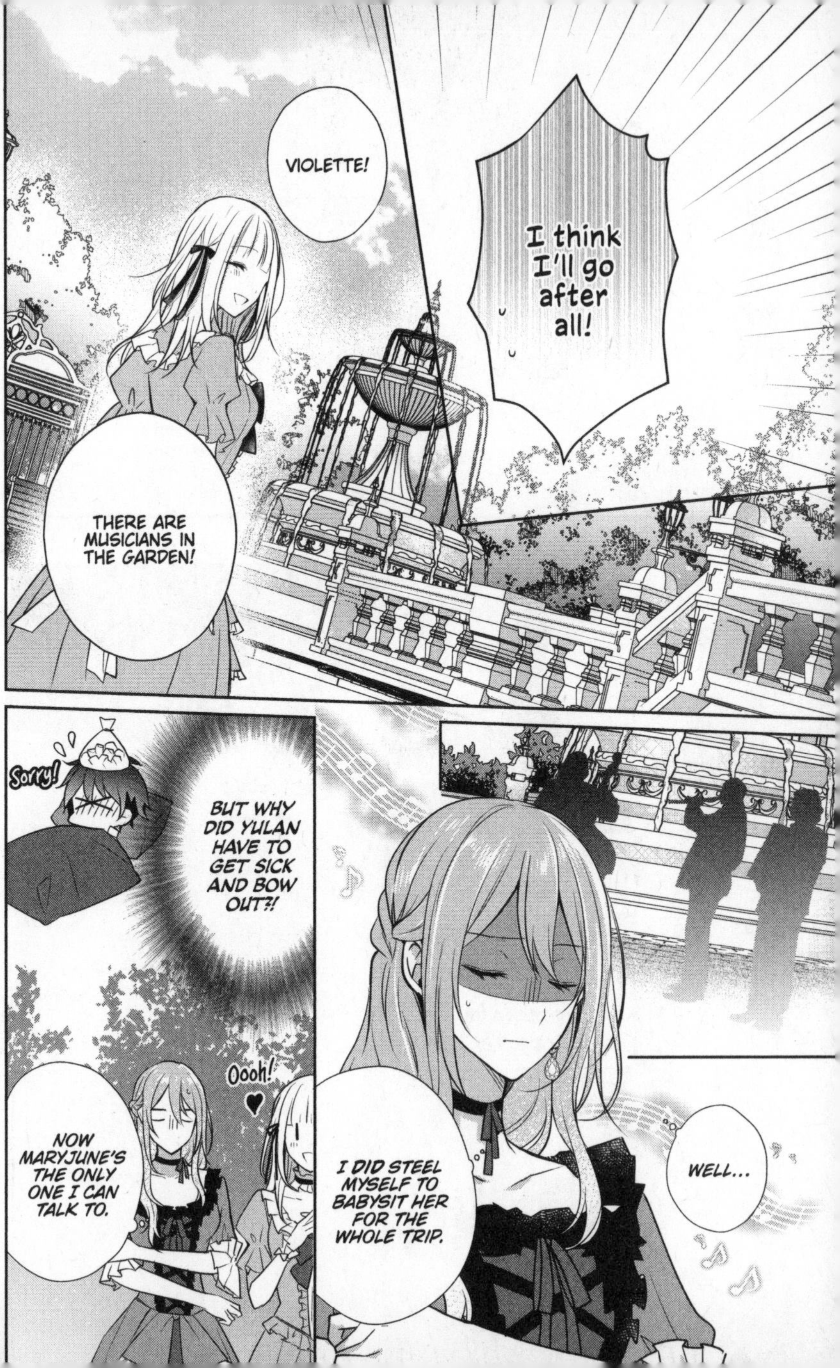

I think I'll go after all!
VIOLETTE!
THERE ARE MUSICIANS IN THE GARDEN!
WELL...
I DID STEEL MYSELF TO BABYSIT HER FOR THE WHOLE TRIP.
BUT WHY DID YULAN HAVE TO GET SICK AND BOW OUT?!
Sorry!
Oooh!
NOW MARYJUNE'S THE ONLY ONE I CAN TALK TO.

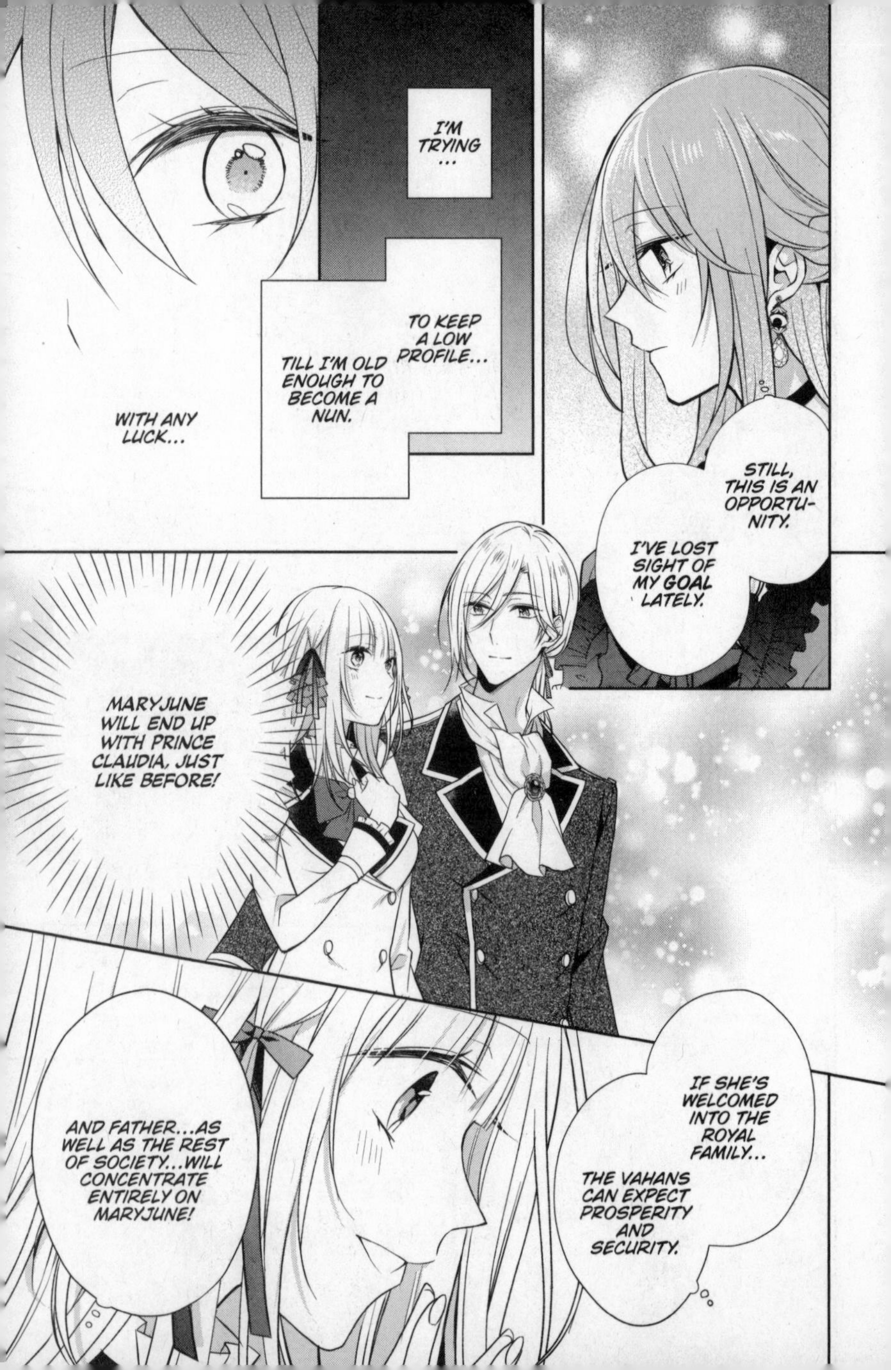
STILL, THIS IS AN OPPORTU-NITY.
I'VE LOST SIGHT OF MY GOAL LATELY.
I'M TRYING...
TO KEEP A LOW PROFILE...
TILL I'M OLD ENOUGH TO BECOME A NUN.
WITH ANY LUCK...
MARYJUNE WILL END UP WITH PRINCE CLAUDIA, JUST LIKE BEFORE!
IF SHE'S WELCOMED INTO THE ROYAL FAMILY...
THE VAHANS CAN EXPECT PROSPERITY AND SECURITY.
AND FATHER...AS WELL AS THE REST OF SOCIETY...WILL CONCENTRATE ENTIRELY ON MARYJUNE!

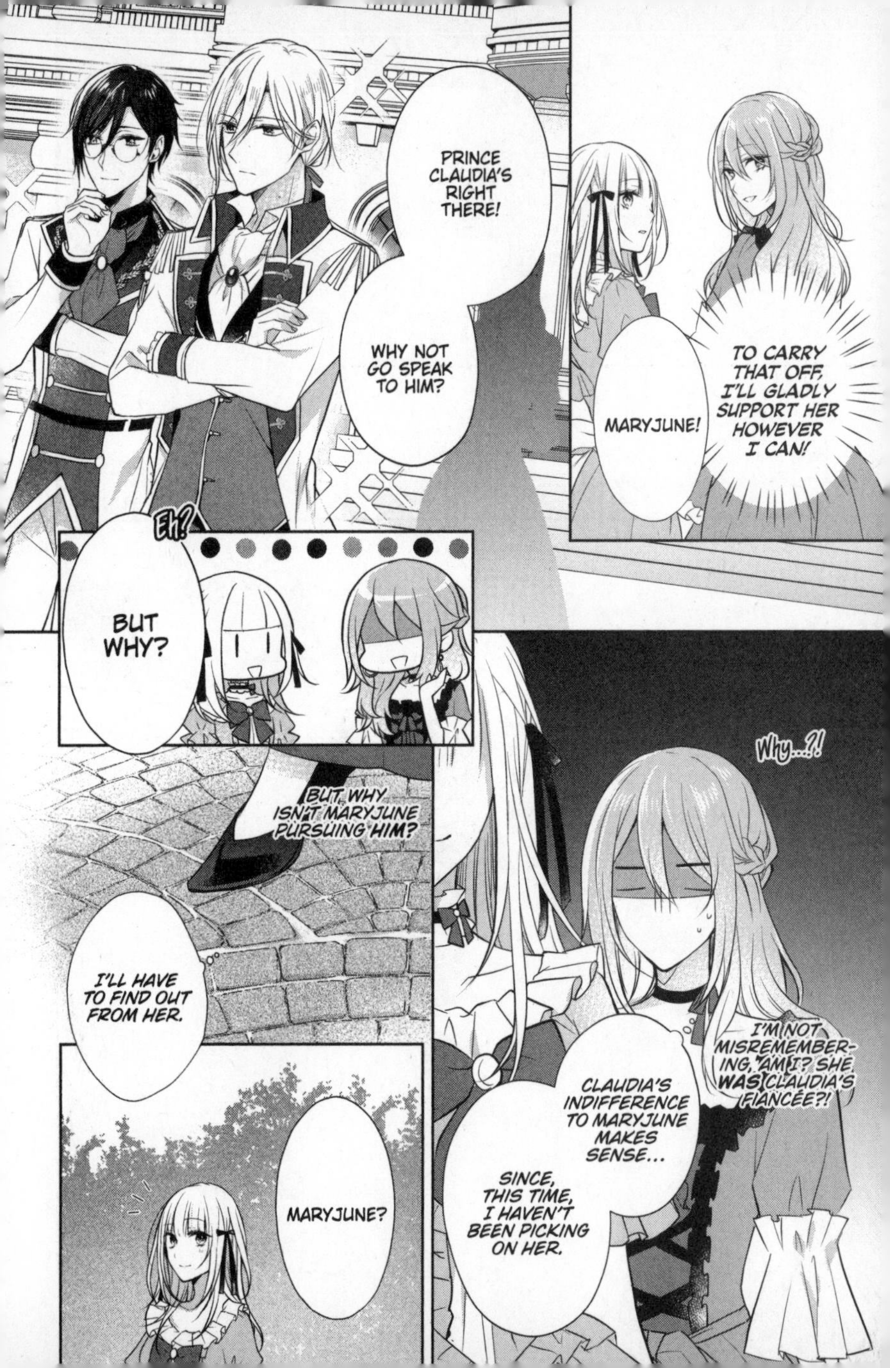
TO CARRY THAT OFF, I'LL GLADLY SUPPORT HER HOWEVER I CAN!
MARYJUNE!
PRINCE CLAUDIA'S RIGHT THERE!
WHY NOT GO SPEAK TO HIM?
Eh?
BUT WHY?
Why...?!
I'M NOT MISREMEMBERING, AM I? SHE WAS CLAUDIA'S FIANCÉE?!
CLAUDIA'S INDIFFERENCE TO MARYJUNE MAKES SENSE...
SINCE, THIS TIME, I HAVEN'T BEEN PICKING ON HER.
BUT WHY ISN'T MARYJUNE PURSUING HIM?
I'LL HAVE TO FIND OUT FROM HER.
MARYJUNE?

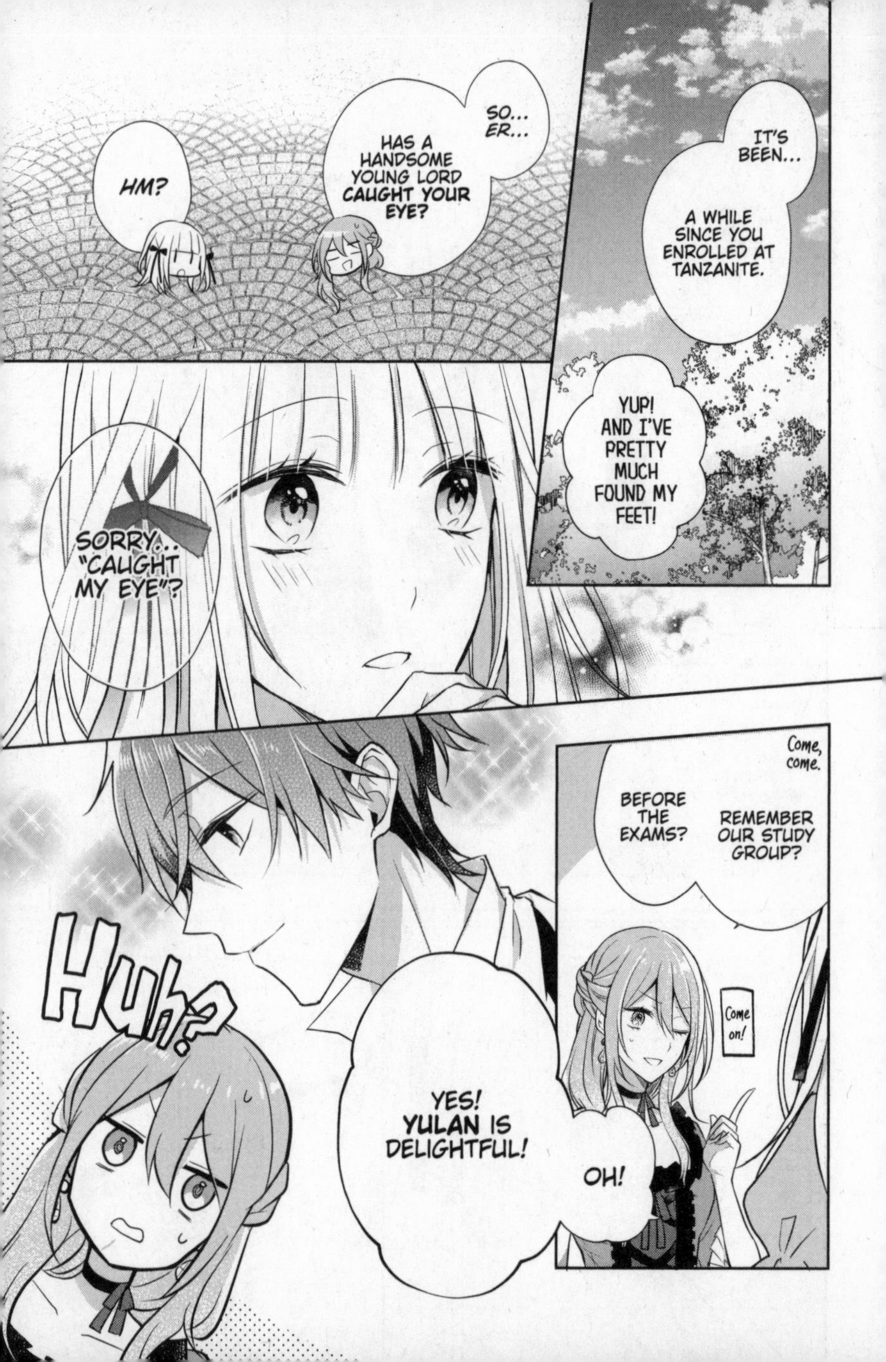
IT'S BEEN...
A WHILE SINCE YOU ENROLLED AT TANZANITE.
YUP! AND I'VE PRETTY MUCH FOUND MY FEET!
SO... ER...
HAS A HANDSOME YOUNG LORD CAUGHT YOUR EYE?
HM?
SORRY... "CAUGHT MY EYE"?
Come, come.
REMEMBER OUR STUDY GROUP?
BEFORE THE EXAMS?
Come on!
OH!
YES! YULAN IS DELIGHTFUL!
Huh?

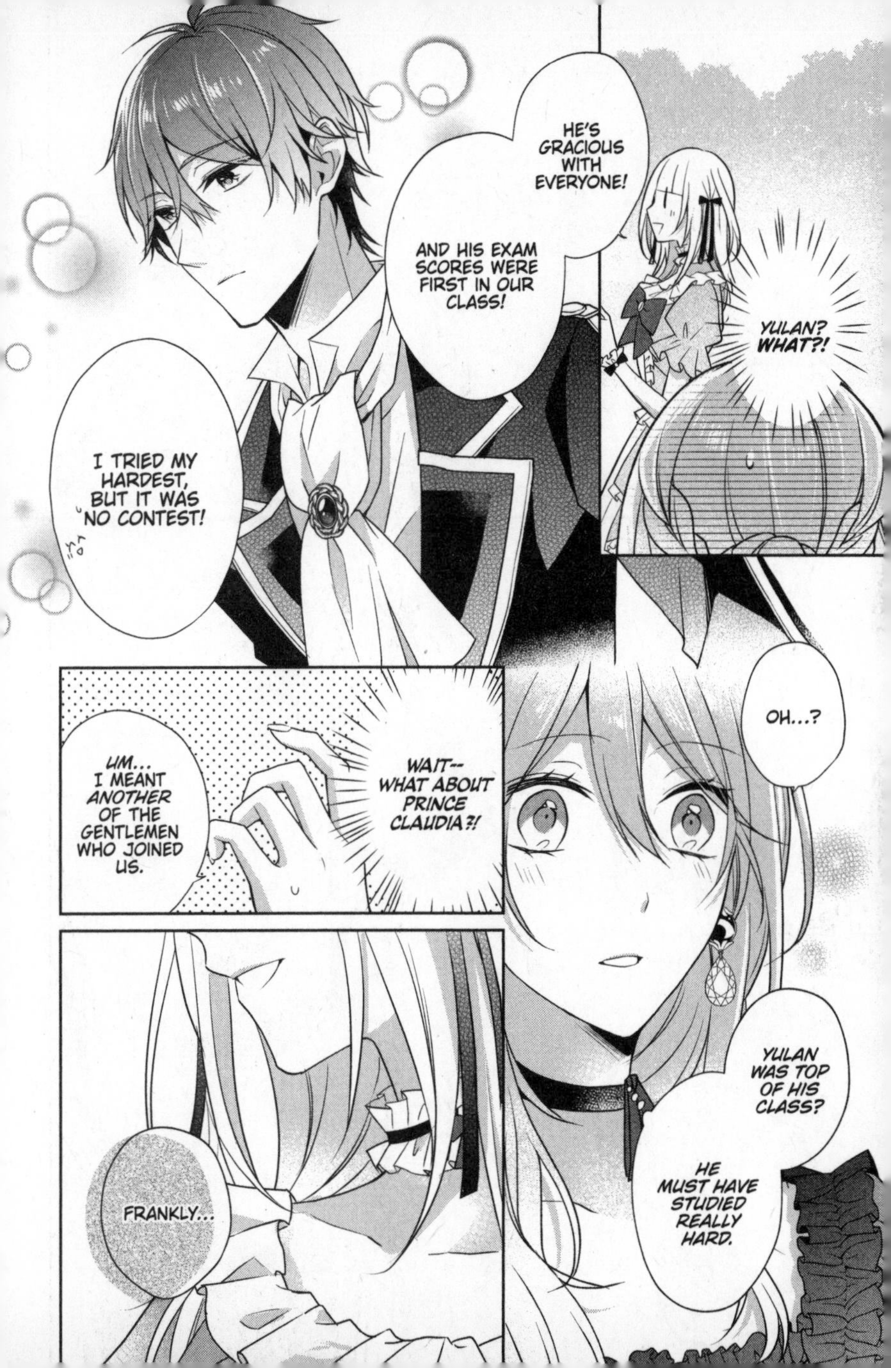
HE'S GRACIOUS WITH EVERYONE!
AND HIS EXAM SCORES WERE FIRST IN OUR CLASS!
YULAN? WHAT?!
I TRIED MY HARDEST, BUT IT WAS NO CONTEST!
OH...?
WAIT-- WHAT ABOUT PRINCE CLAUDIA?!
UM... I MEANT ANOTHER OF THE GENTLEMEN WHO JOINED US.
YULAN WAS TOP OF HIS CLASS?
HE MUST HAVE STUDIED REALLY HARD.
FRANKLY...

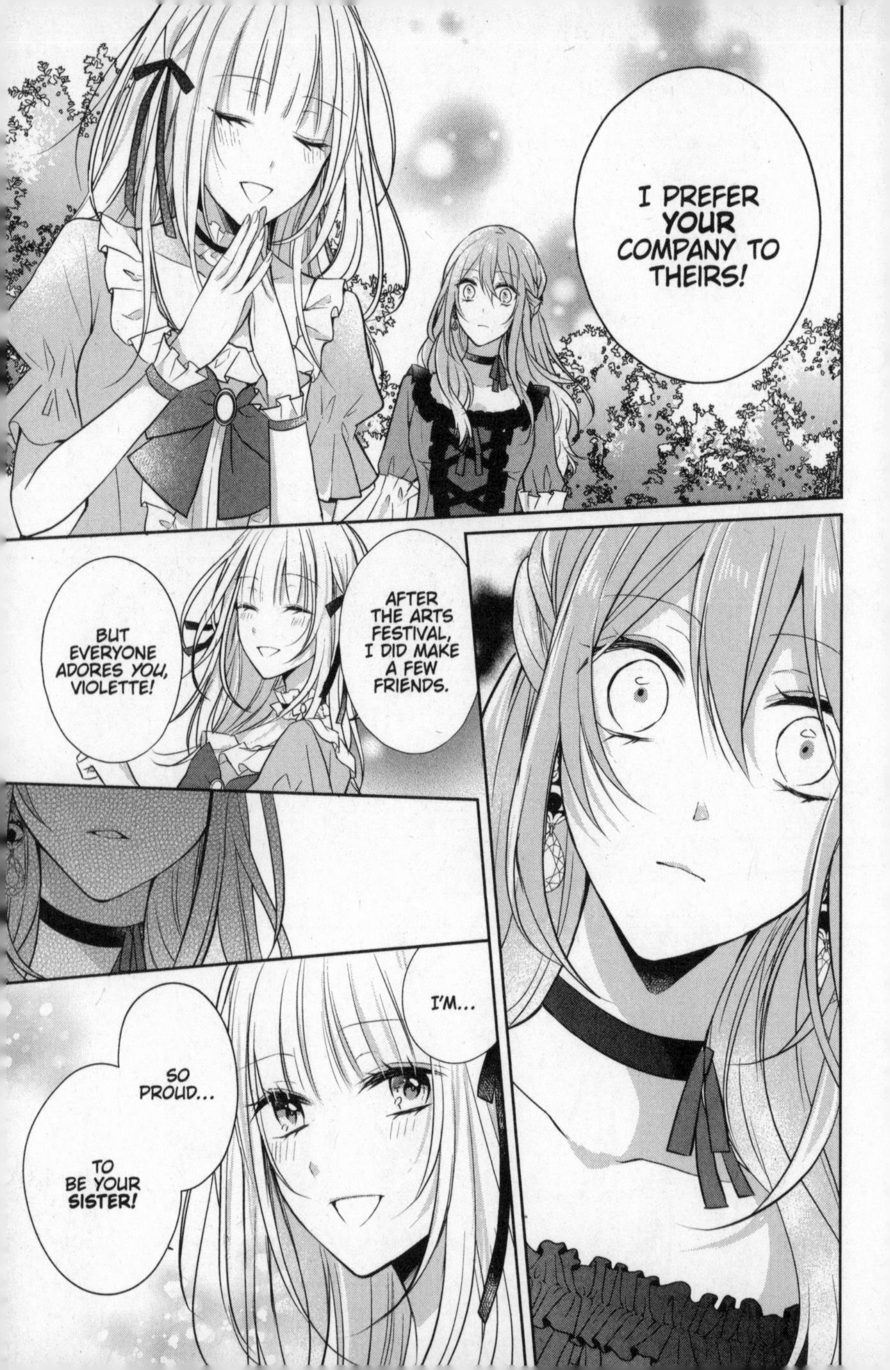
I PREFER YOUR COMPANY TO THEIRS!
AFTER THE ARTS FESTIVAL, I DID MAKE A FEW FRIENDS.
BUT EVERYONE ADORES YOU, VIOLETTE!
I'M...
SO PROUD...
TO BE YOUR SISTER!

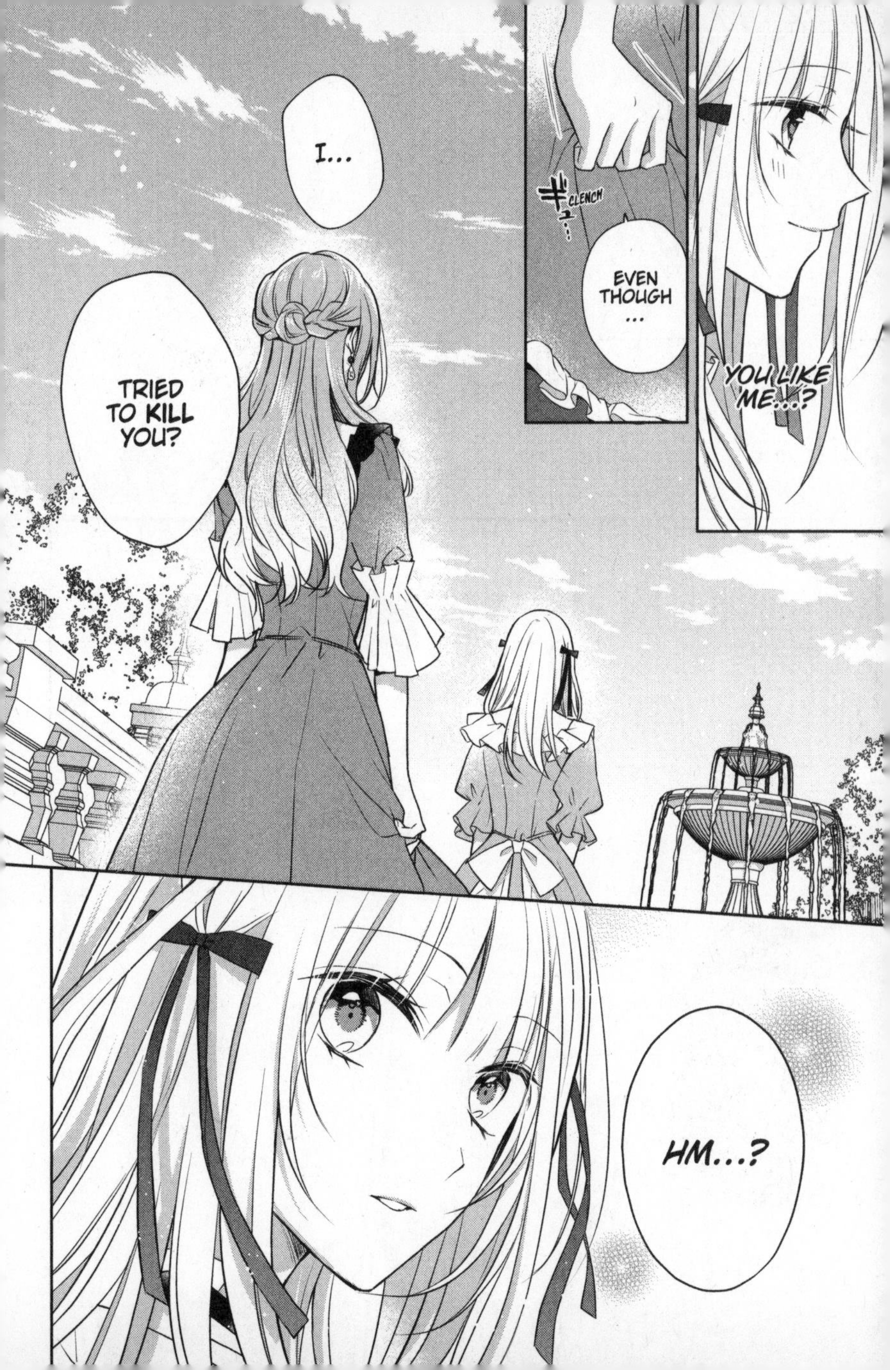
YOU LIKE ME...?
CLENCH
EVEN THOUGH ...
I...
TRIED TO KILL YOU?
HM...?

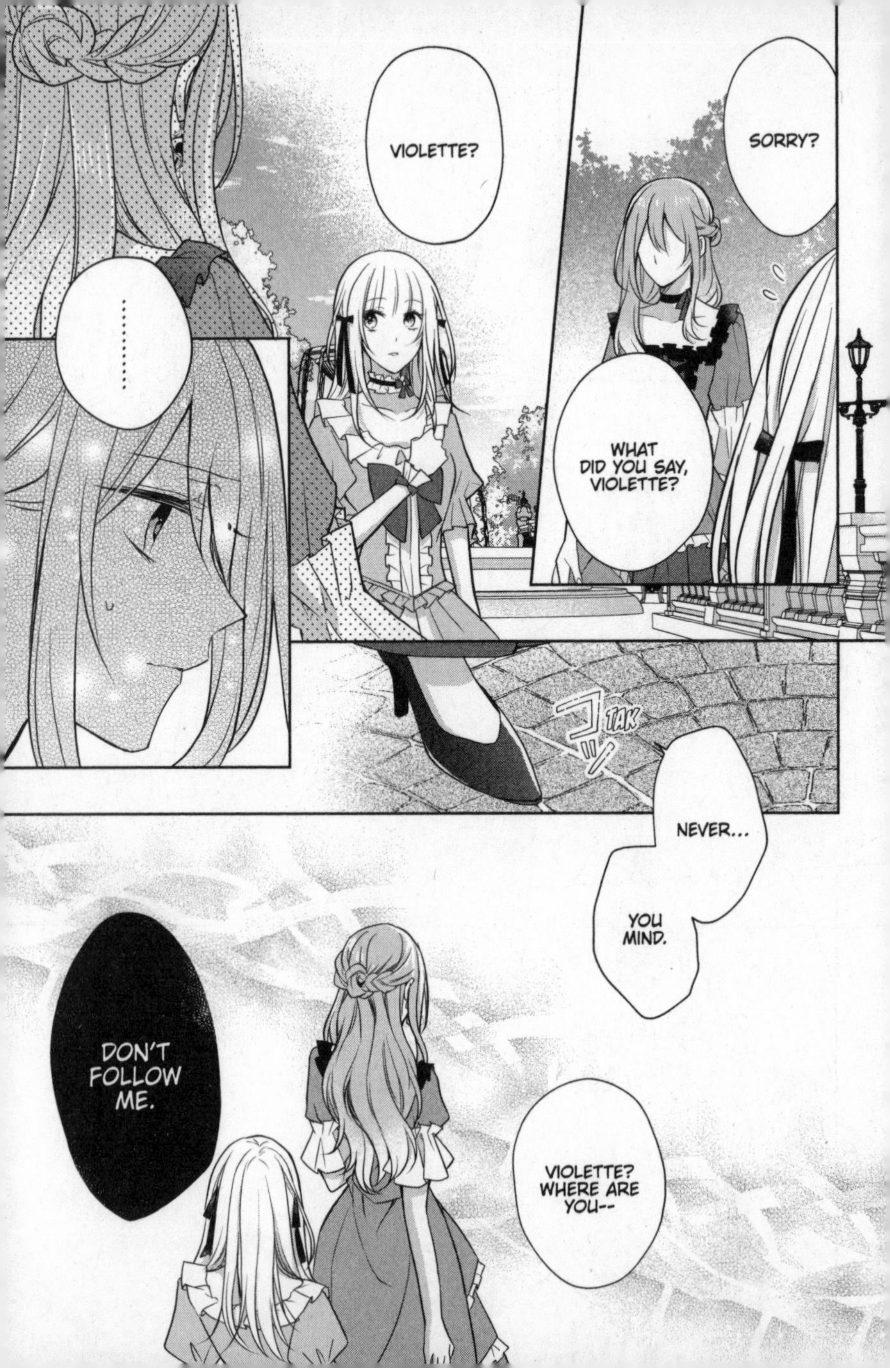
SORRY?
WHAT DID YOU SAY, VIOLETTE?
VIOLETTE?
......
TAK
NEVER...
YOU MIND.
VIOLETTE? WHERE ARE YOU--
DON'T FOLLOW ME.

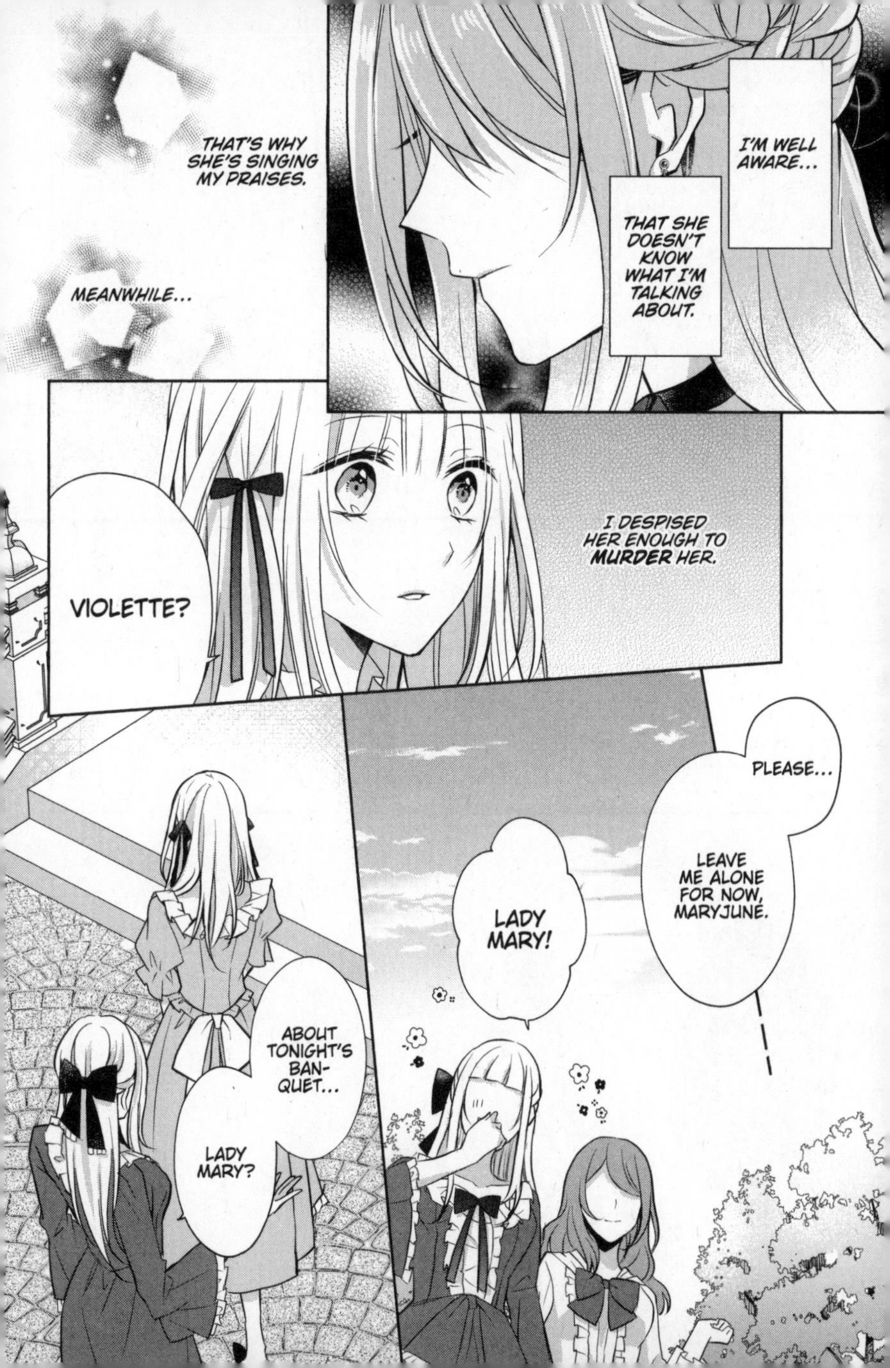
I'M WELL AWARE...
THAT SHE DOESN'T KNOW WHAT I'M TALKING ABOUT.
THAT'S WHY SHE'S SINGING MY PRAISES.
MEANWHILE...
I DESPISED HER ENOUGH TO MURDER HER.
VIOLETTE?
PLEASE...
LEAVE ME ALONE FOR NOW, MARYJUNE.
LADY MARY!
ABOUT TONIGHT'S BAN-QUET...
LADY MARY?

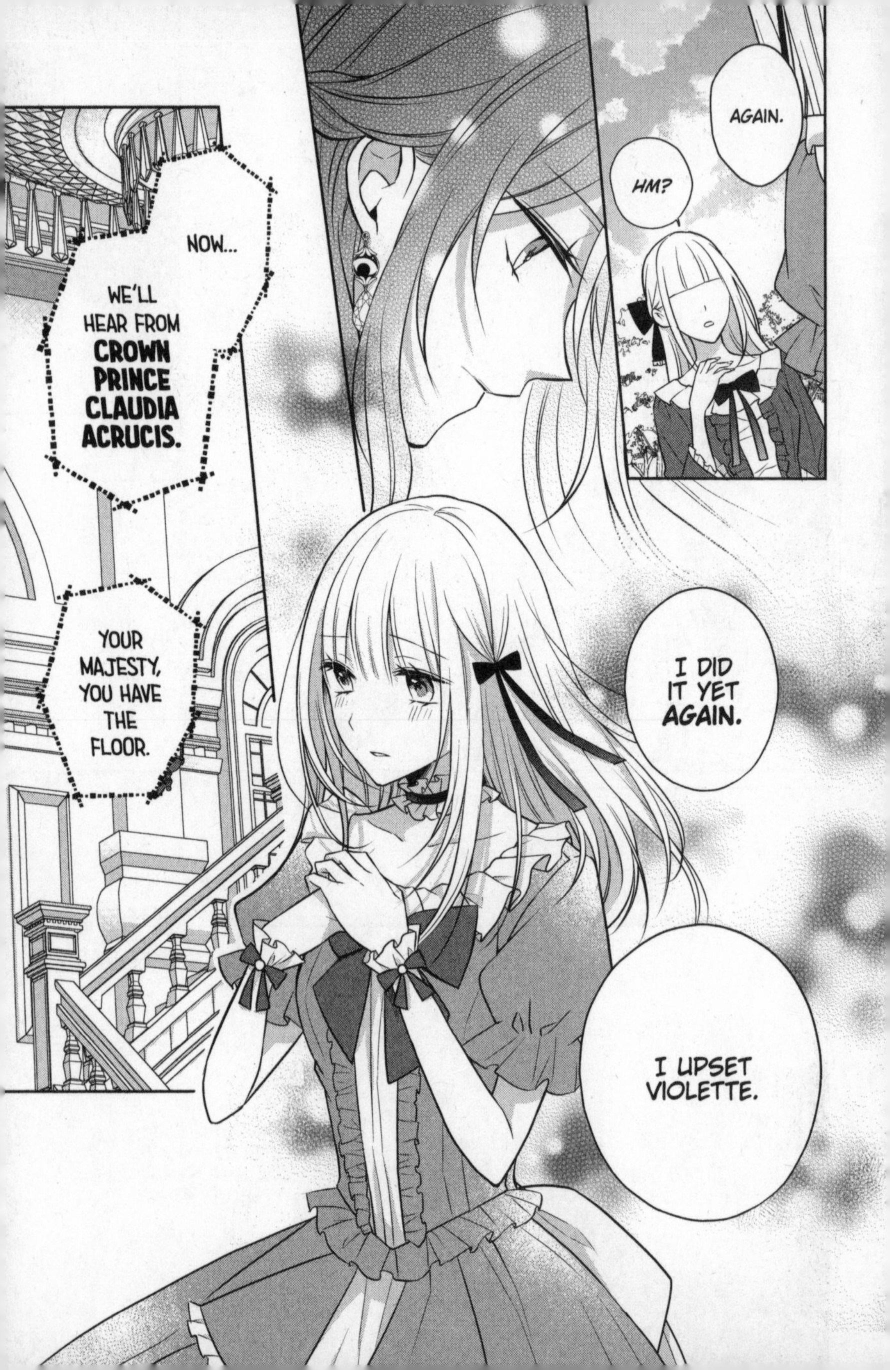
AGAIN.
HM?
I DID IT YET AGAIN.
I UPSET VIOLETTE.
NOW...
WE'LL HEAR FROM CROWN PRINCE CLAUDIA ACRUCIS.
YOUR MAJESTY, YOU HAVE THE FLOOR.

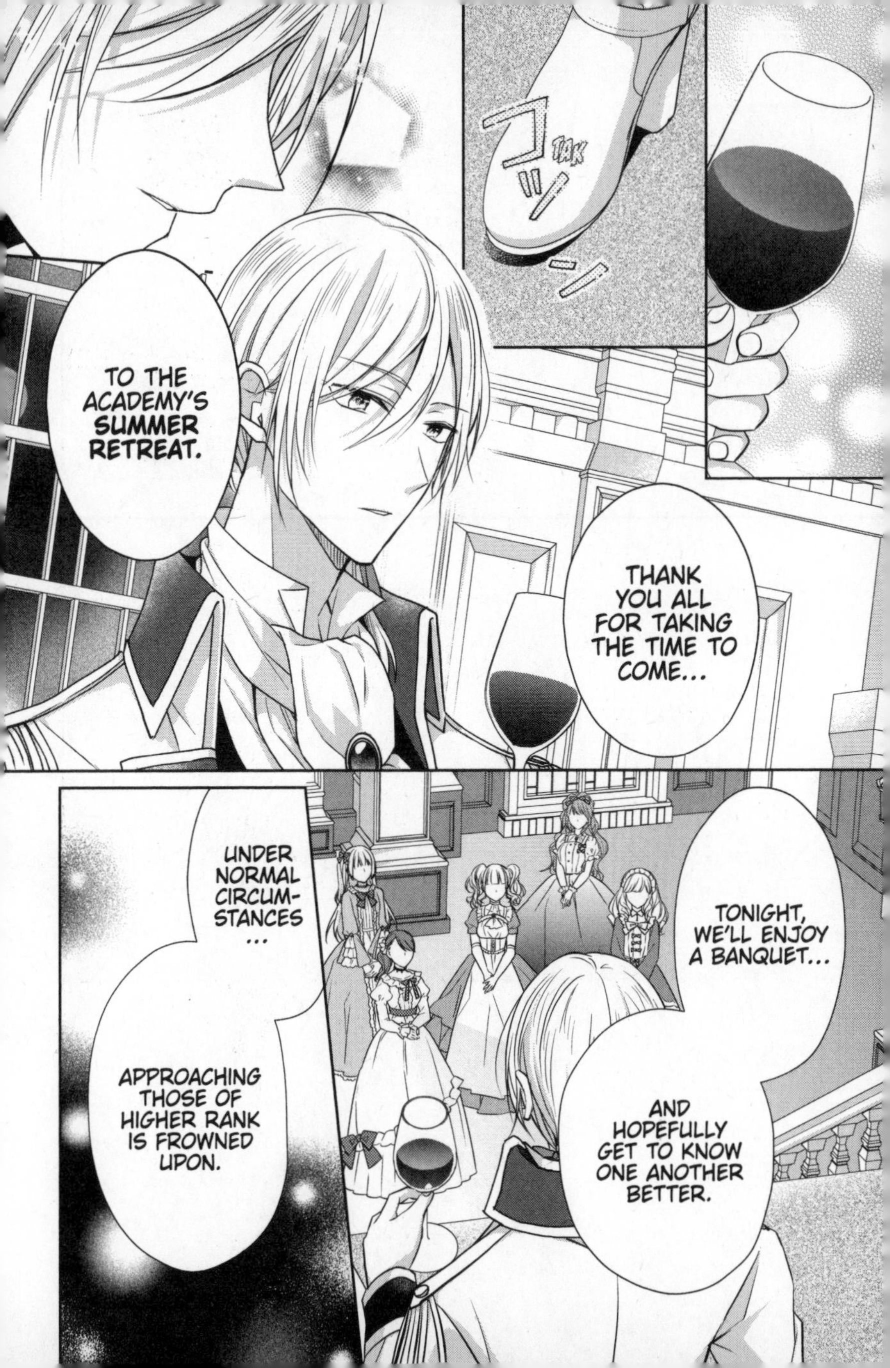
TAK
THANK YOU ALL FOR TAKING THE TIME TO COME...
TO THE ACADEMY'S SUMMER RETREAT.
TONIGHT, WE'LL ENJOY A BANQUET...
AND HOPEFULLY GET TO KNOW ONE ANOTHER BETTER.
UNDER NORMAL CIRCUM-STANCES...
APPROACHING THOSE OF HIGHER RANK IS FROWNED UPON.

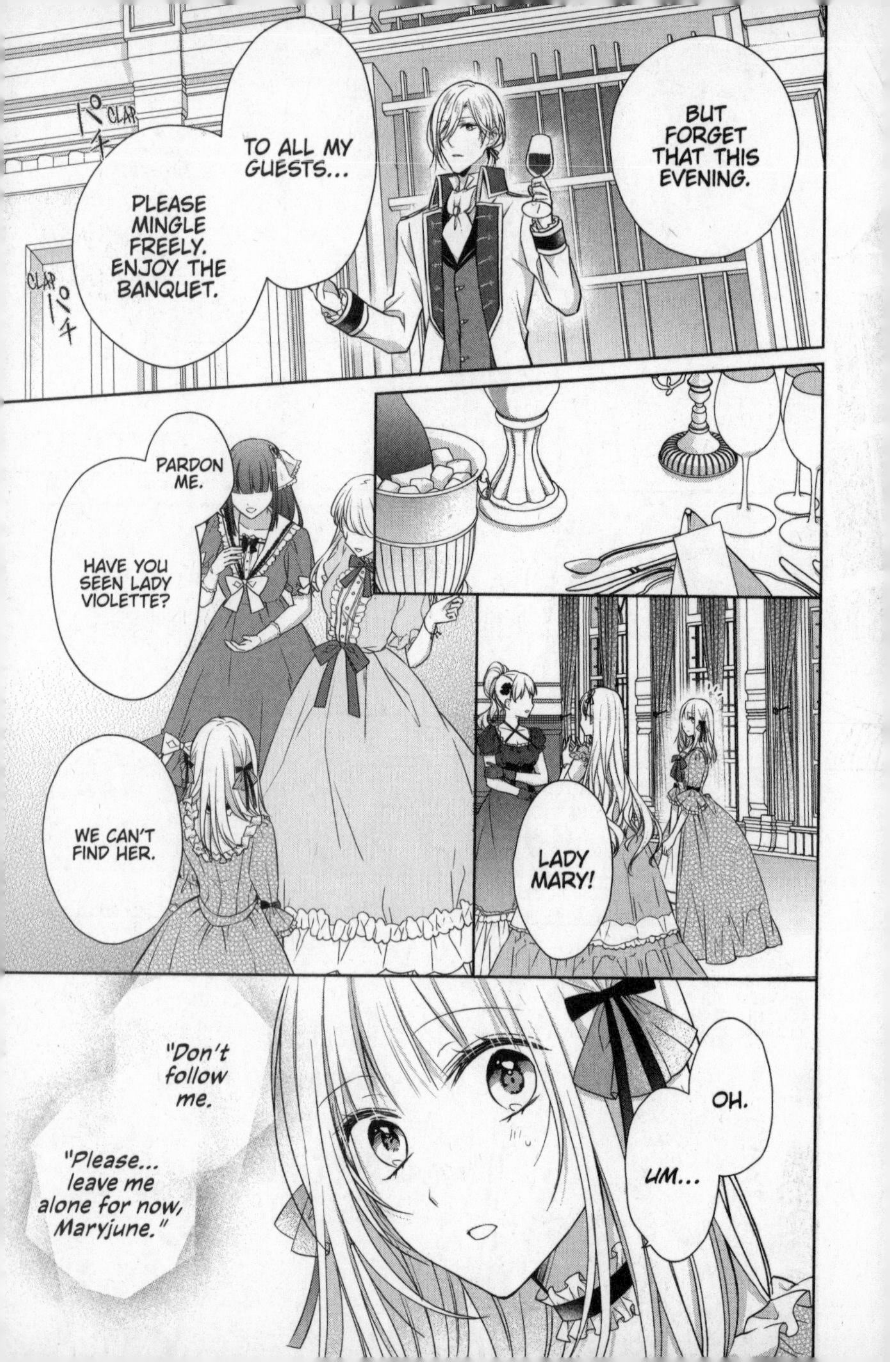

BUT FORGET THAT THIS EVENING.
TO ALL MY GUESTS...
PLEASE MINGLE FREELY. ENJOY THE BANQUET.
パチ CLAP
CLAP パチ
LADY MARY!
PARDON ME.
HAVE YOU SEEN LADY VIOLETTE?
WE CAN'T FIND HER.
OH.
UM...
"Don't follow me.
"Please... leave me alone for now, Maryjune."

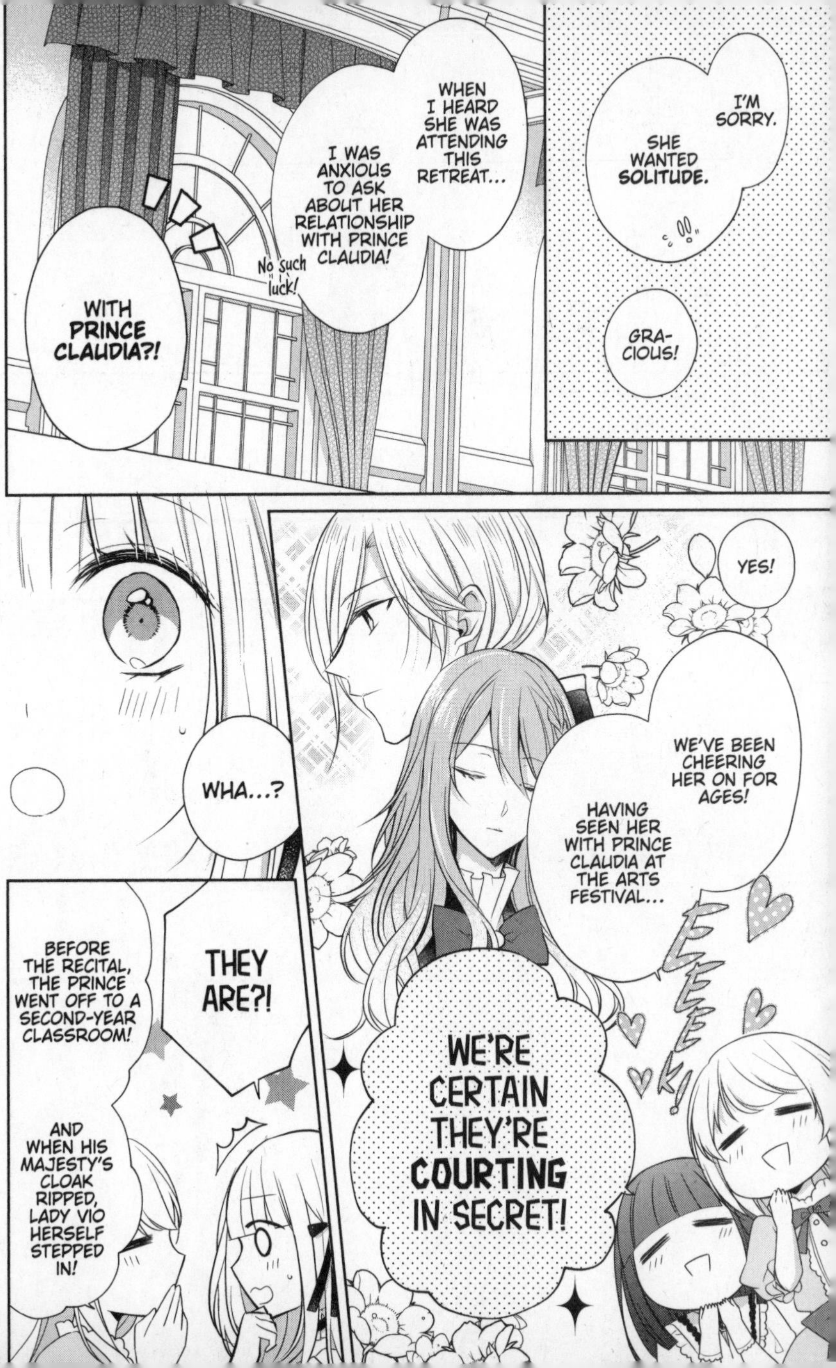

I'M SORRY.
SHE WANTED SOLITUDE.
GRA-CIOUS!
WHEN I HEARD SHE WAS ATTENDING THIS RETREAT...
I WAS ANXIOUS TO ASK ABOUT HER RELATIONSHIP WITH PRINCE CLAUDIA!
No such luck!
WITH PRINCE CLAUDIA?!
YES!
WE'VE BEEN CHEERING HER ON FOR AGES!
HAVING SEEN HER WITH PRINCE CLAUDIA AT THE ARTS FESTIVAL...
EEEEK!
WE'RE CERTAIN THEY'RE COURTING IN SECRET!
WHA...?
THEY ARE?!
BEFORE THE RECITAL, THE PRINCE WENT OFF TO A SECOND-YEAR CLASSROOM!
AND WHEN HIS MAJESTY'S CLOAK RIPPED, LADY VIO HERSELF STEPPED IN!

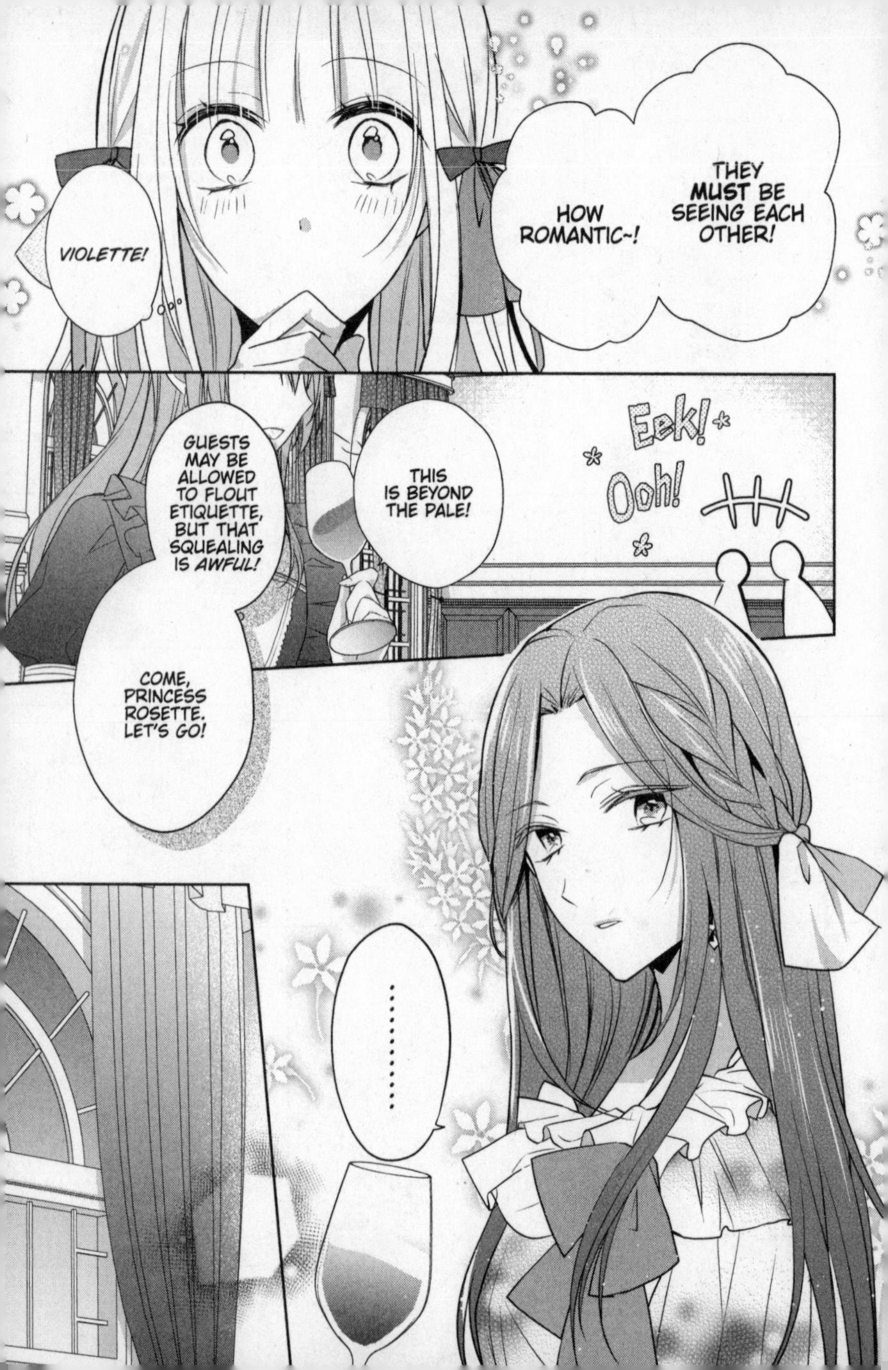
THEY MUST BE SEEING EACH OTHER!
HOW ROMANTIC~!
VIOLETTE!
Eek!
Ooh!
THIS IS BEYOND THE PALE!
GUESTS MAY BE ALLOWED TO FLOUT ETIQUETTE, BUT THAT SQUEALING IS *AWFUL!*
COME, PRINCESS ROSETTE. LET'S GO!
......

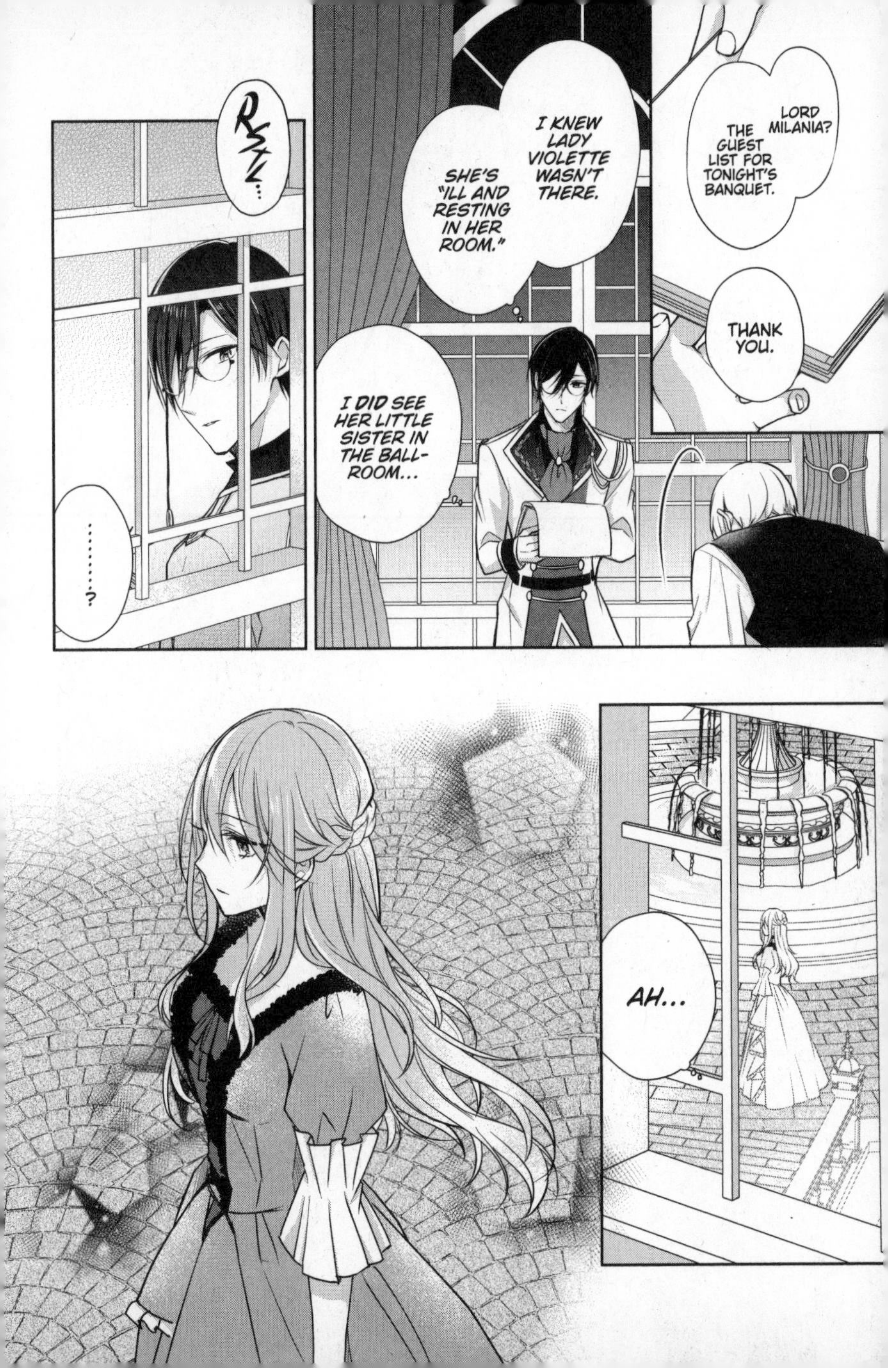
LORD MILANIA? THE GUEST LIST FOR TONIGHT'S BANQUET.
THANK YOU.
I KNEW LADY VIOLETTE WASN'T THERE.
SHE'S "ILL AND RESTING IN HER ROOM."
I DID SEE HER LITTLE SISTER IN THE BALL-ROOM...
RSTL...
......?
AH...

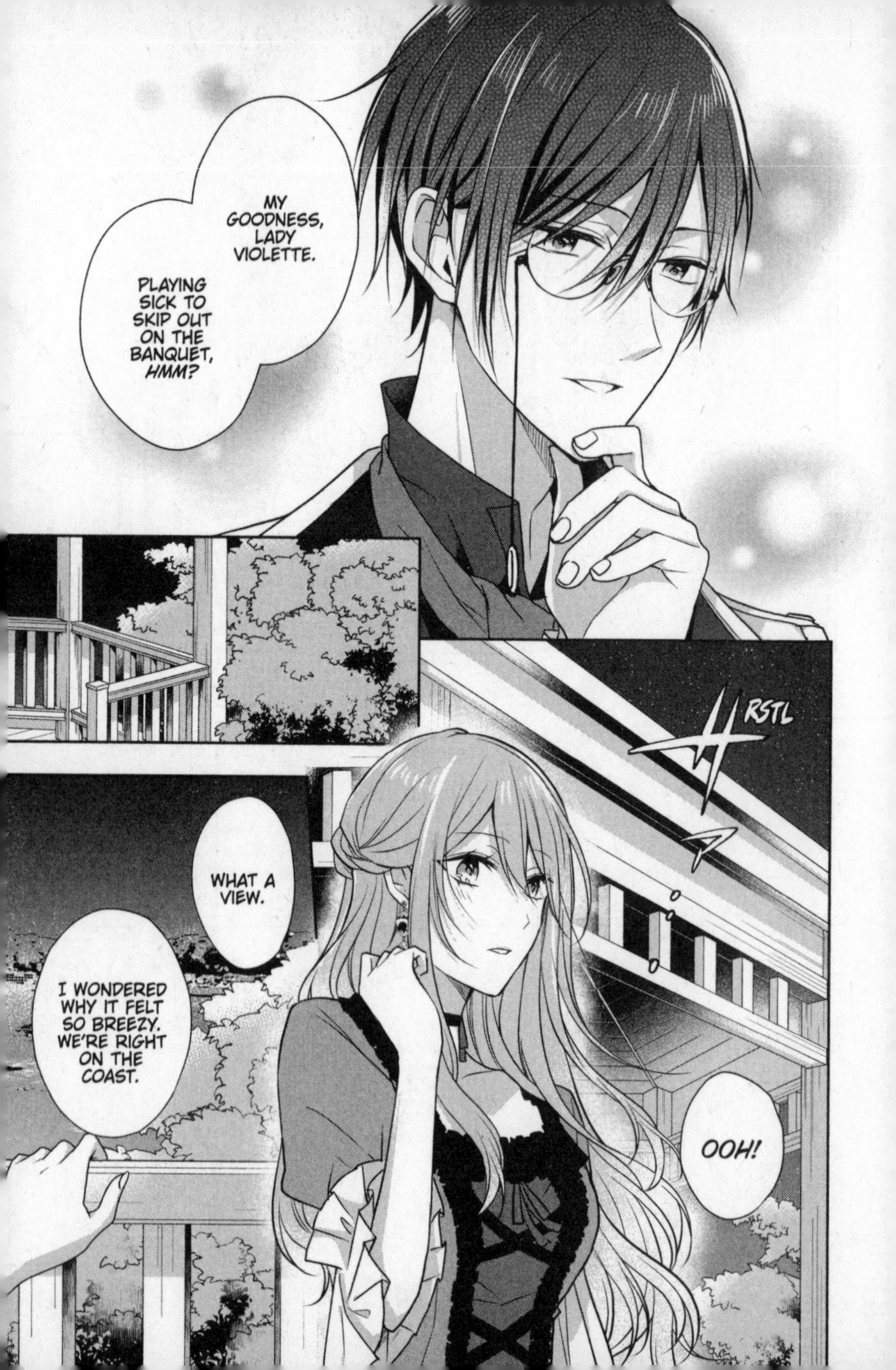
MY GOODNESS, LADY VIOLETTE.
PLAYING SICK TO SKIP OUT ON THE BANQUET, HMM?
RSTL
OOH!
WHAT A VIEW.
I WONDERED WHY IT FELT SO BREEZY. WE'RE RIGHT ON THE COAST.

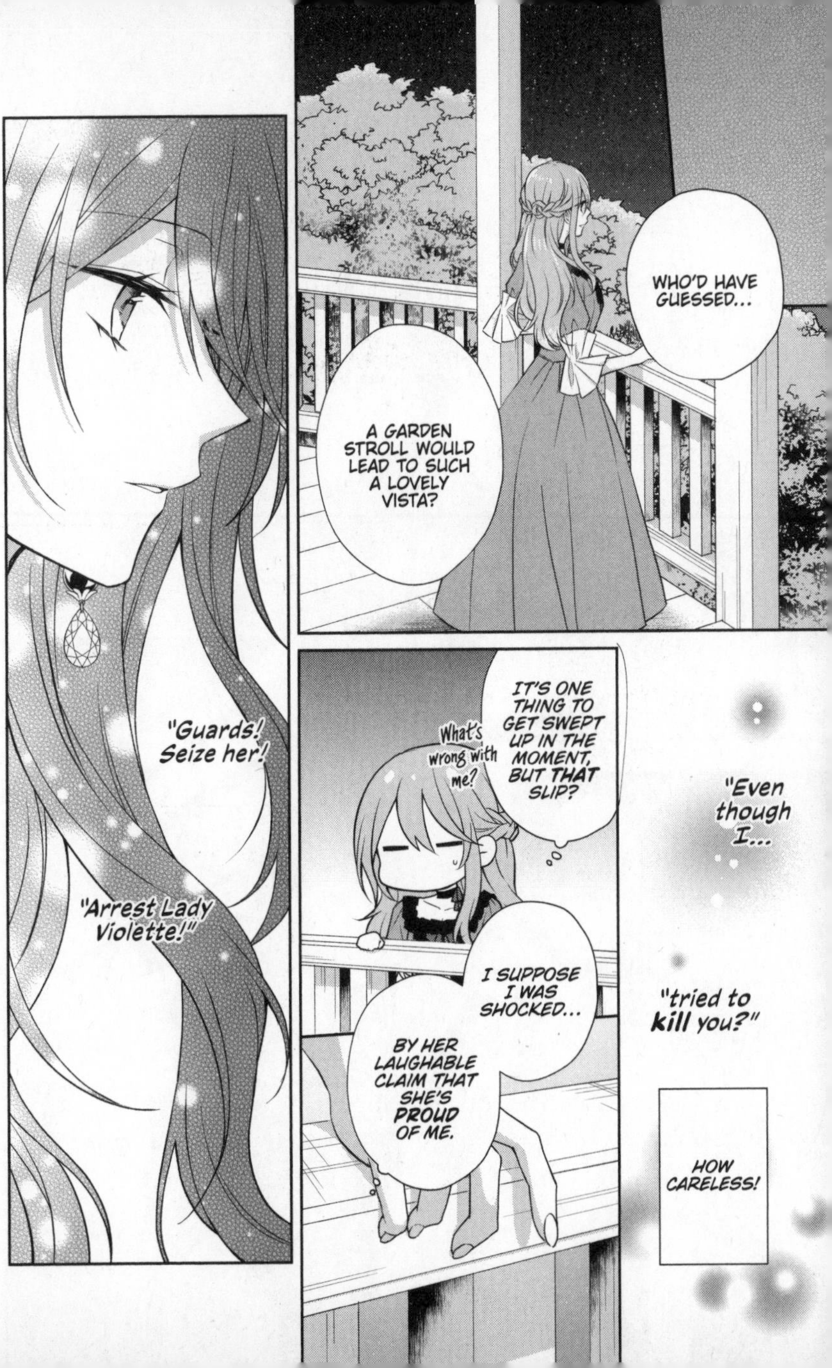
WHO'D HAVE GUESSED...
A GARDEN STROLL WOULD LEAD TO SUCH A LOVELY VISTA?
"Even though I...
"tried to kill you?"
HOW CARELESS!
IT'S ONE THING TO GET SWEPT UP IN THE MOMENT, BUT THAT SLIP?
What's wrong with me?
I SUPPOSE I WAS SHOCKED...
BY HER LAUGHABLE CLAIM THAT SHE'S PROUD OF ME.
"Guards! Seize her!
"Arrest Lady Violette!"

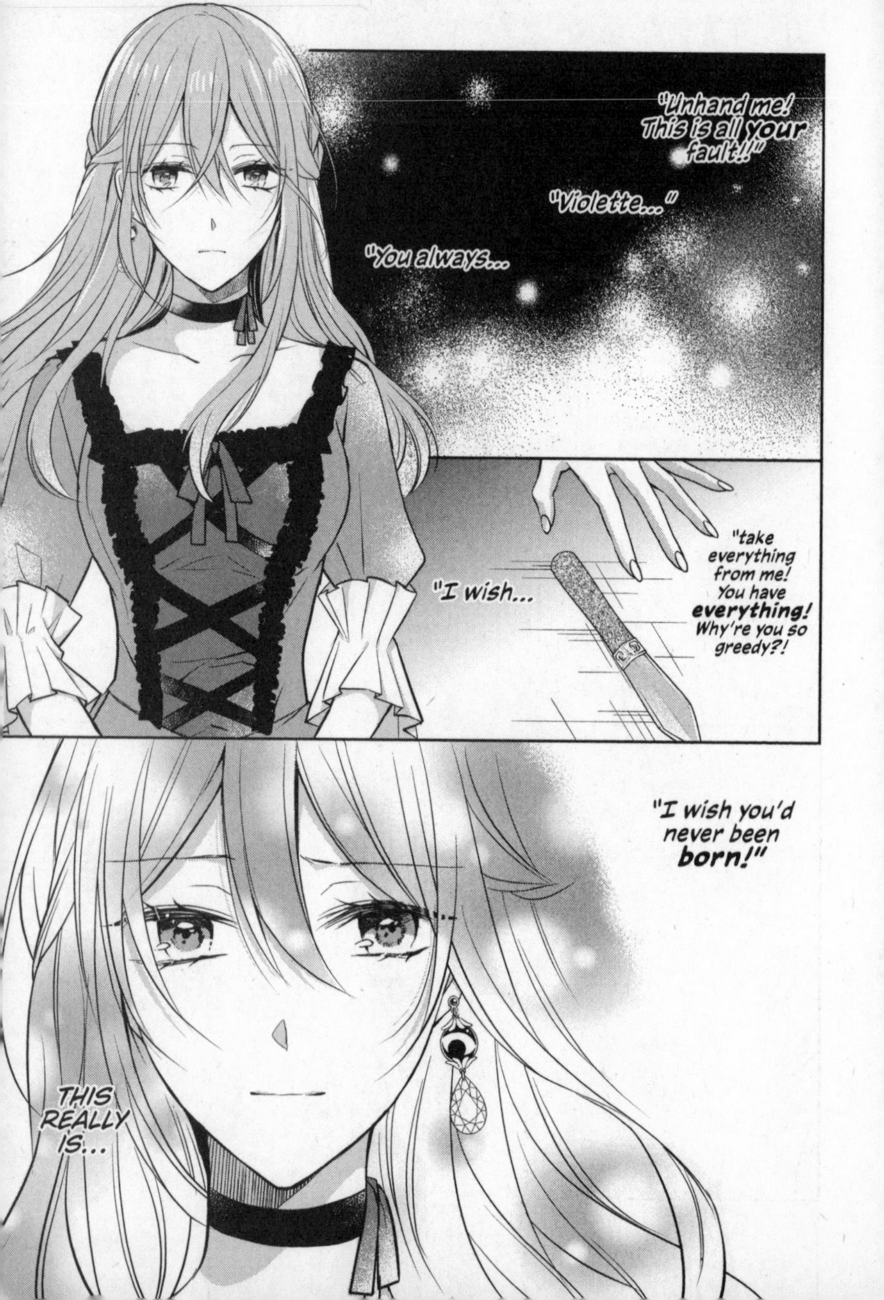
"Unhand me! This is all your fault!!"
"Violette..."
"You always...
"take everything from me! You have everything! Why're you so greedy?!
"I wish...
"I wish you'd never been born!"
THIS REALLY IS...

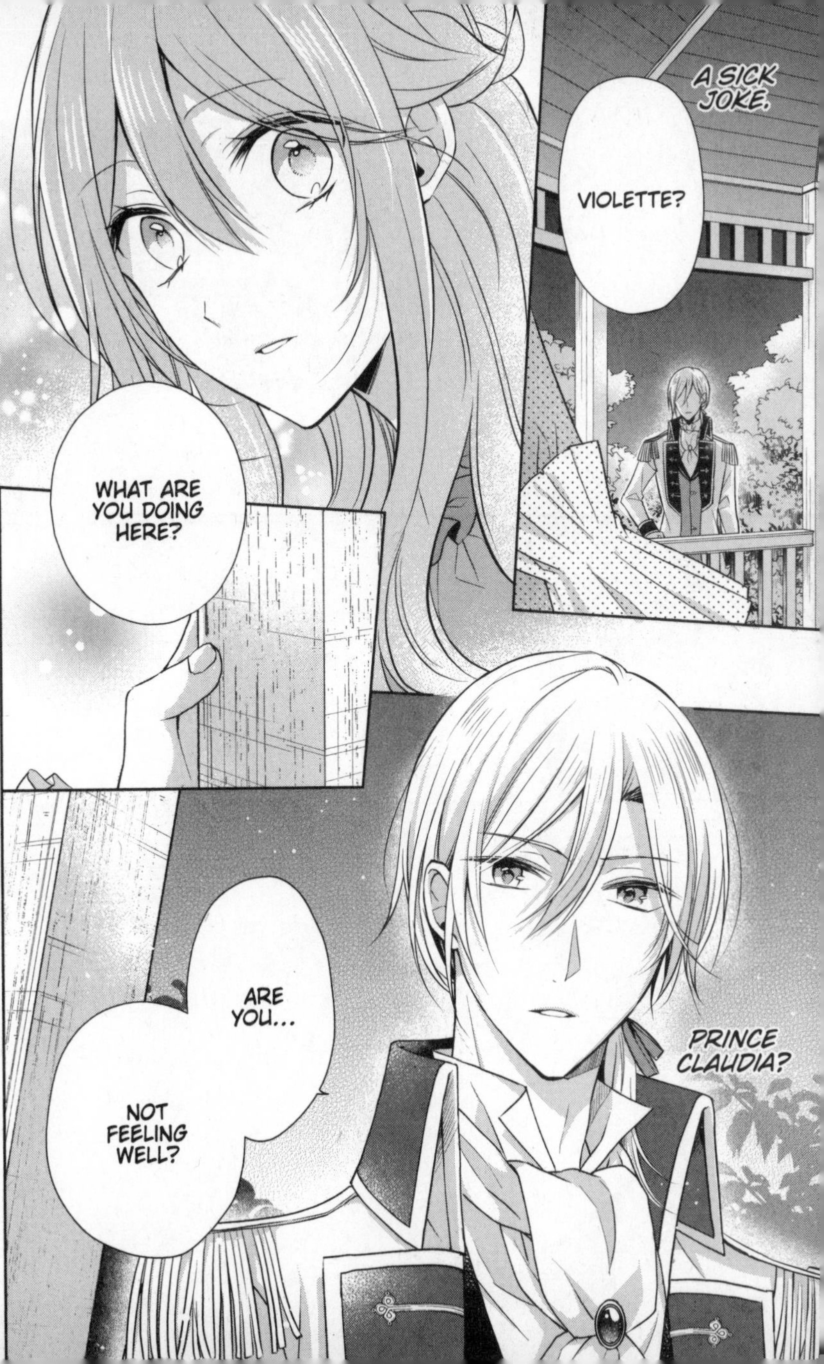

A SICK JOKE.
VIOLETTE?
WHAT ARE YOU DOING HERE?
PRINCE CLAUDIA?
ARE YOU...
NOT FEELING WELL?

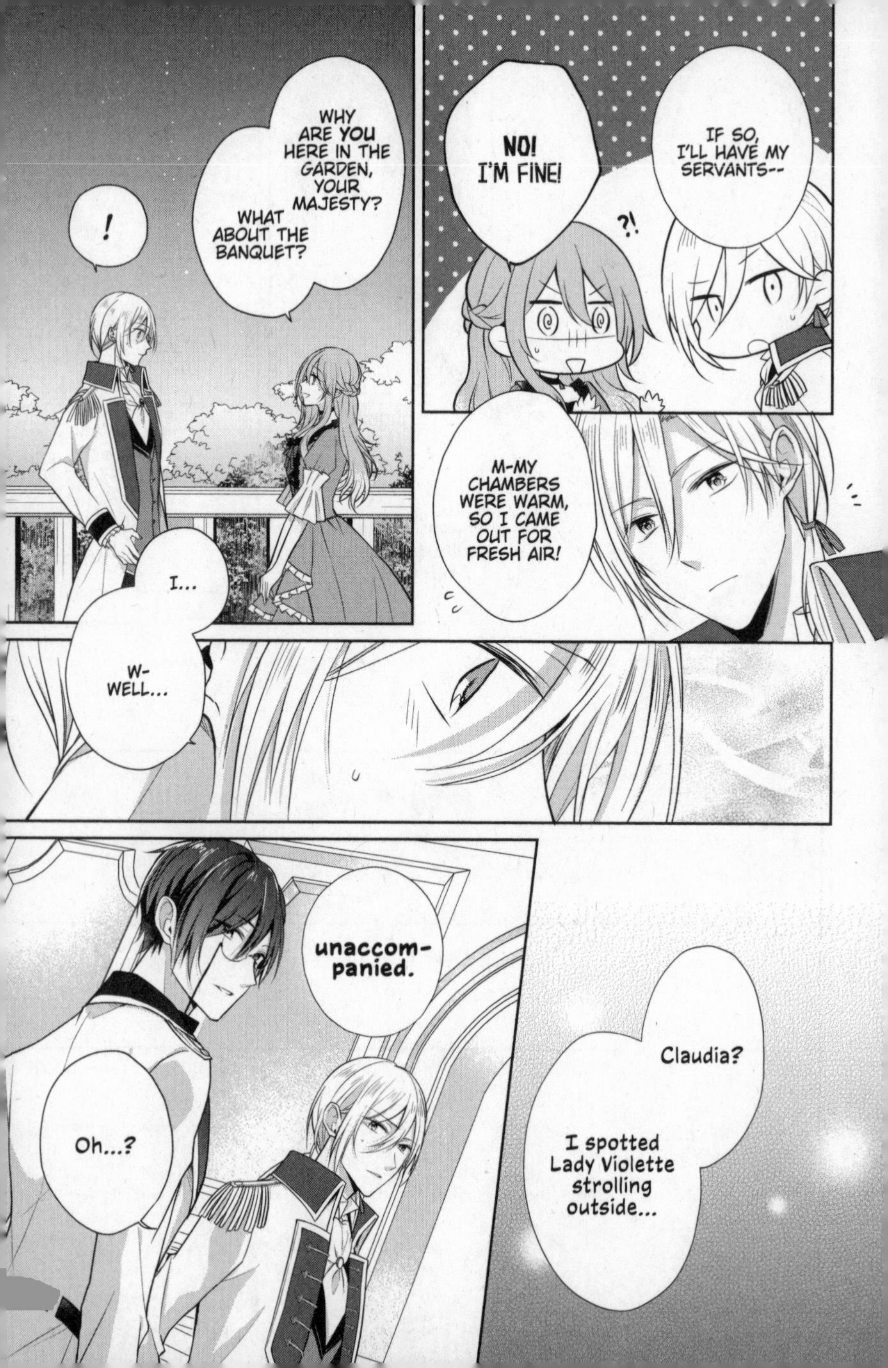
!
WHY ARE YOU HERE IN THE GARDEN, YOUR MAJESTY?
WHAT ABOUT THE BANQUET?
I...
W-WELL...
M-MY CHAMBERS WERE WARM, SO I CAME OUT FOR FRESH AIR!
IF SO, I'LL HAVE MY SERVANTS--
?!
NO! I'M FINE!
Claudia?
I spotted Lady Violette strolling outside...
unaccompanied.
Oh...?

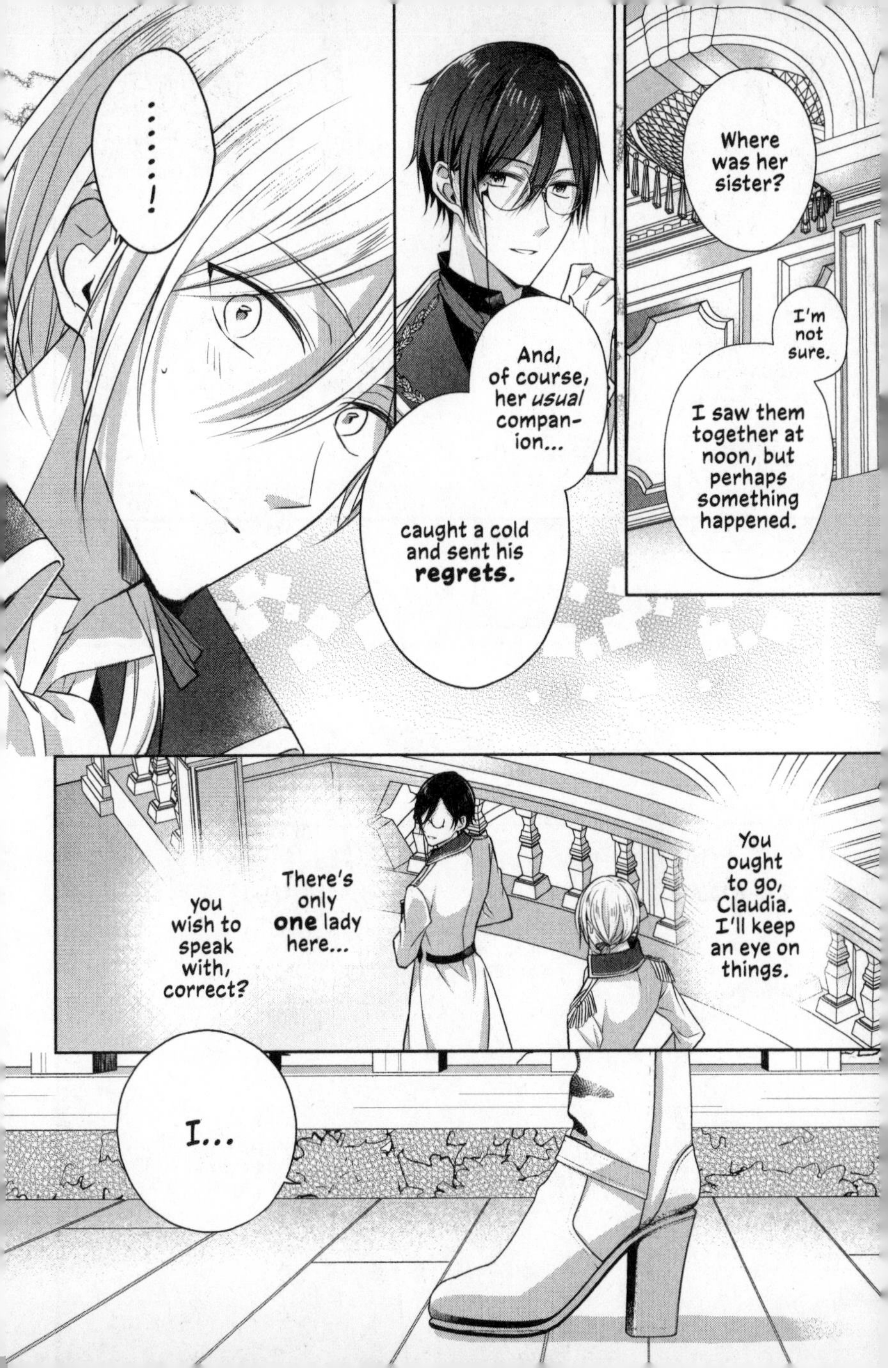
Where was her sister?
I'm not sure.
I saw them together at noon, but perhaps something happened.
And, of course, her *usual* companion...
caught a cold and sent his **regrets.**
......!
You ought to go, Claudia. I'll keep an eye on things.
There's only **one** lady here...
you wish to speak with, correct?
I...

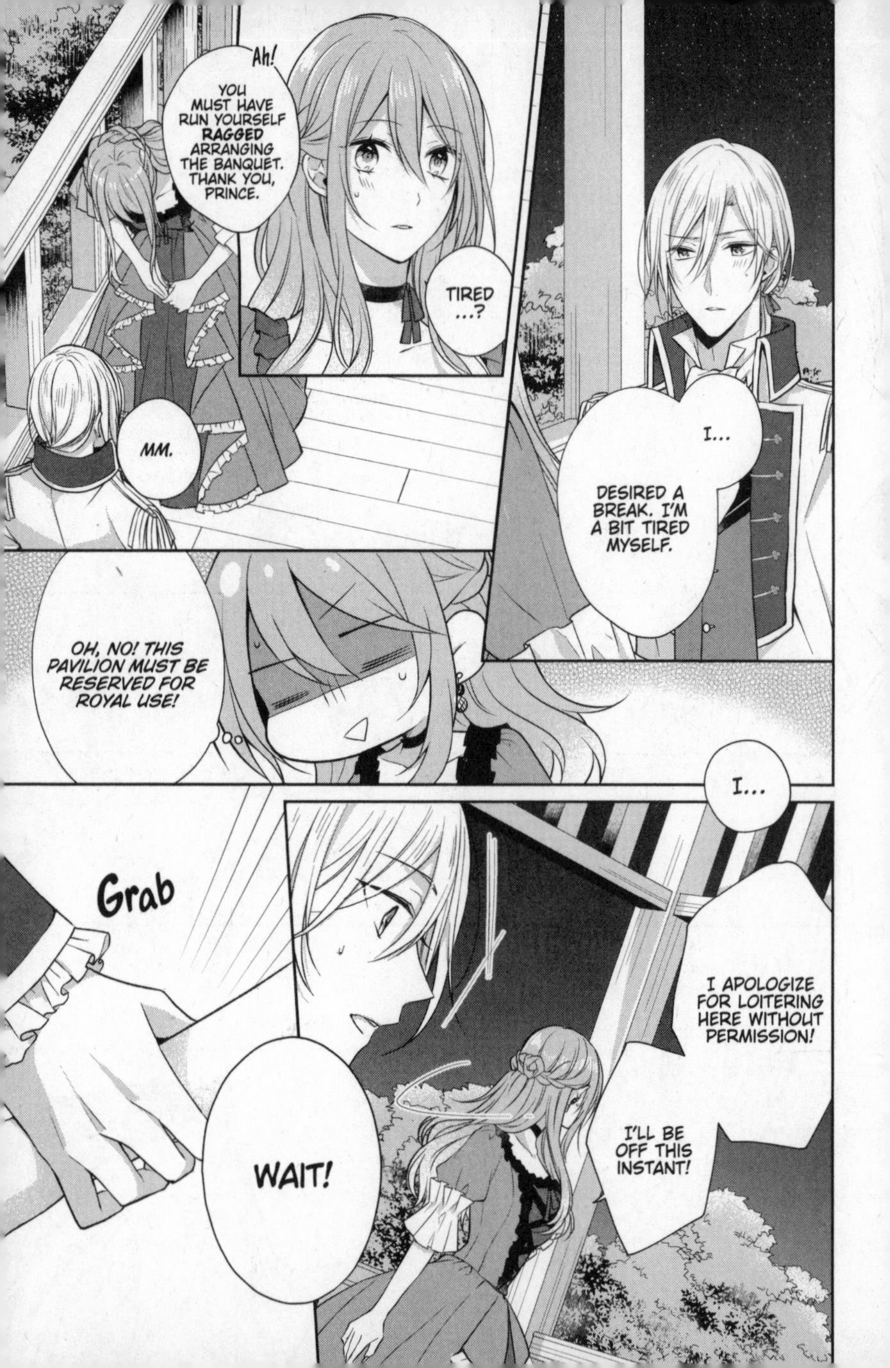
Ah!
YOU MUST HAVE RUN YOURSELF RAGGED ARRANGING THE BANQUET. THANK YOU, PRINCE.
MM.
TIRED ...?
I...
DESIRED A BREAK. I'M A BIT TIRED MYSELF.
OH, NO! THIS PAVILION MUST BE RESERVED FOR ROYAL USE!
I...
I APOLOGIZE FOR LOITERING HERE WITHOUT PERMISSION!
I'LL BE OFF THIS INSTANT!
Grab
WAIT!

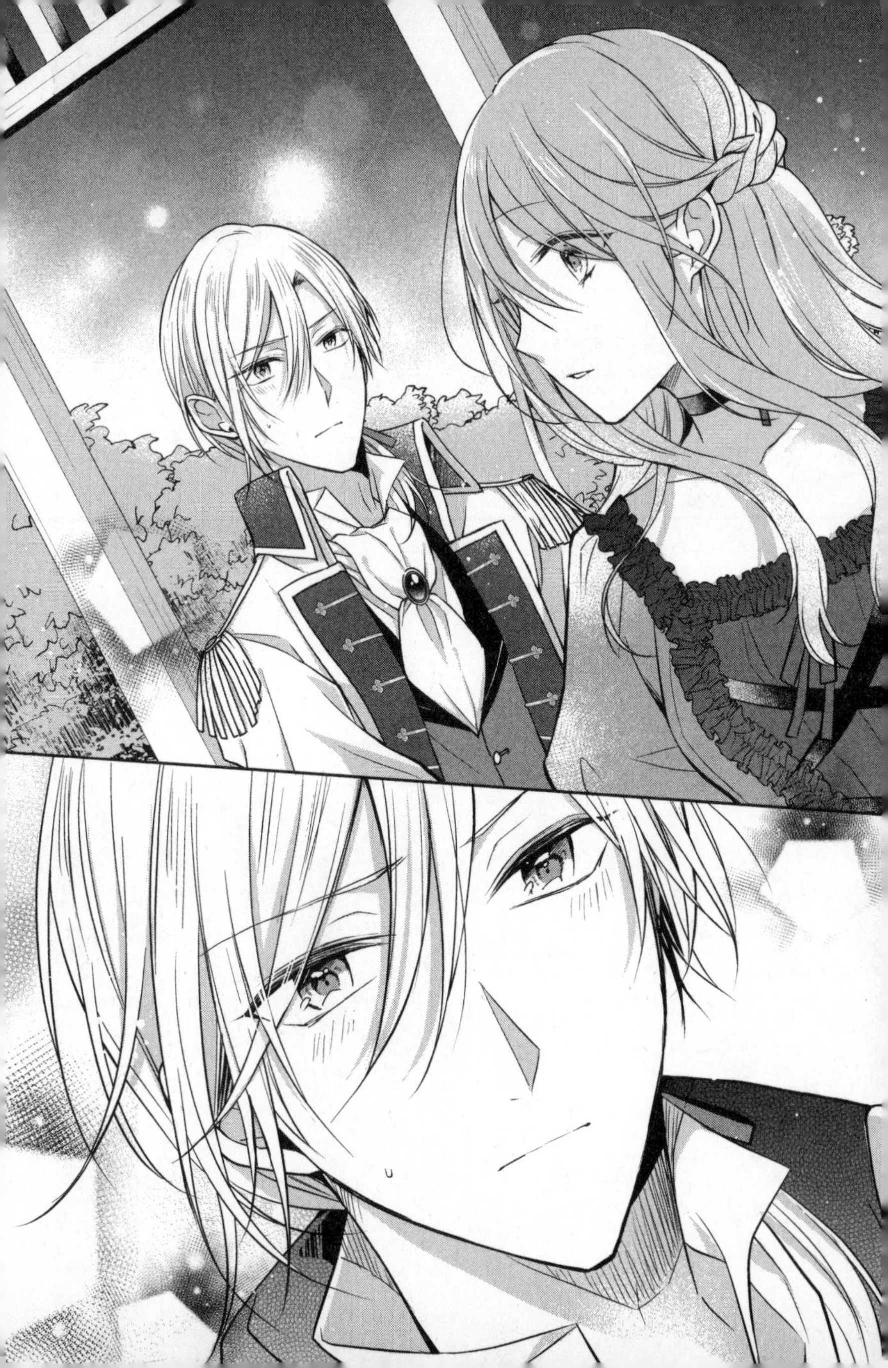

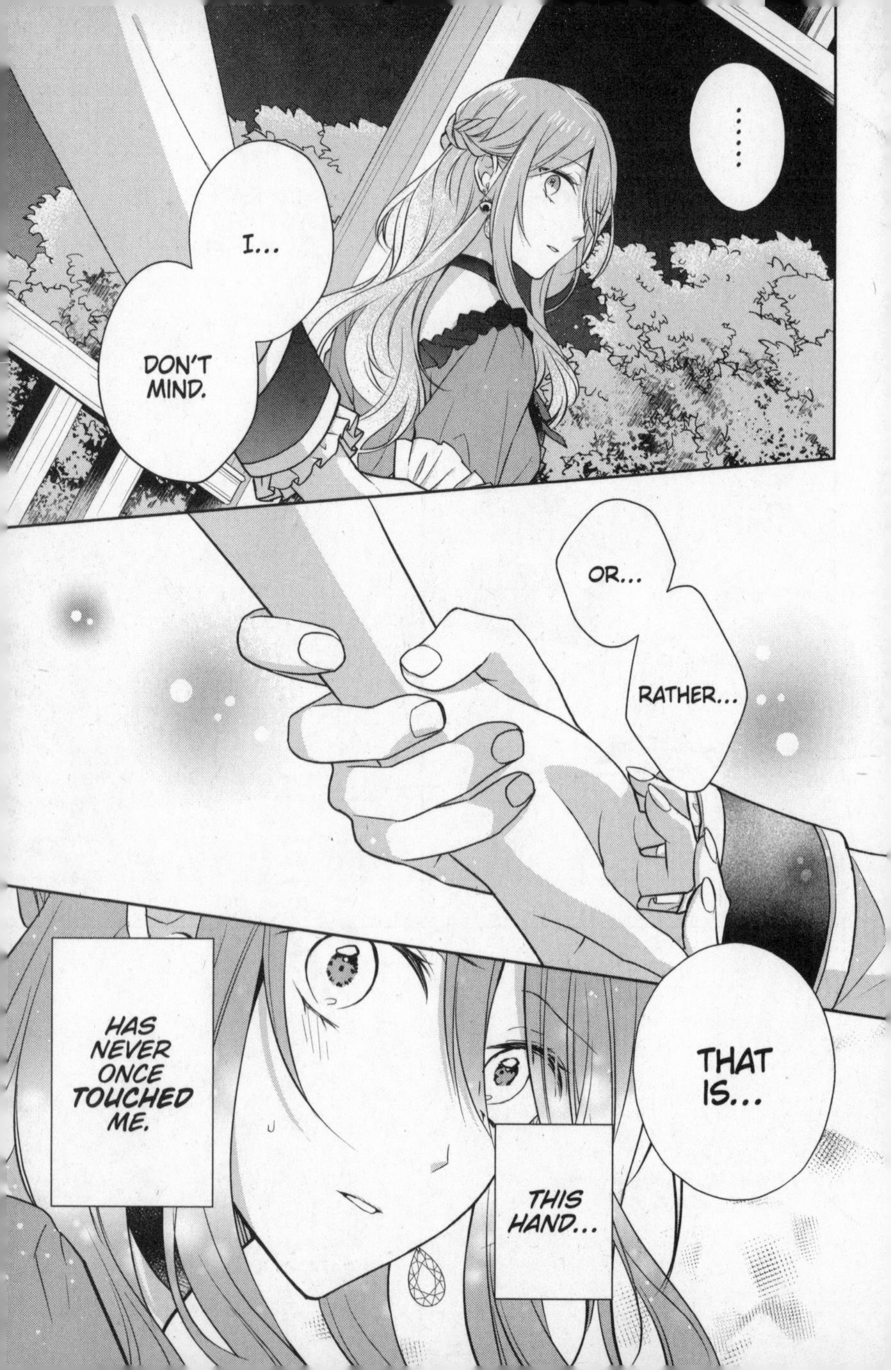
......
I... DON'T MIND.
OR... RATHER...
THAT IS...
THIS HAND...
HAS NEVER ONCE TOUCHED ME.

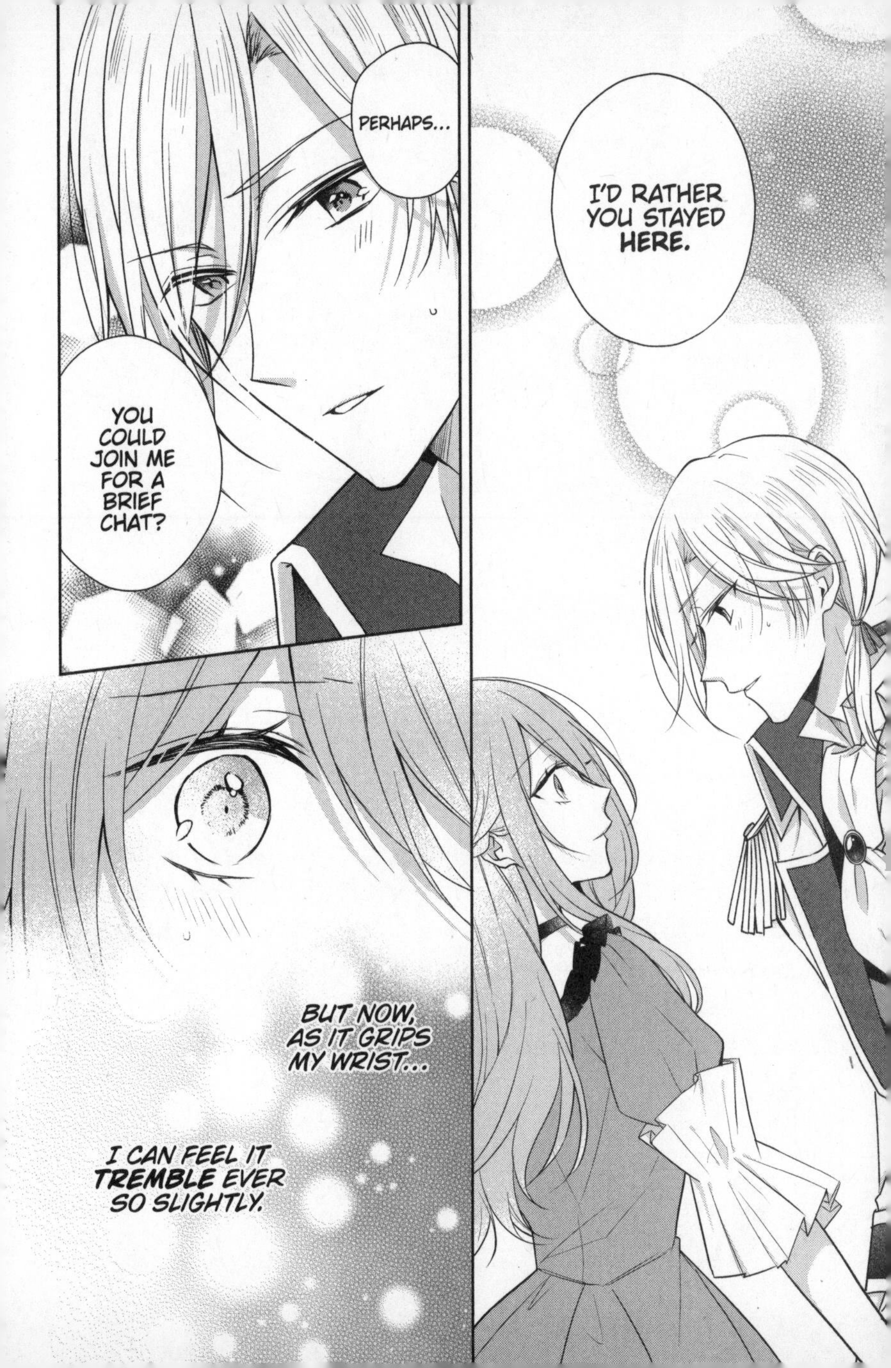
I'D RATHER YOU STAYED HERE.
PERHAPS...
YOU COULD JOIN ME FOR A BRIEF CHAT?
BUT NOW, AS IT GRIPS MY WRIST...
I CAN FEEL IT TREMBLE EVER SO SLIGHTLY.

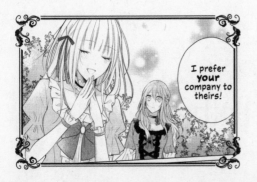

I prefer **your** company to theirs!

# I Swear I Won't Bother You AGAIN!

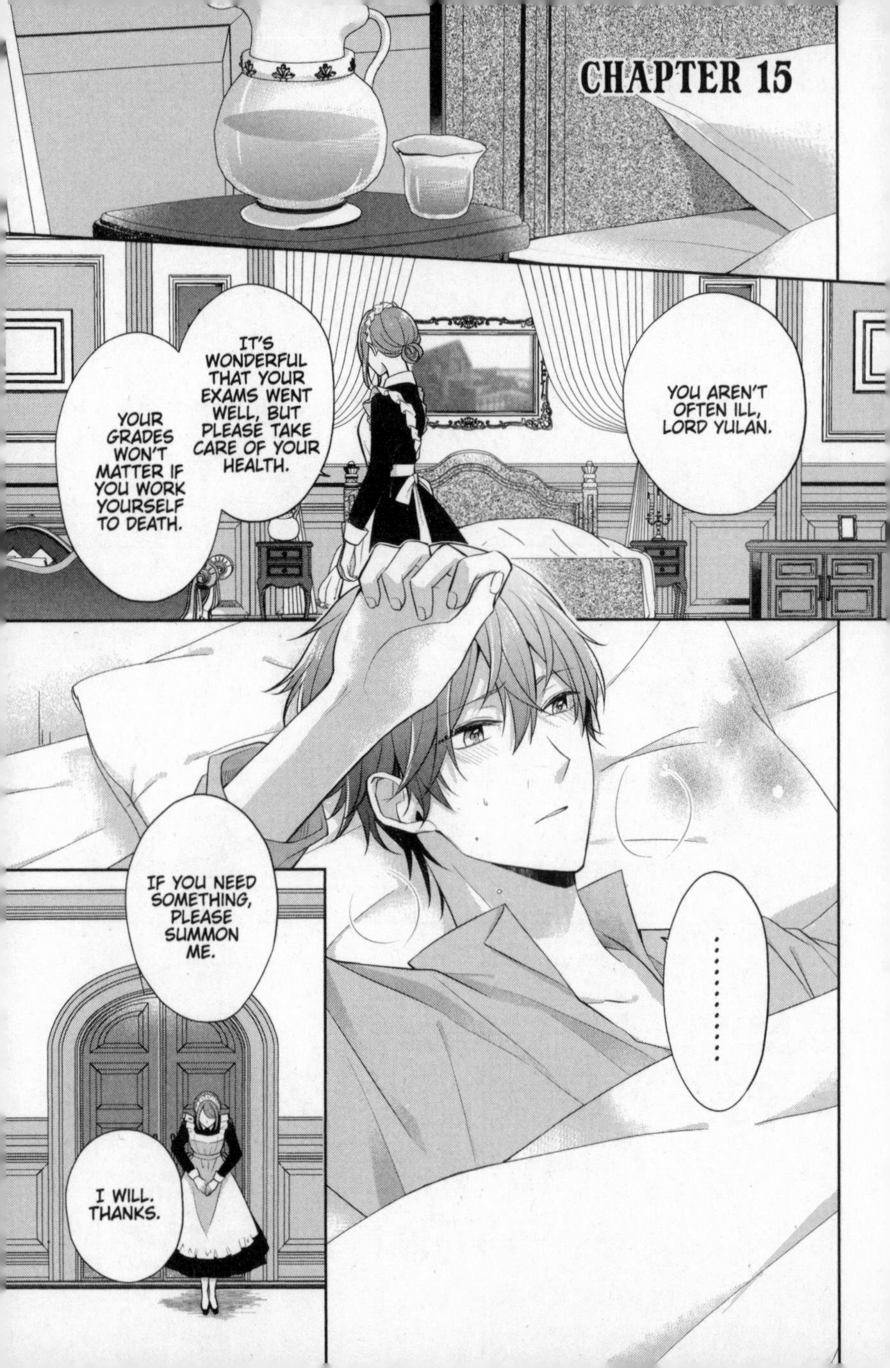
CHAPTER 15
YOU AREN'T OFTEN ILL, LORD YULAN.
IT'S WONDERFUL THAT YOUR EXAMS WENT WELL, BUT PLEASE TAKE CARE OF YOUR HEALTH.
YOUR GRADES WON'T MATTER IF YOU WORK YOURSELF TO DEATH.
......
IF YOU NEED SOMETHING, PLEASE SUMMON ME.
I WILL. THANKS.

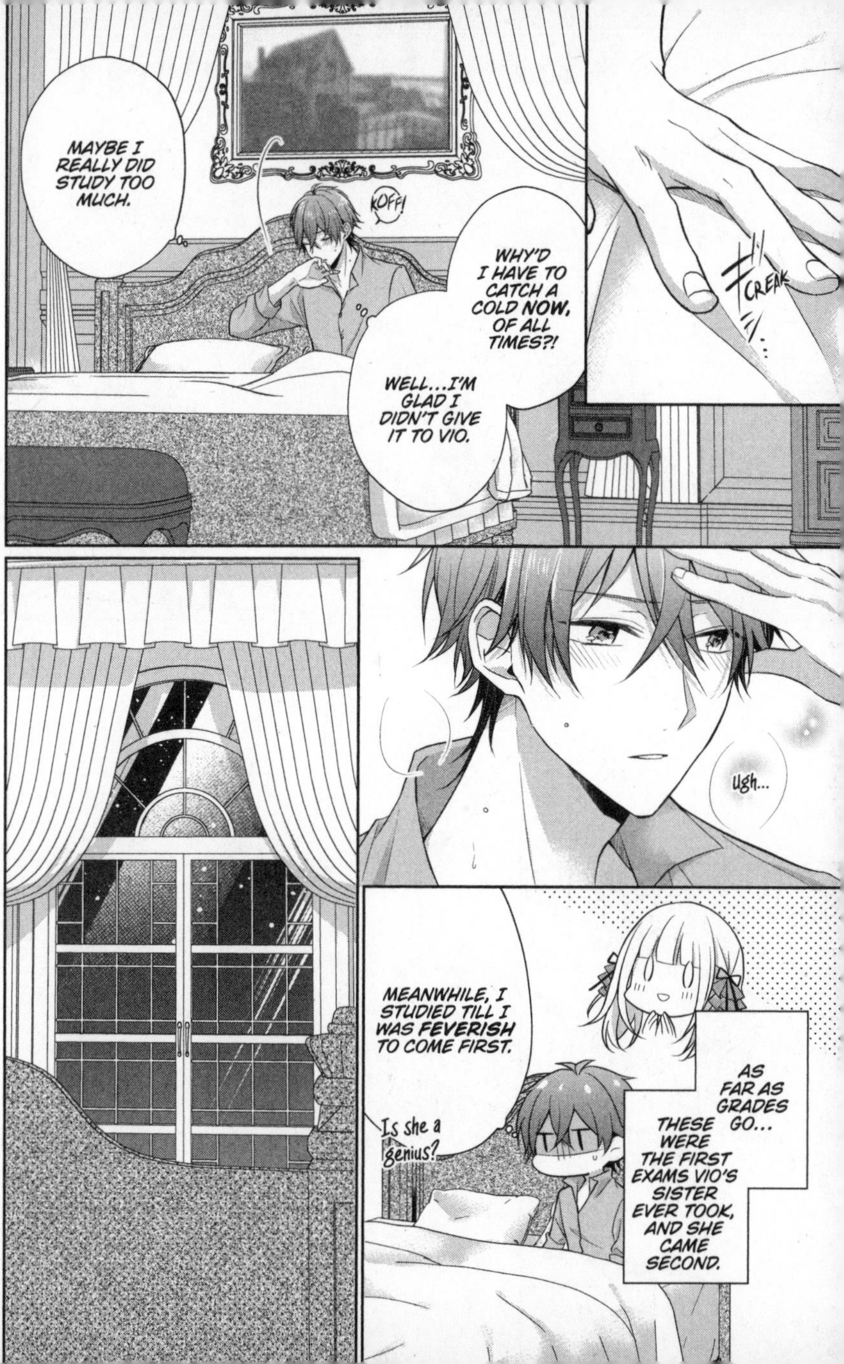
CREAK
KOFF!
WHY'D I HAVE TO CATCH A COLD NOW, OF ALL TIMES?!
WELL...I'M GLAD I DIDN'T GIVE IT TO VIO.
MAYBE I REALLY DID STUDY TOO MUCH.
Ugh...
AS FAR AS GRADES GO... THESE WERE THE FIRST EXAMS VIO'S SISTER EVER TOOK, AND SHE CAME SECOND.
MEANWHILE, I STUDIED TILL I WAS FEVERISH TO COME FIRST.
Is she a genius?

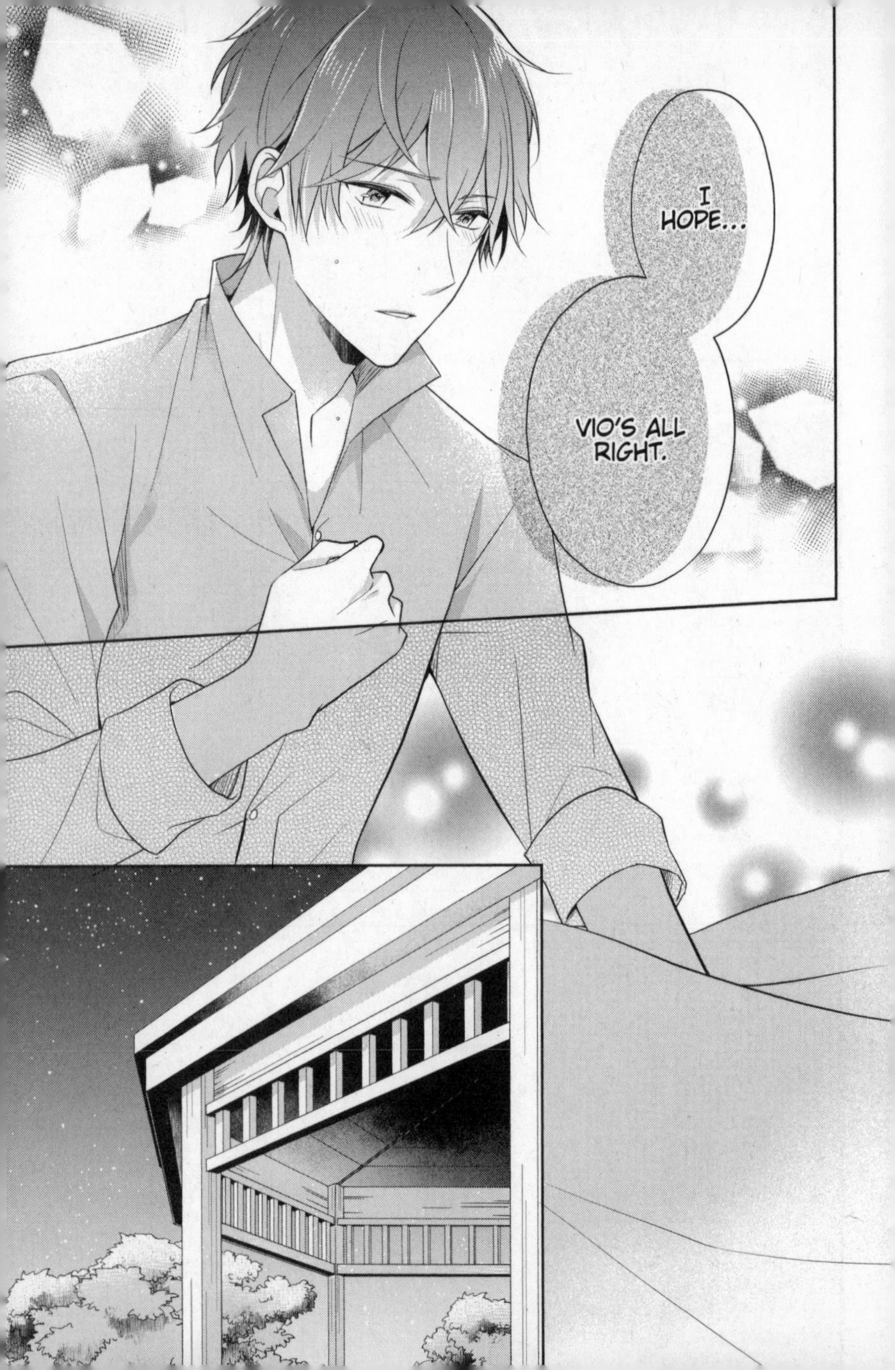
I HOPE...
VIO'S ALL RIGHT.

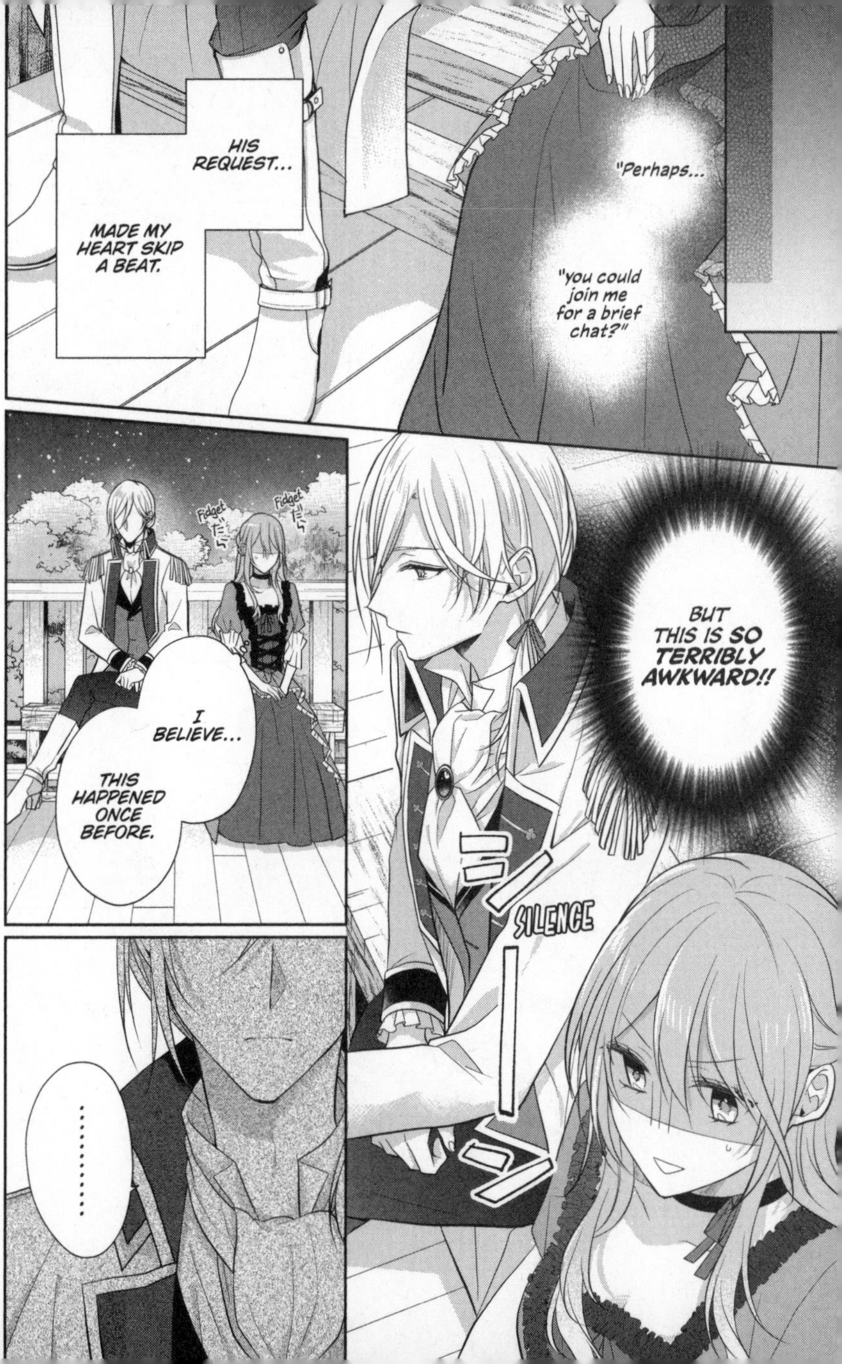

"Perhaps...
"you could join me for a brief chat?"
HIS REQUEST...
MADE MY HEART SKIP A BEAT.
BUT THIS IS SO TERRIBLY AWKWARD!!
SILENCE
Fidget
Fidget
I BELIEVE...
THIS HAPPENED ONCE BEFORE.
............

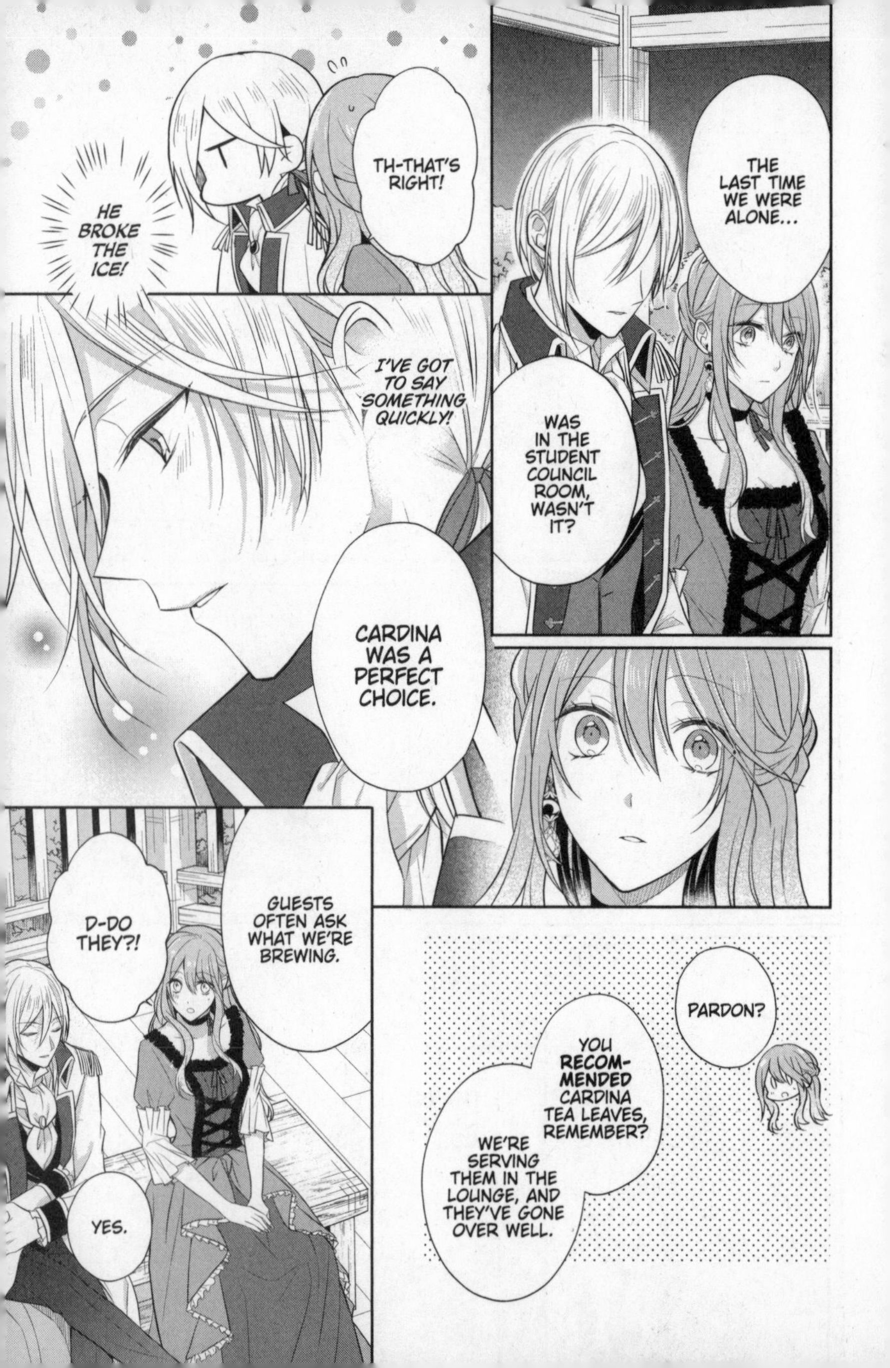
THE LAST TIME WE WERE ALONE...
WAS IN THE STUDENT COUNCIL ROOM, WASN'T IT?
TH-THAT'S RIGHT!
HE BROKE THE ICE!
I'VE GOT TO SAY SOMETHING QUICKLY!
CARDINA WAS A PERFECT CHOICE.
PARDON?
YOU RECOM-MENDED CARDINA TEA LEAVES, REMEMBER?
WE'RE SERVING THEM IN THE LOUNGE, AND THEY'VE GONE OVER WELL.
GUESTS OFTEN ASK WHAT WE'RE BREWING.
D-DO THEY?!
YES.

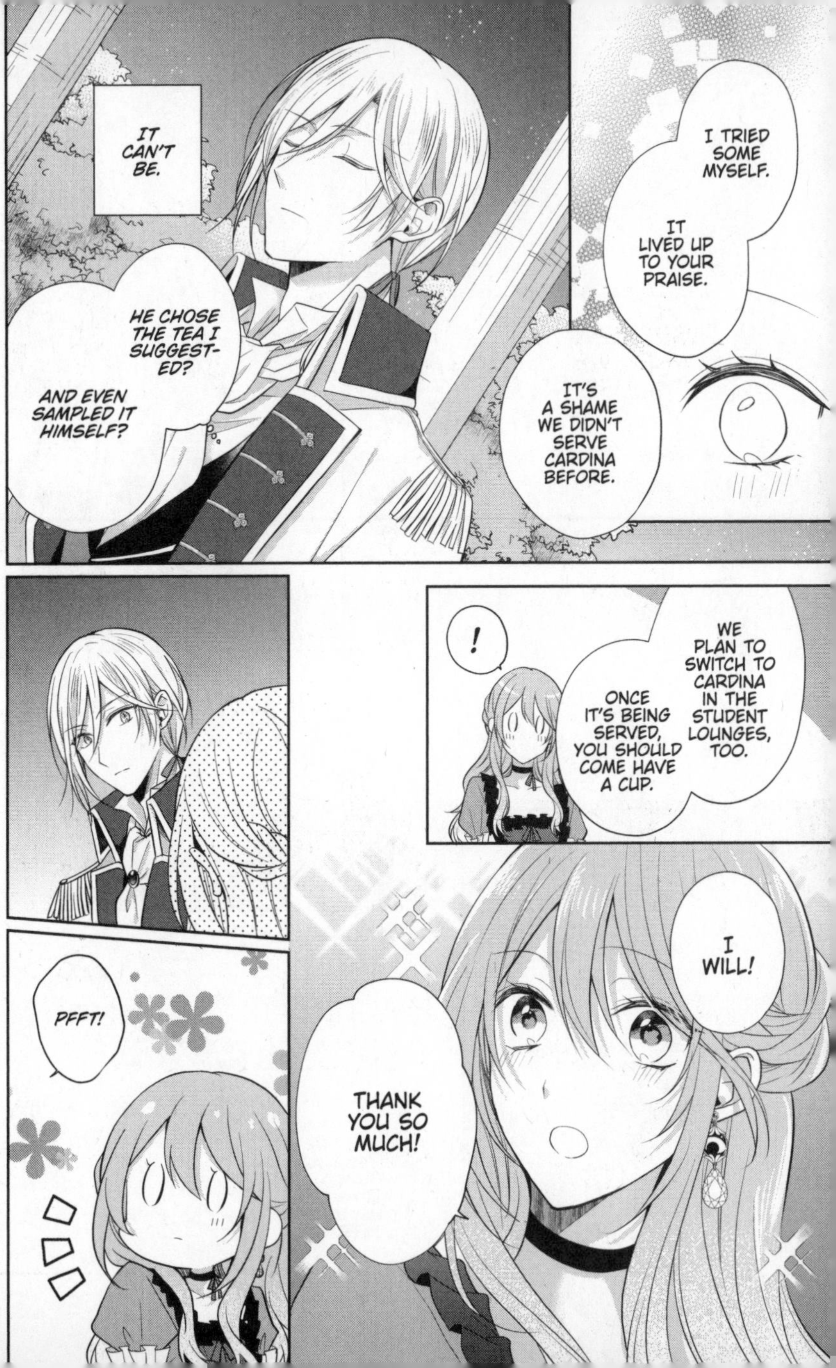
I TRIED SOME MYSELF.
IT LIVED UP TO YOUR PRAISE.
IT'S A SHAME WE DIDN'T SERVE CARDINA BEFORE.
IT CAN'T BE.
HE CHOSE THE TEA I SUGGEST-ED?
AND EVEN SAMPLED IT HIMSELF?
!
WE PLAN TO SWITCH TO CARDINA IN THE STUDENT LOUNGES, TOO.
ONCE IT'S BEING SERVED, YOU SHOULD COME HAVE A CUP.
I WILL!
THANK YOU SO MUCH!
PFFT!

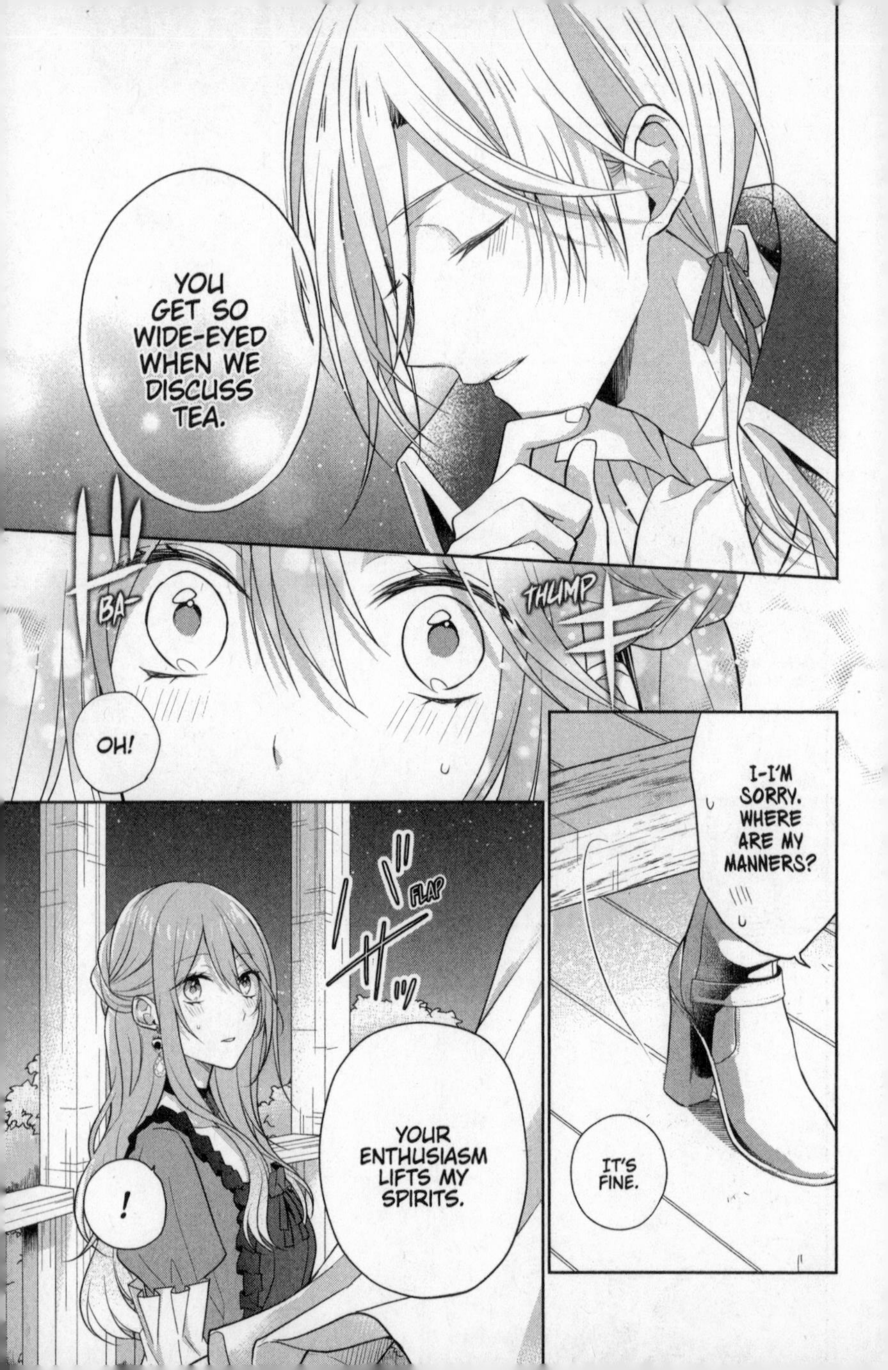
YOU GET SO WIDE-EYED WHEN WE DISCUSS TEA.
BA-
THUMP
OH!
I-I'M SORRY. WHERE ARE MY MANNERS?
IT'S FINE.
FLAP
YOUR ENTHUSIASM LIFTS MY SPIRITS.
!

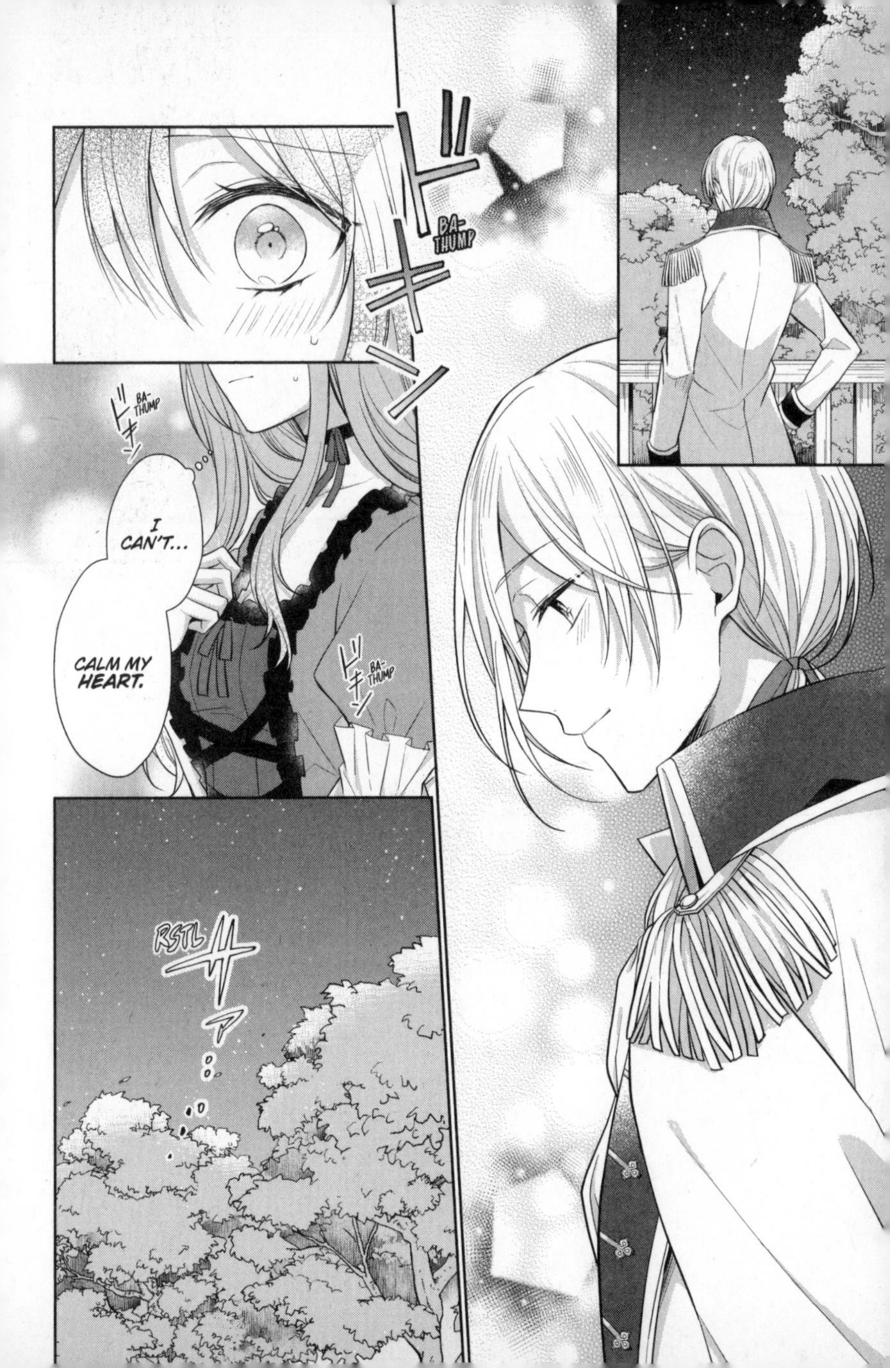
BA-THUMP
BA-THUMP
I CAN'T... CALM MY HEART.
BA-THUMP
RSTL

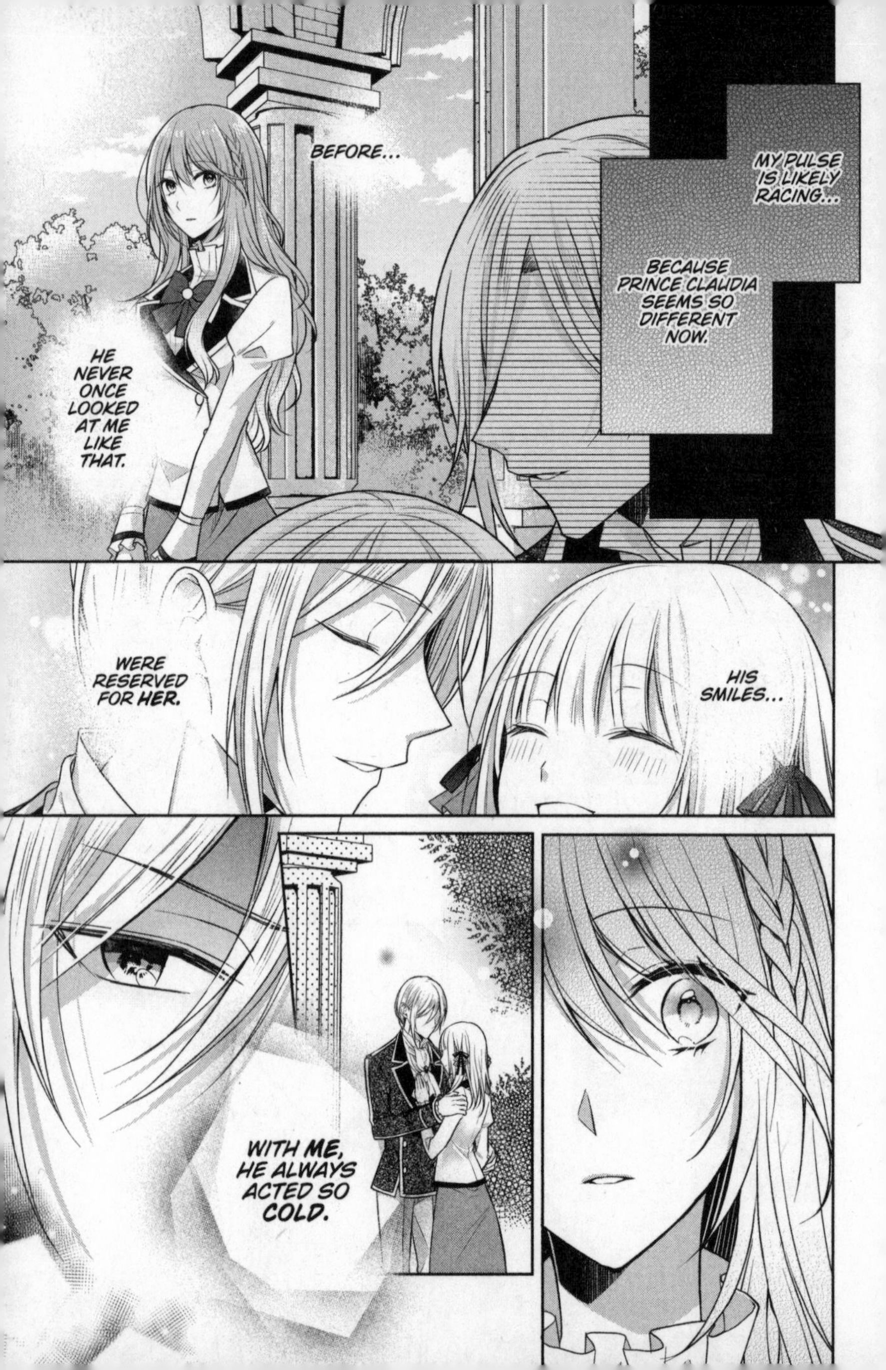
MY PULSE IS LIKELY RACING...
BECAUSE PRINCE CLAUDIA SEEMS SO DIFFERENT NOW.
BEFORE...
HE NEVER ONCE LOOKED AT ME LIKE THAT.
HIS SMILES...
WERE RESERVED FOR HER.
WITH ME, HE ALWAYS ACTED SO COLD.

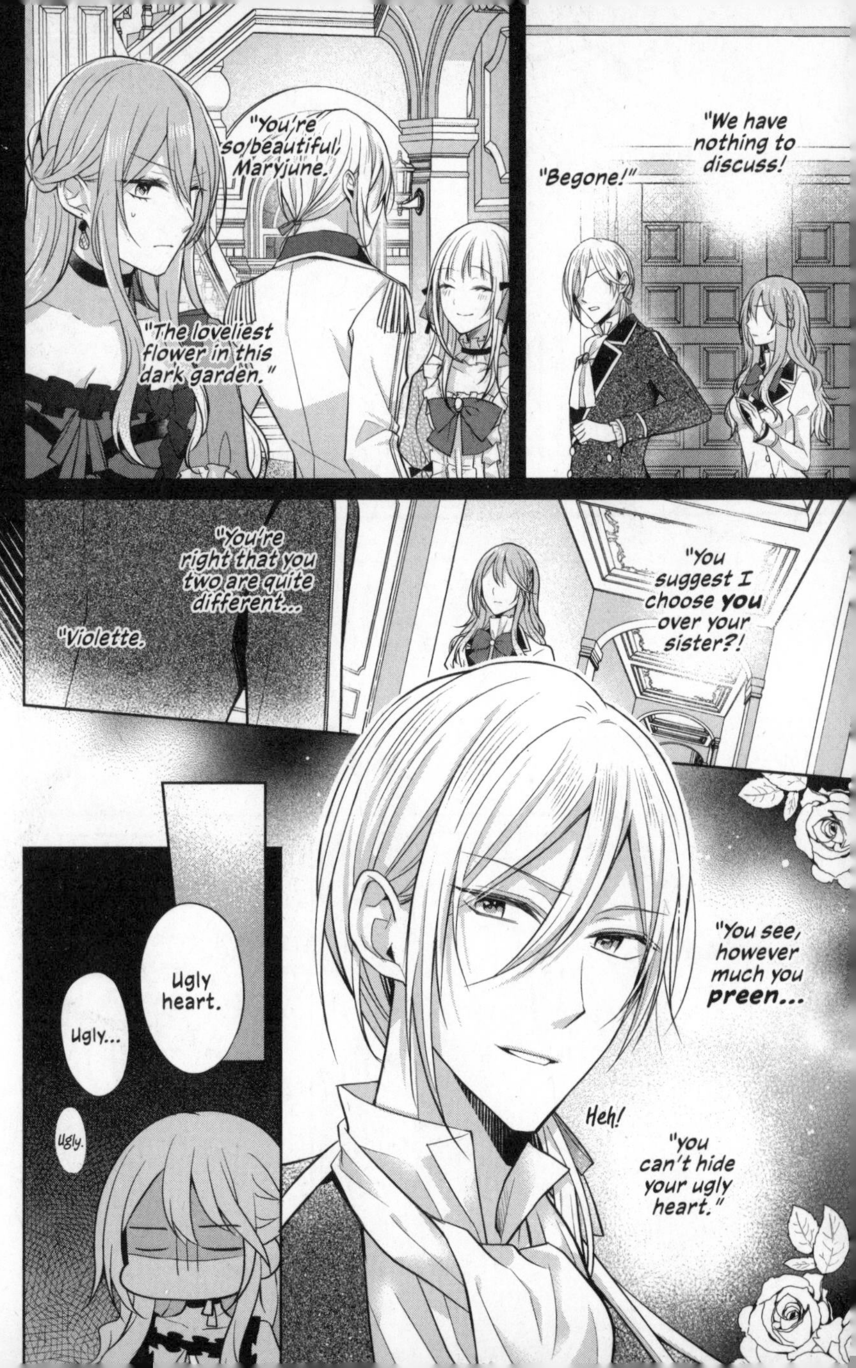
"We have nothing to discuss!
"Begone!"
"You're so beautiful, Maryjune.
"The loveliest flower in this dark garden."
"You suggest I choose **you** over your sister?!
"You're right that you two are quite different...
"Violette.
"You see, however much you **preen...**
Heh!
"you can't hide your ugly heart."
Ugly heart.
Ugly...
Ugly.

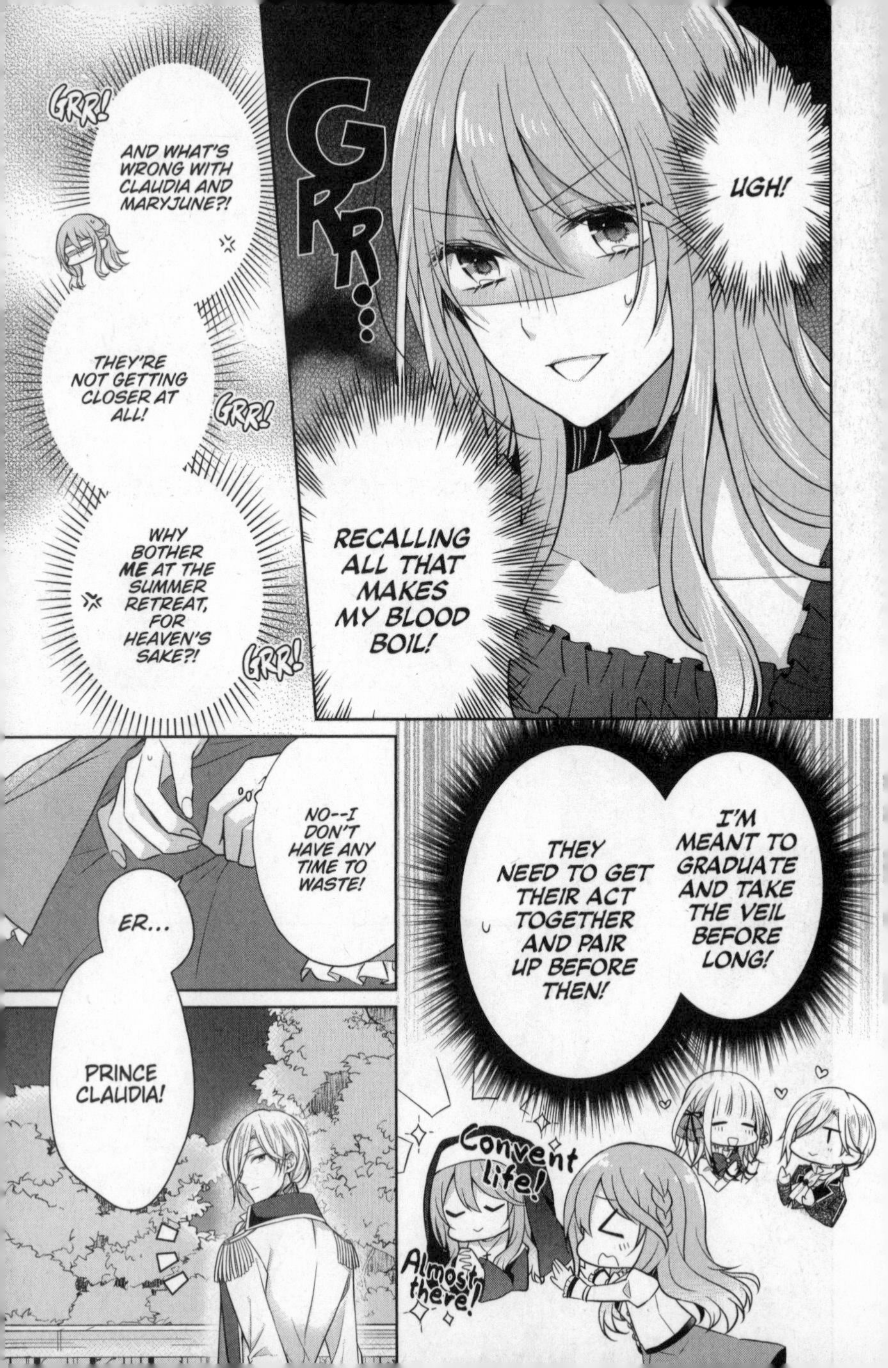
GRR...
UGH!
RECALLING ALL THAT MAKES MY BLOOD BOIL!
GRR!
AND WHAT'S WRONG WITH CLAUDIA AND MARYJUNE?!
THEY'RE NOT GETTING CLOSER AT ALL!
GRR!
WHY BOTHER ME AT THE SUMMER RETREAT, FOR HEAVEN'S SAKE?!
GRR!
I'M MEANT TO GRADUATE AND TAKE THE VEIL BEFORE LONG!
THEY NEED TO GET THEIR ACT TOGETHER AND PAIR UP BEFORE THEN!
Convent life!
Almost there!
NO--I DON'T HAVE ANY TIME TO WASTE!
ER...
PRINCE CLAUDIA!

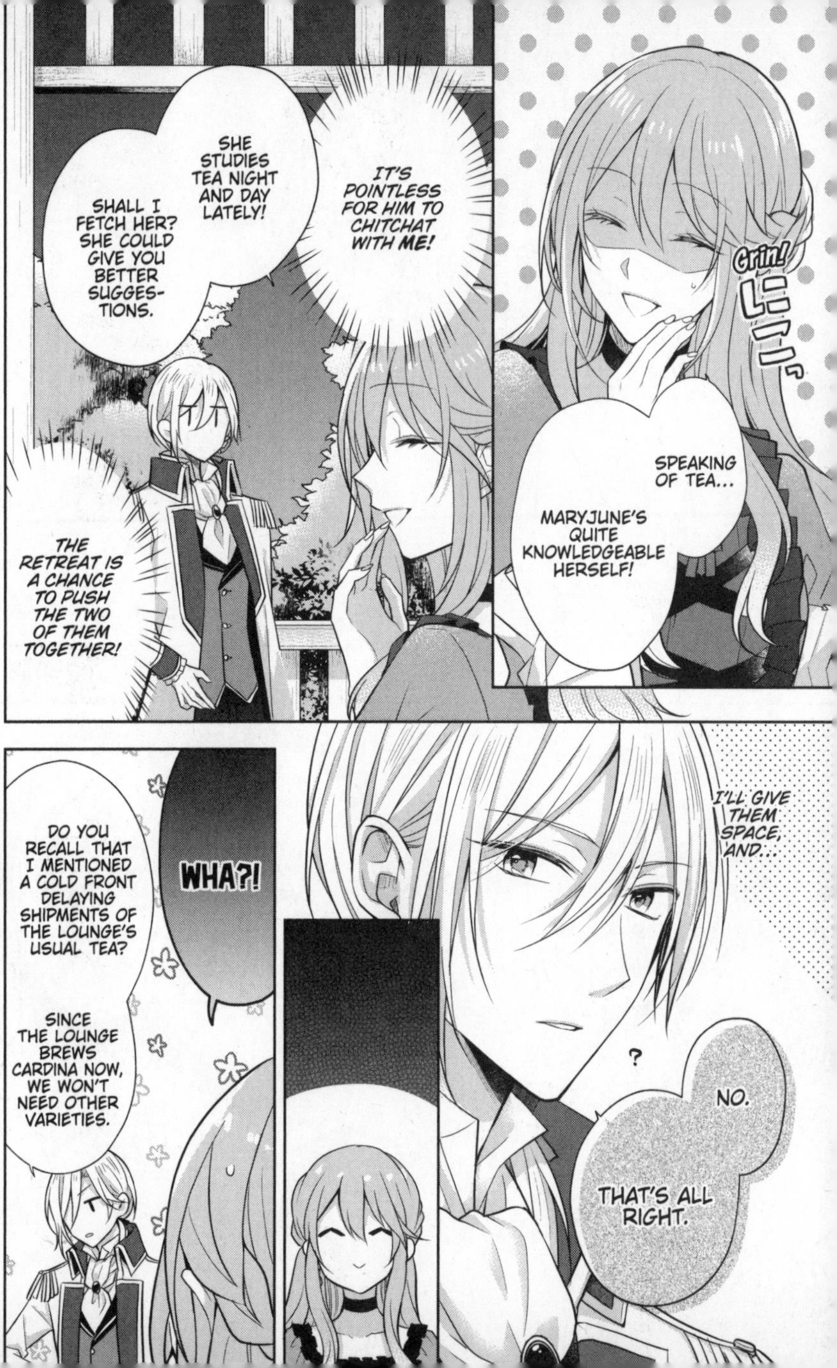
Grin!
SPEAKING OF TEA...
MARYJUNE'S QUITE KNOWLEDGEABLE HERSELF!
IT'S POINTLESS FOR HIM TO CHITCHAT WITH ME!
SHE STUDIES TEA NIGHT AND DAY LATELY!
SHALL I FETCH HER? SHE COULD GIVE YOU BETTER SUGGES-TIONS.
THE RETREAT IS A CHANCE TO PUSH THE TWO OF THEM TOGETHER!
I'LL GIVE THEM SPACE, AND...
?
NO.
THAT'S ALL RIGHT.
WHA?!
DO YOU RECALL THAT I MENTIONED A COLD FRONT DELAYING SHIPMENTS OF THE LOUNGE'S USUAL TEA?
SINCE THE LOUNGE BREWS CARDINA NOW, WE WON'T NEED OTHER VARIETIES.

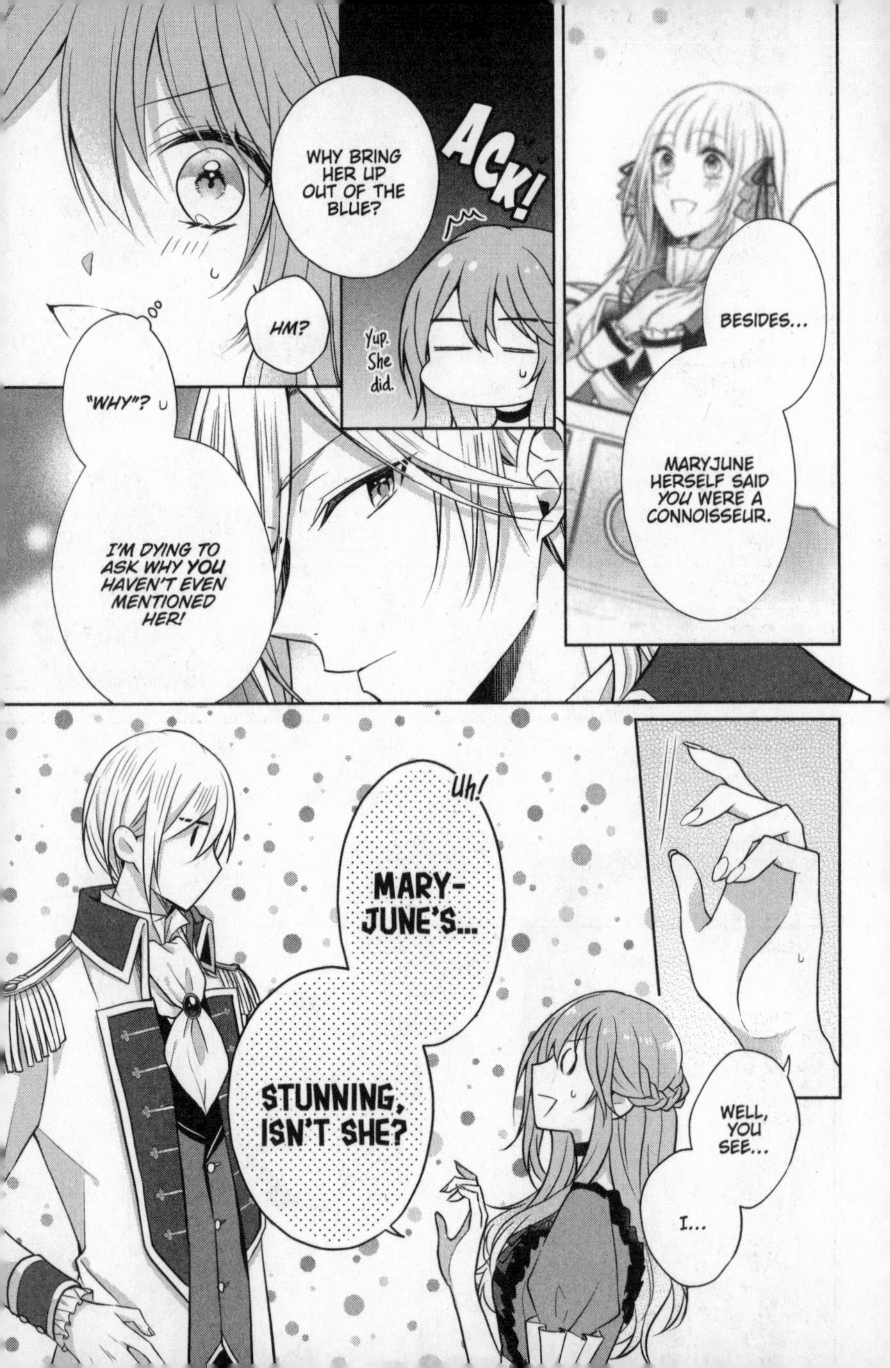
BESIDES...
MARYJUNE HERSELF SAID YOU WERE A CONNOISSEUR.
WHY BRING HER UP OUT OF THE BLUE?
ACK!
Yup. She did.
HM?
"WHY"?
I'M DYING TO ASK WHY YOU HAVEN'T EVEN MENTIONED HER!
MARY-JUNE'S...
STUNNING, ISN'T SHE?
Uh!
WELL, YOU SEE...
I...

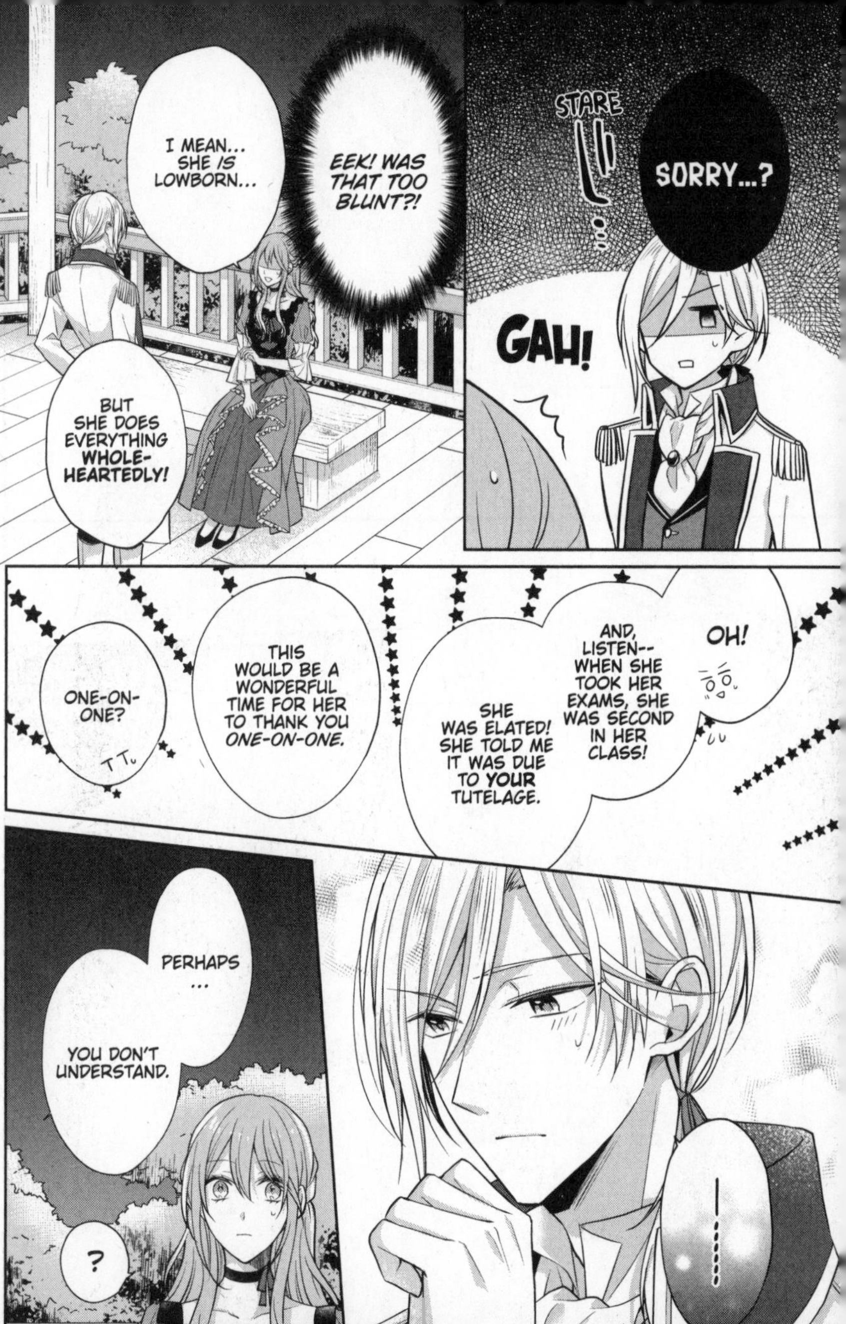
STARE
SORRY...?
GAH!
I MEAN... SHE *IS* LOWBORN...
EEK! WAS THAT TOO BLUNT?!
BUT SHE DOES EVERYTHING WHOLE-HEARTEDLY!
OH!
AND, LISTEN-- WHEN SHE TOOK HER EXAMS, SHE WAS SECOND IN HER CLASS!
SHE WAS ELATED! SHE TOLD ME IT WAS DUE TO **YOUR** TUTELAGE.
THIS WOULD BE A WONDERFUL TIME FOR HER TO THANK YOU *ONE-ON-ONE*.
ONE-ON-ONE?
......
PERHAPS ...
YOU DON'T UNDERSTAND.
?

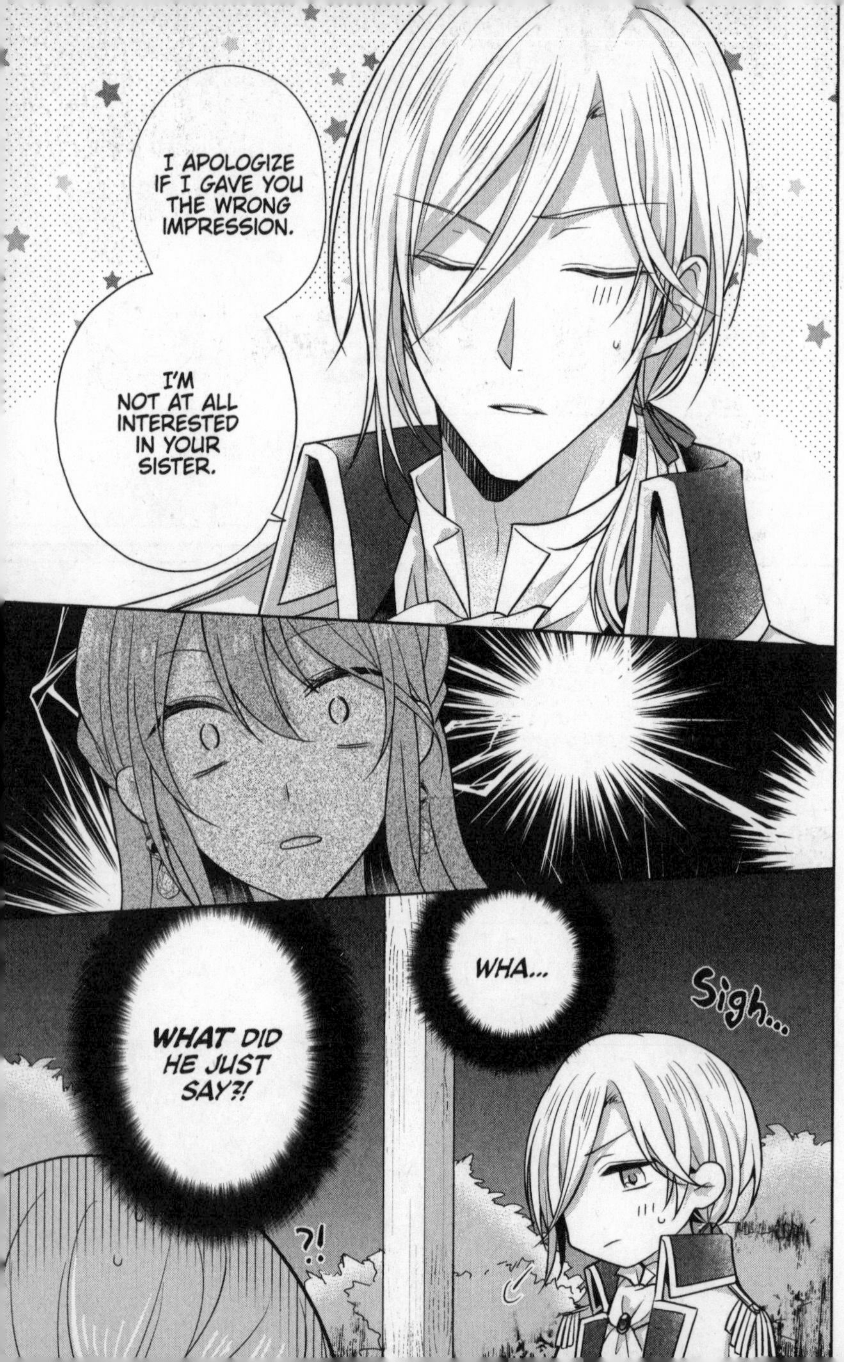
I APOLOGIZE IF I GAVE YOU THE WRONG IMPRESSION.
I'M NOT AT ALL INTERESTED IN YOUR SISTER.
Sigh...
WHA...
WHAT DID HE JUST SAY?!
?!

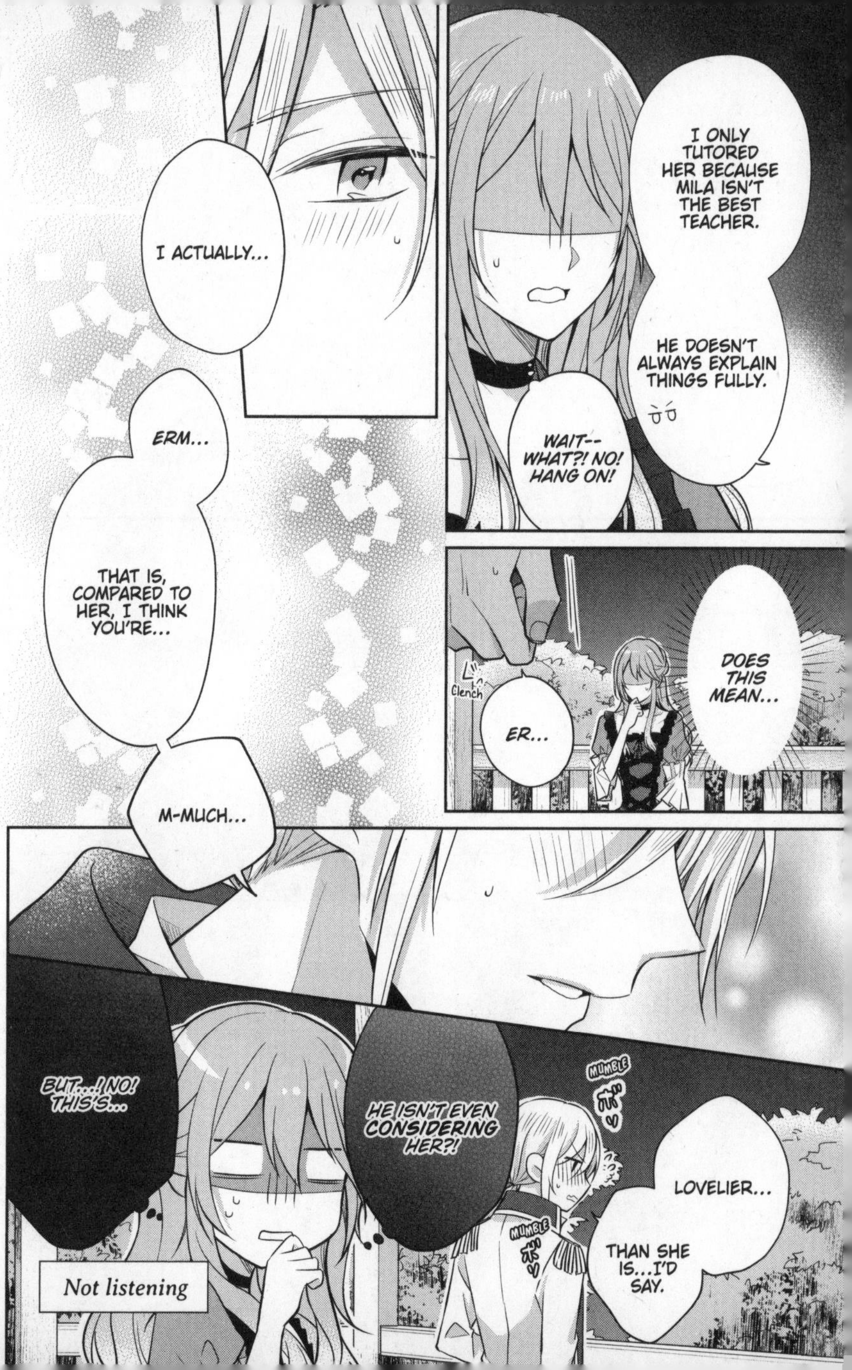
I ONLY TUTORED HER BECAUSE MILA ISN'T THE BEST TEACHER.
HE DOESN'T ALWAYS EXPLAIN THINGS FULLY.
WAIT-- WHAT?! NO! HANG ON!
DOES THIS MEAN...
Clench
ER...
I ACTUALLY...
ERM...
THAT IS, COMPARED TO HER, I THINK YOU'RE...
M-MUCH...
MUMBLE
LOVELIER...
THAN SHE IS...I'D SAY.
MUMBLE
HE ISN'T EVEN CONSIDERING HER?!
BUT...! NO! THIS'S...
Not listening

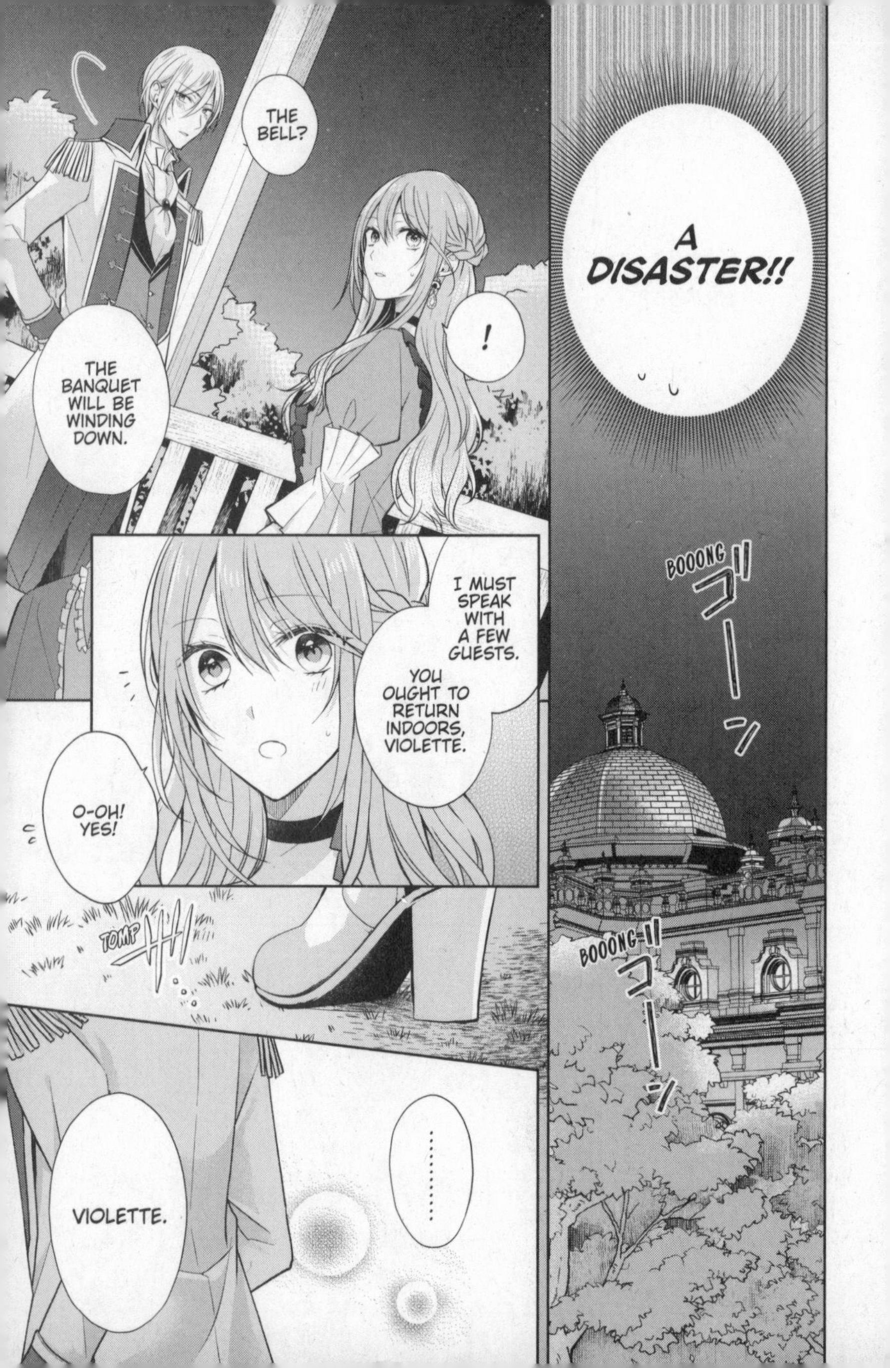
A DISASTER!!
BOOONG
BOOONG
THE BELL?
!
THE BANQUET WILL BE WINDING DOWN.
I MUST SPEAK WITH A FEW GUESTS.
YOU OUGHT TO RETURN INDOORS, VIOLETTE.
O-OH! YES!
TOMP
……
VIOLETTE.

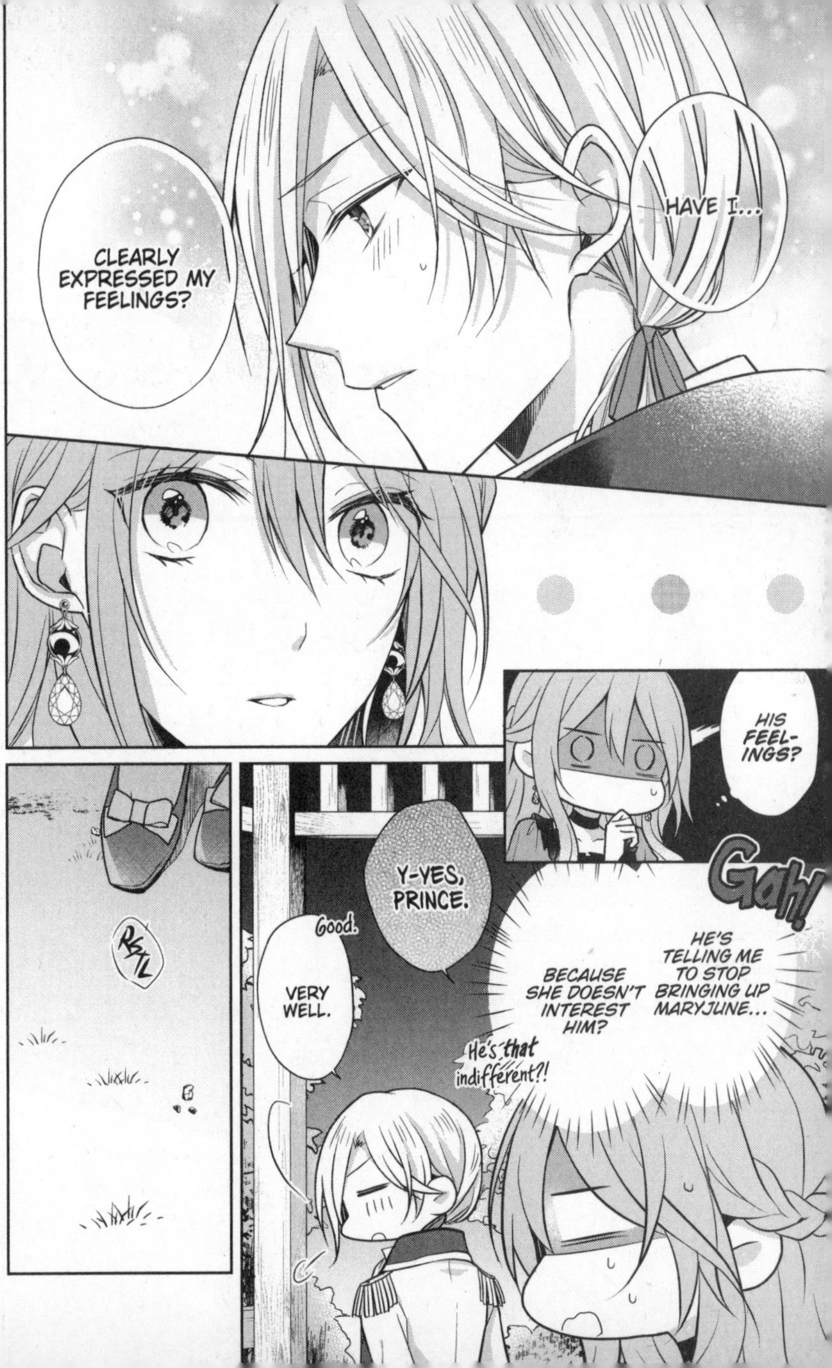

HAVE I...
CLEARLY EXPRESSED MY FEELINGS?
HIS FEELINGS?
Gah!
HE'S TELLING ME TO STOP BRINGING UP MARYJUNE...
BECAUSE SHE DOESN'T INTEREST HIM?
He's that indifferent?!
Y-YES, PRINCE.
Good.
VERY WELL.
RSTL

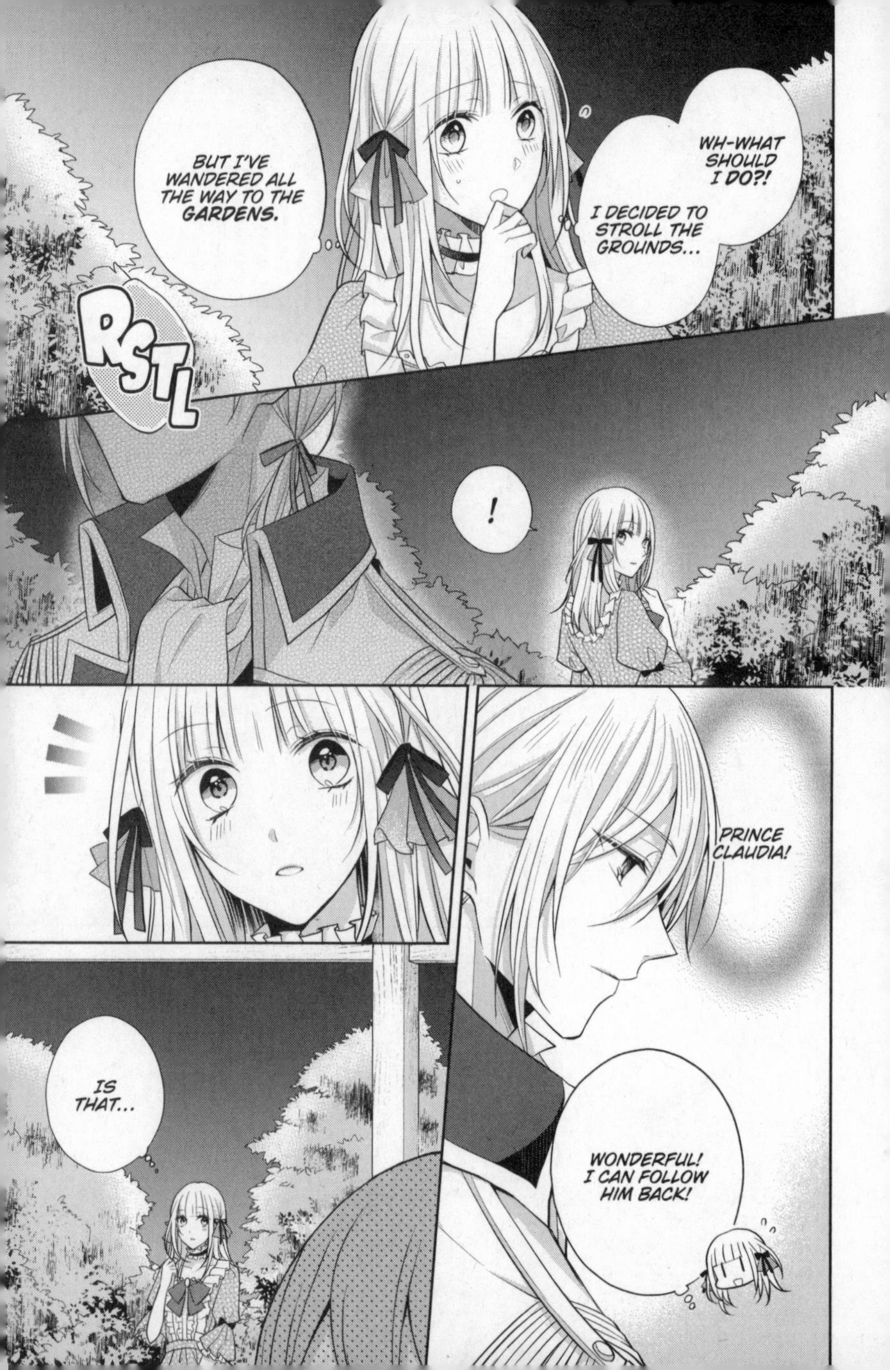
WH-WHAT SHOULD I DO?!
I DECIDED TO STROLL THE GROUNDS...
BUT I'VE WANDERED ALL THE WAY TO THE GARDENS.
RSTL
!
PRINCE CLAUDIA!
WONDERFUL! I CAN FOLLOW HIM BACK!
IS THAT...

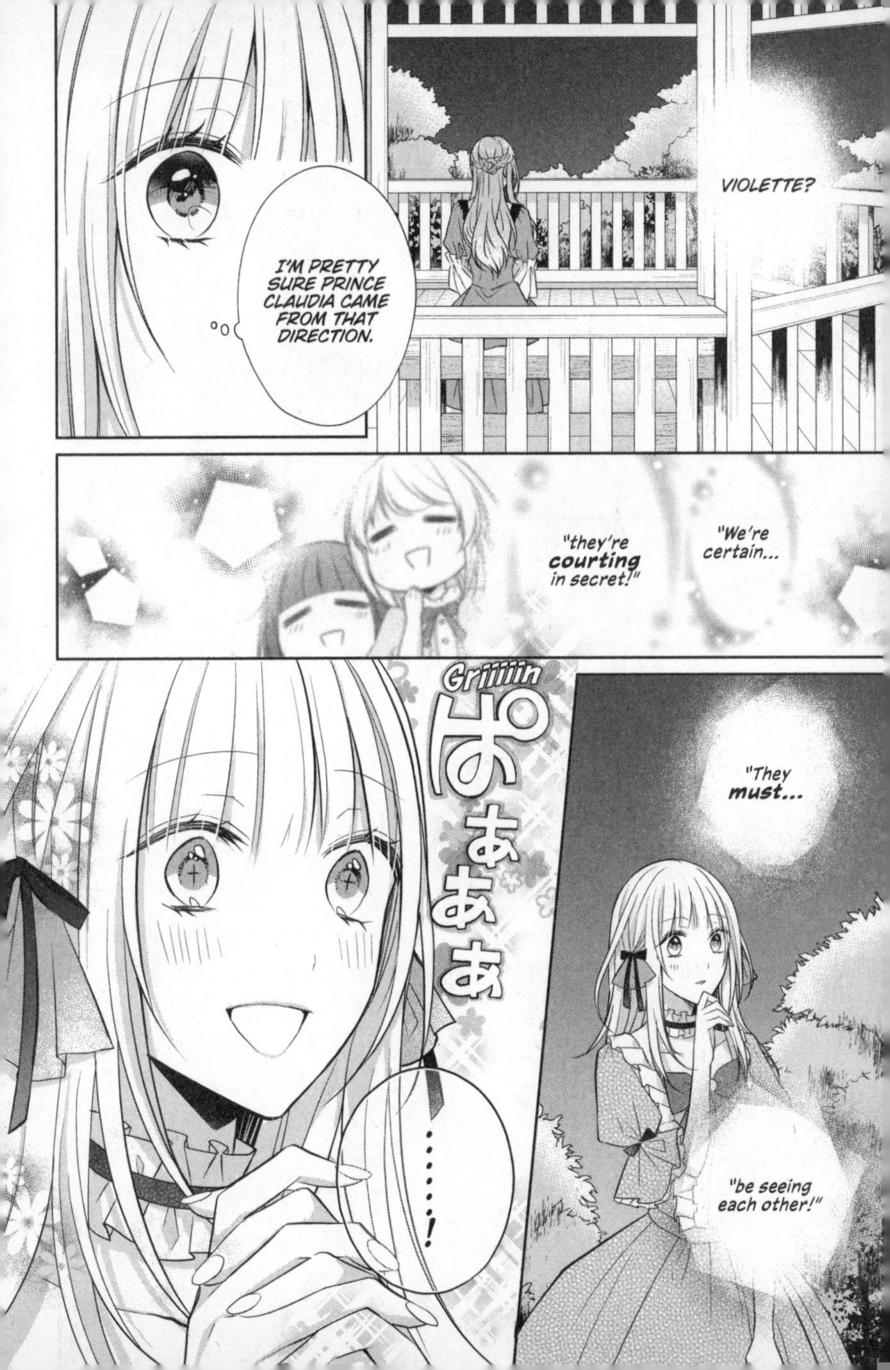
VIOLETTE?
I'M PRETTY SURE PRINCE CLAUDIA CAME FROM THAT DIRECTION.
"We're certain...
"they're courting in secret!"
"They must...
"be seeing each other!"
Griiiiin
ぱぁぁぁ
......!

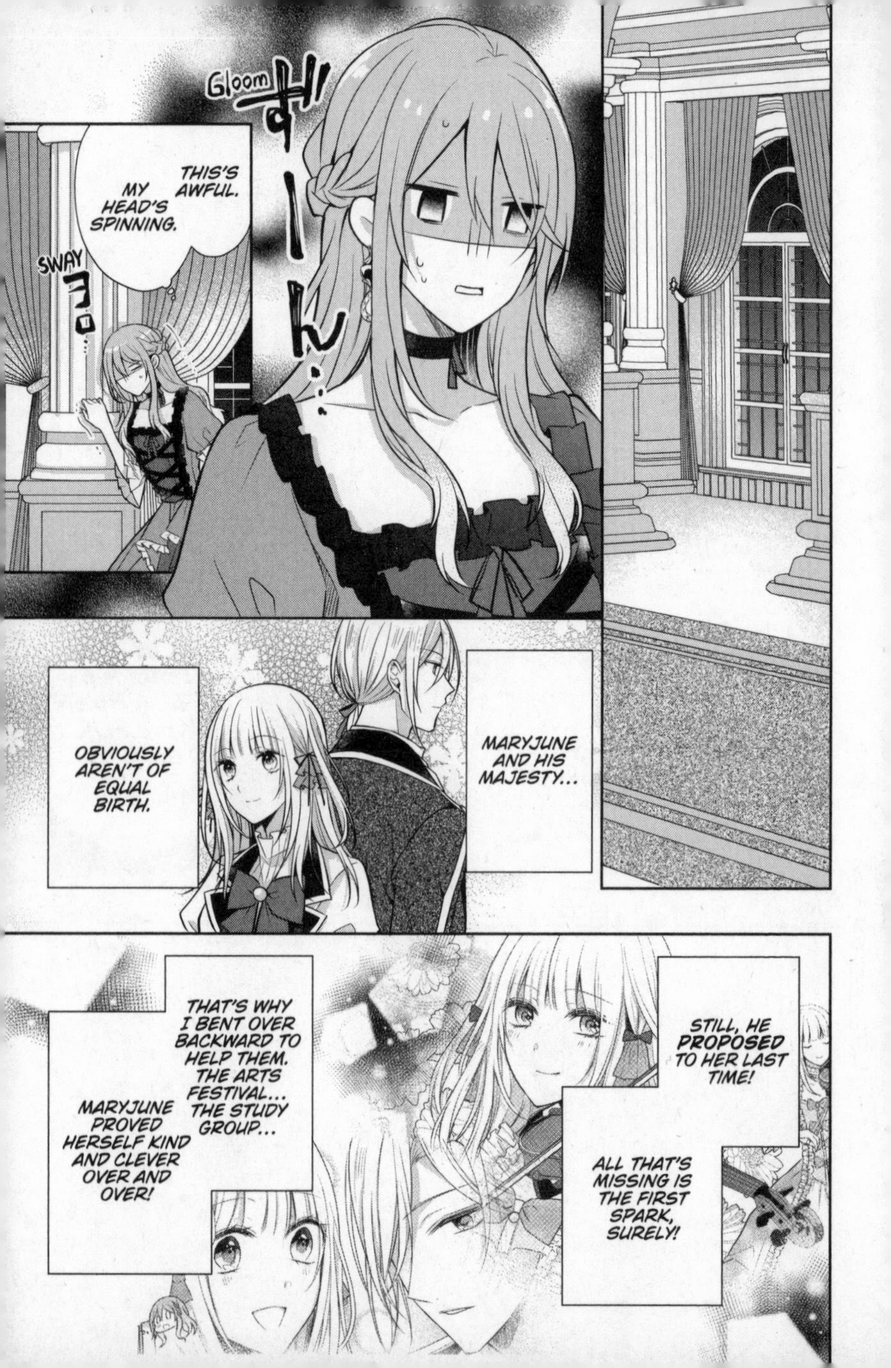
Gloom
THIS'S AWFUL. MY HEAD'S SPINNING.
SWAY
MARYJUNE AND HIS MAJESTY...
OBVIOUSLY AREN'T OF EQUAL BIRTH.
STILL, HE PROPOSED TO HER LAST TIME!
ALL THAT'S MISSING IS THE FIRST SPARK, SURELY!
THAT'S WHY I BENT OVER BACKWARD TO HELP THEM. THE ARTS FESTIVAL... THE STUDY GROUP...
MARYJUNE PROVED HERSELF KIND AND CLEVER OVER AND OVER!

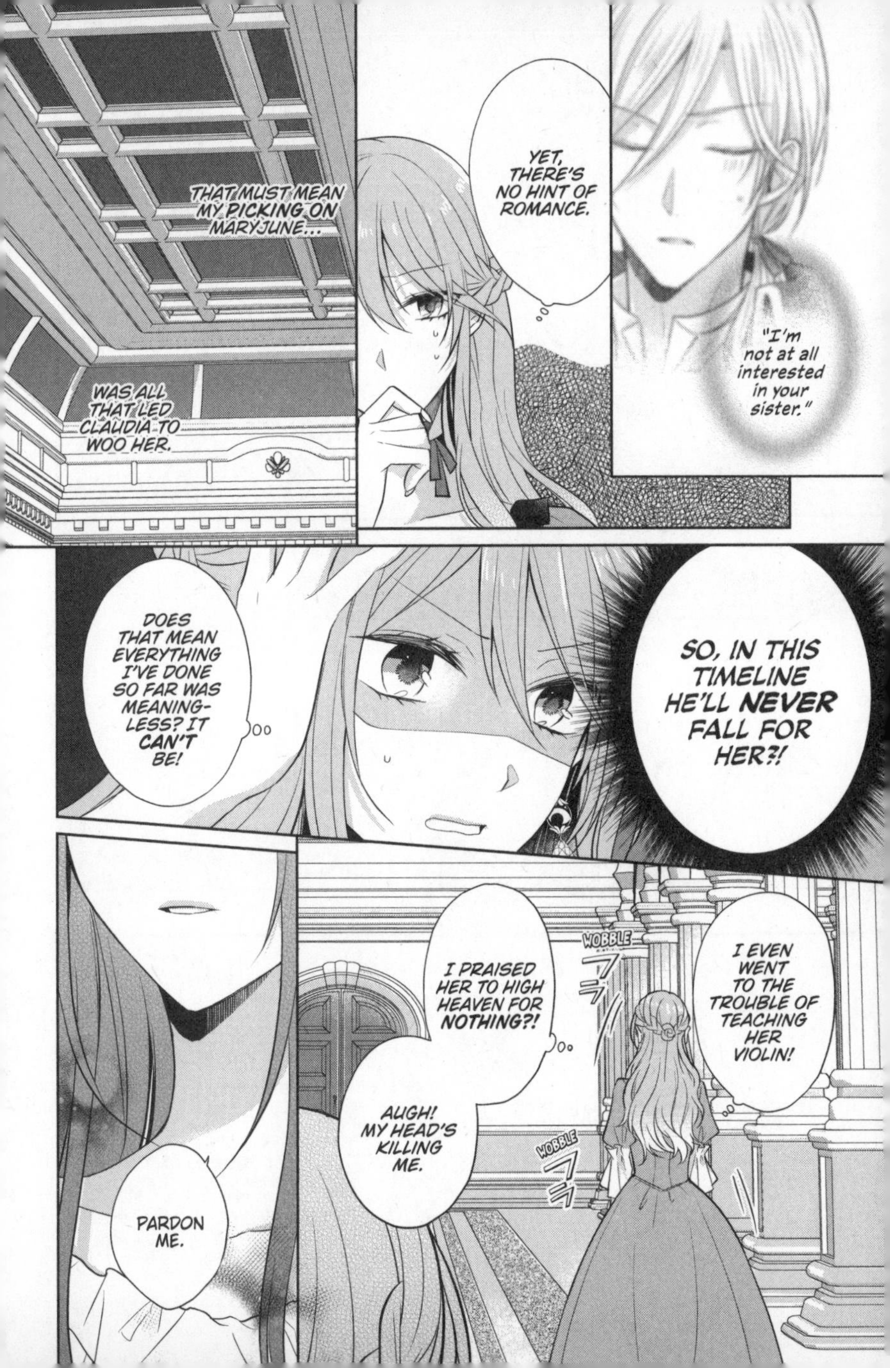
"I'm not at all interested in your sister."
YET, THERE'S NO HINT OF ROMANCE.
THAT MUST MEAN MY PICKING ON MARYJUNE...
WAS ALL THAT LED CLAUDIA TO WOO HER.
SO, IN THIS TIMELINE HE'LL **NEVER** FALL FOR HER?!
DOES THAT MEAN EVERYTHING I'VE DONE SO FAR WAS MEANING-LESS? IT **CAN'T** BE!
I EVEN WENT TO THE TROUBLE OF TEACHING HER VIOLIN!
WOBBLE
I PRAISED HER TO HIGH HEAVEN FOR **NOTHING?!**
WOBBLE
AUGH! MY HEAD'S KILLING ME.
PARDON ME.

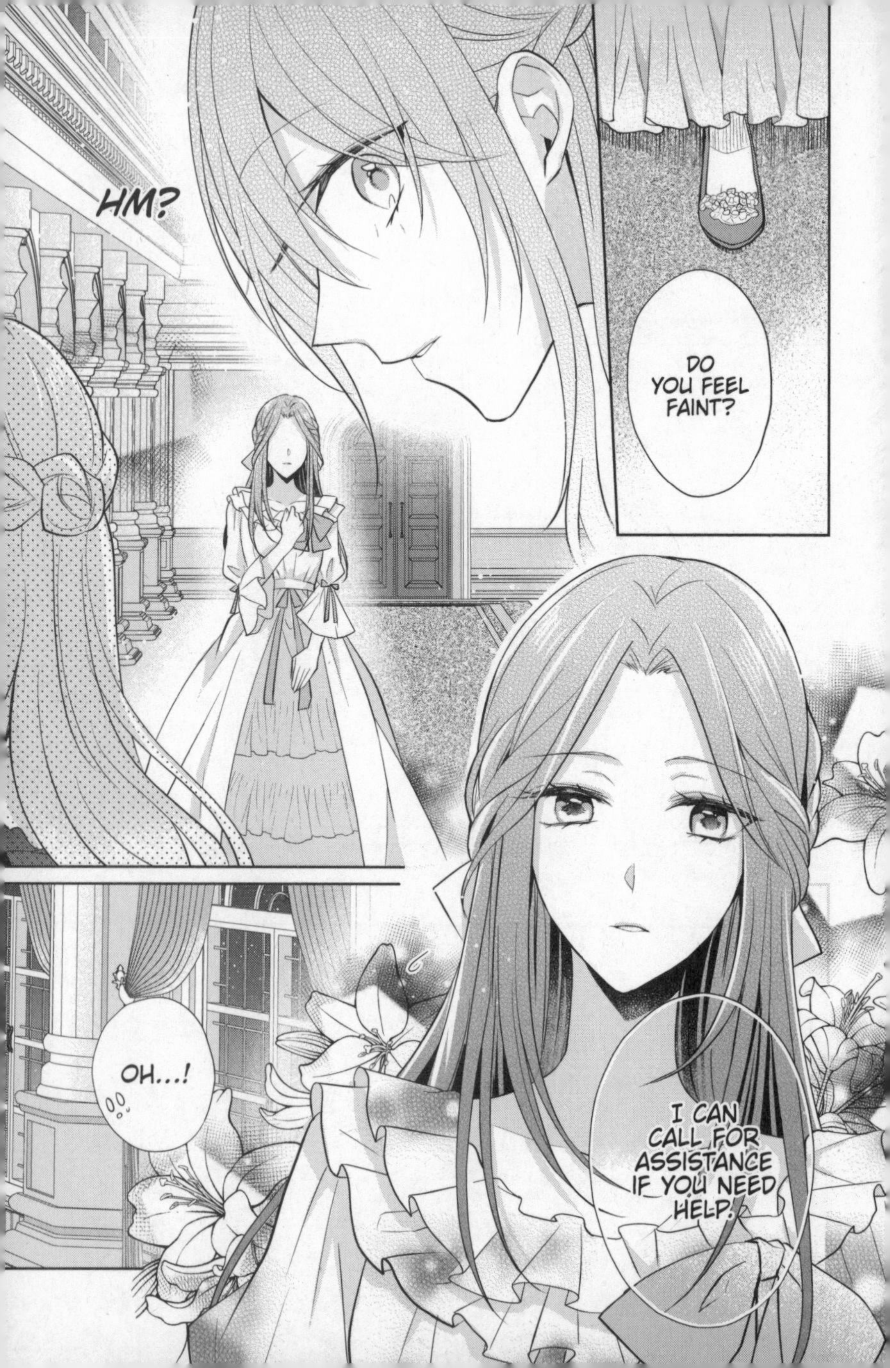
DO YOU FEEL FAINT?
HM?
I CAN CALL FOR ASSISTANCE IF YOU NEED HELP.
OH...!

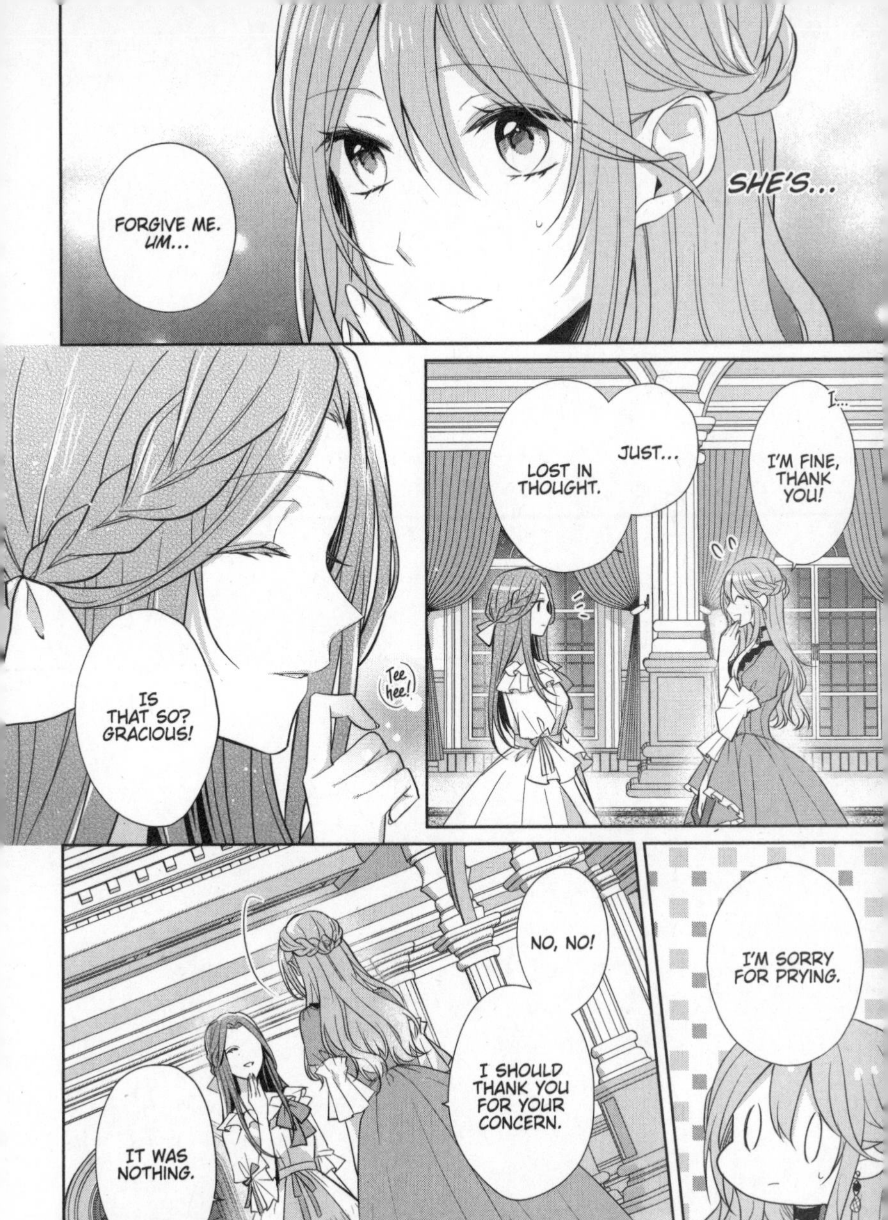
SHE'S...
FORGIVE ME. UM...
I...
I'M FINE, THANK YOU!
JUST...
LOST IN THOUGHT.
Tee hee!
IS THAT SO? GRACIOUS!
I'M SORRY FOR PRYING.
NO, NO!
I SHOULD THANK YOU FOR YOUR CONCERN.
IT WAS NOTHING.

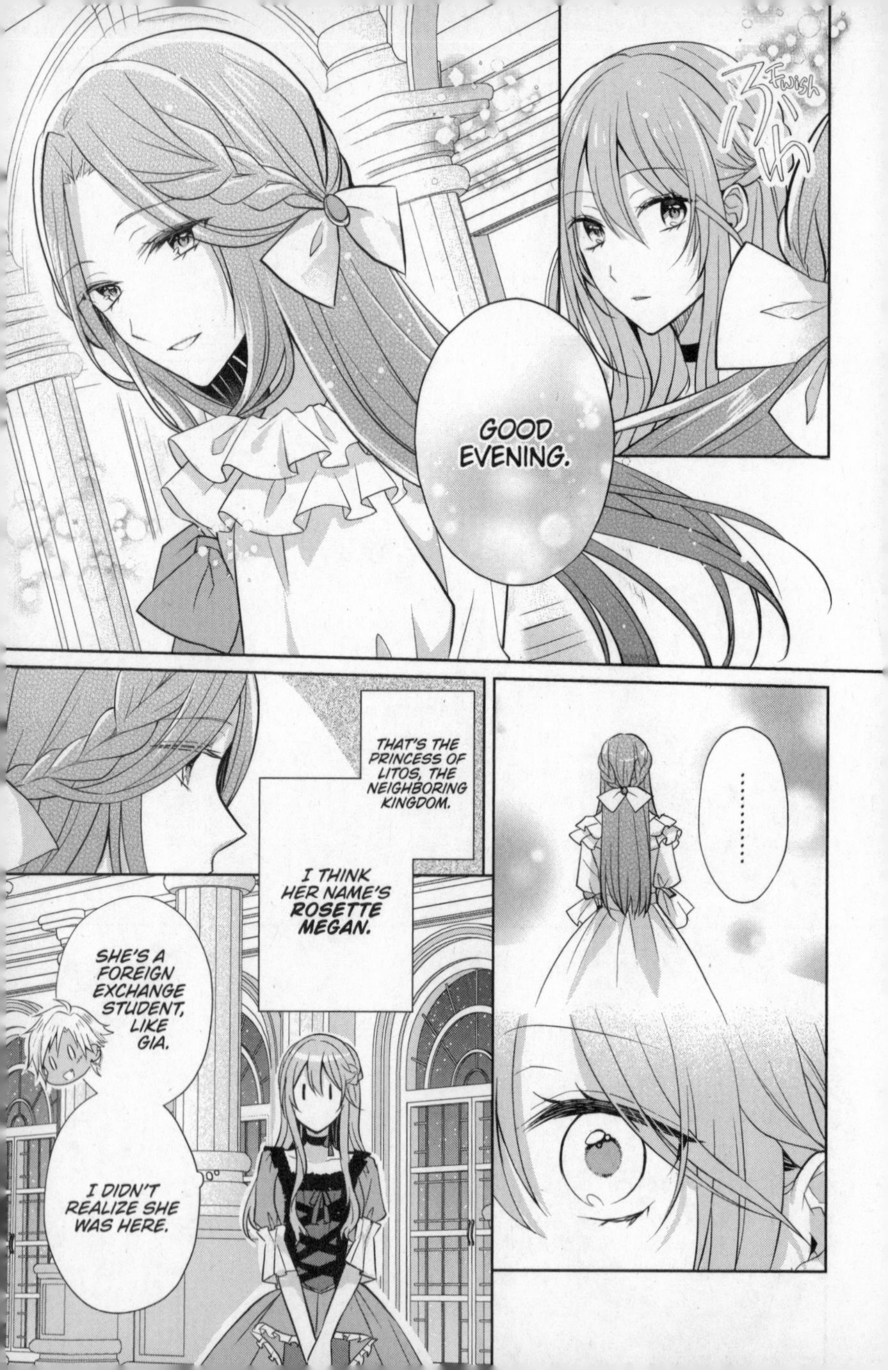
ふわ
FWISH
GOOD EVENING.
......
THAT'S THE PRINCESS OF LITOS, THE NEIGHBORING KINGDOM.
I THINK HER NAME'S ROSETTE MEGAN.
SHE'S A FOREIGN EXCHANGE STUDENT, LIKE GIA.
I DIDN'T REALIZE SHE WAS HERE.

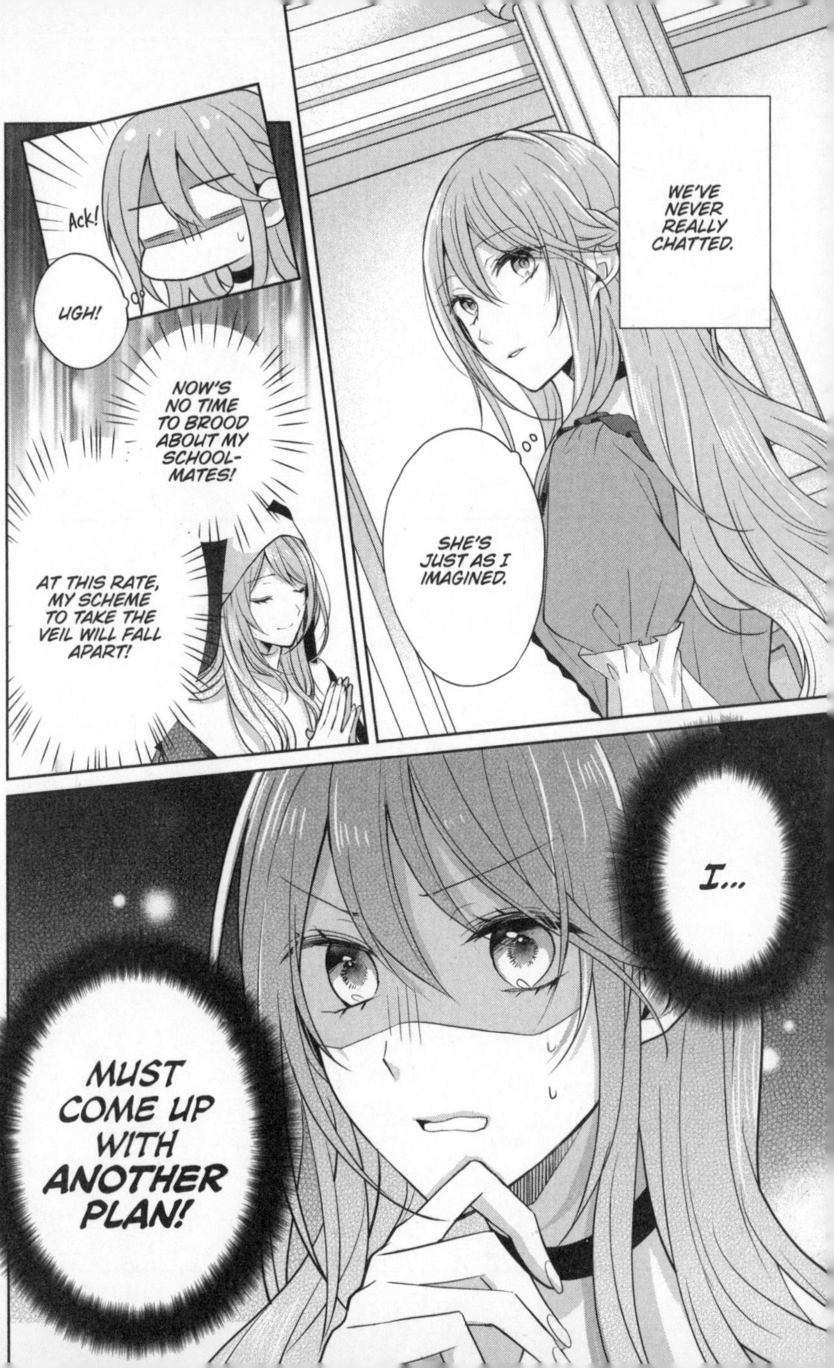
WE'VE NEVER REALLY CHATTED.
SHE'S JUST AS I IMAGINED.
Ack!
UGH!
NOW'S NO TIME TO BROOD ABOUT MY SCHOOL-MATES!
AT THIS RATE, MY SCHEME TO TAKE THE VEIL WILL FALL APART!
I...
MUST COME UP WITH ANOTHER PLAN!

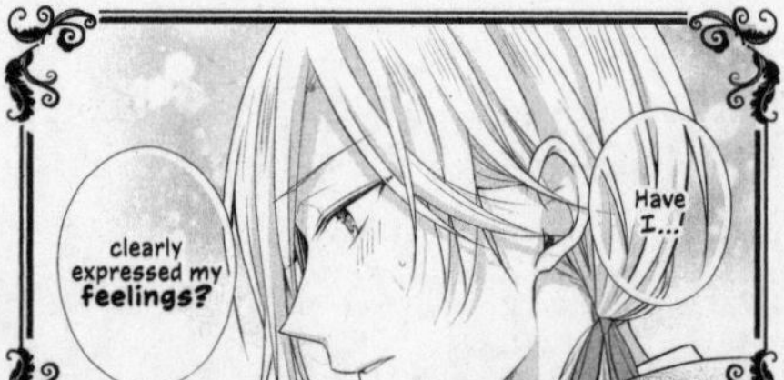
Have I...!
clearly expressed my feelings?

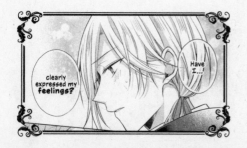

I Swear I Won't
Bother
You AGAIN!

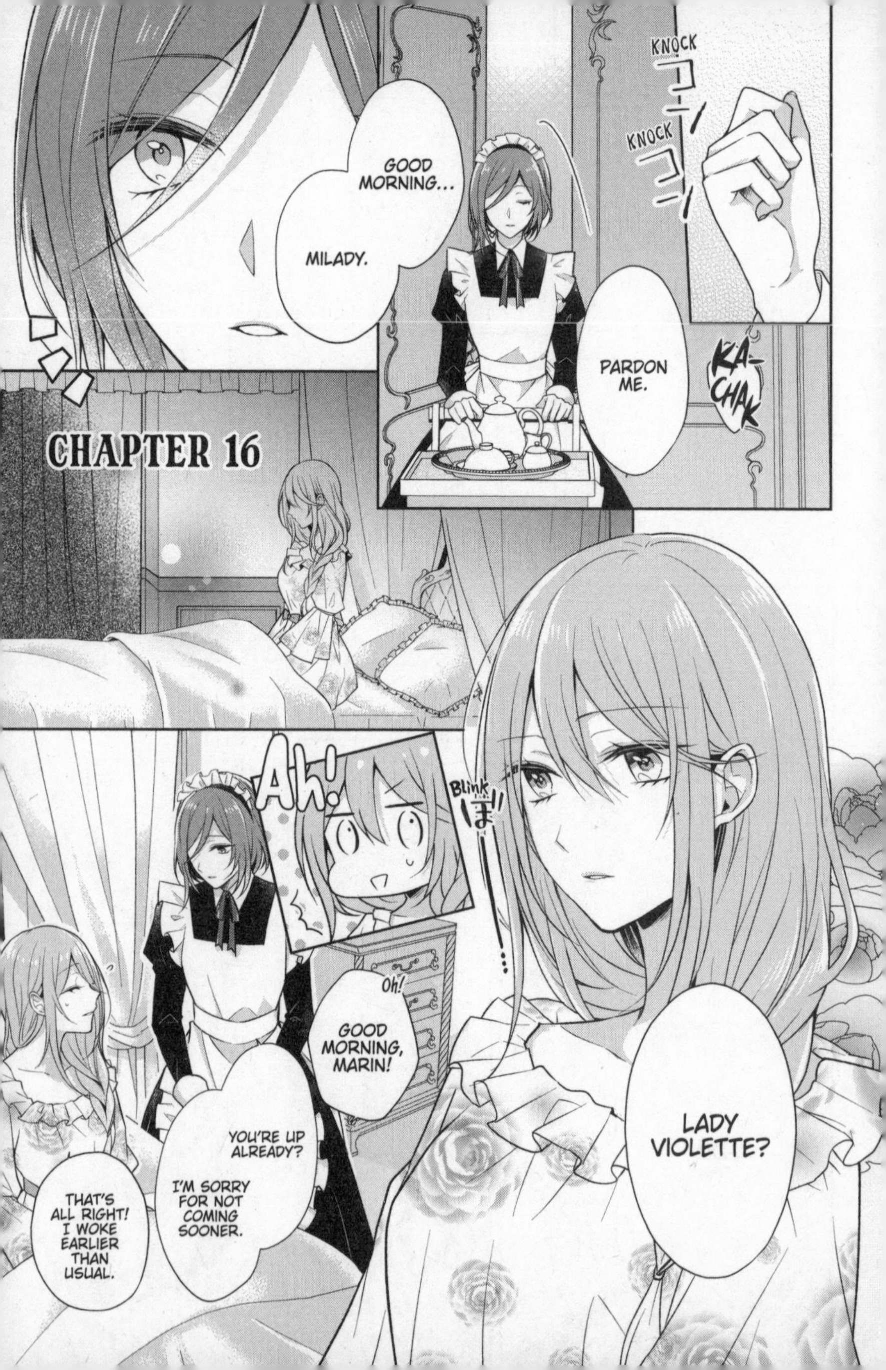
KNOCK
KNOCK
PARDON ME.
KA-CHAK
GOOD MORNING...
MILADY.
CHAPTER 16
Blink
LADY VIOLETTE?
Ah!
Oh!
GOOD MORNING, MARIN!
YOU'RE UP ALREADY?
I'M SORRY FOR NOT COMING SOONER.
THAT'S ALL RIGHT! I WOKE EARLIER THAN USUAL.

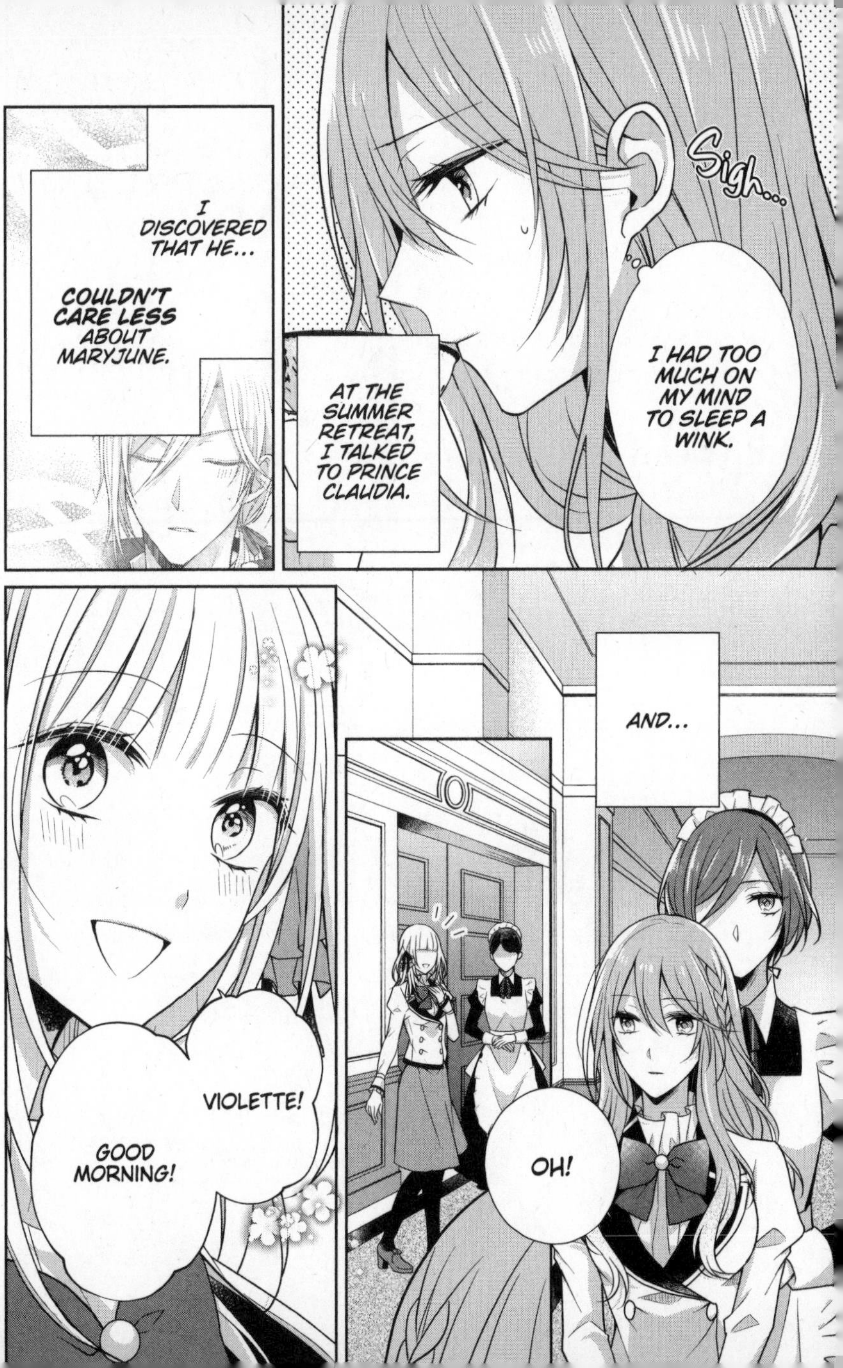

Sigh...
I HAD TOO MUCH ON MY MIND TO SLEEP A WINK.
AT THE SUMMER RETREAT, I TALKED TO PRINCE CLAUDIA.
I DISCOVERED THAT HE...
COULDN'T CARE LESS ABOUT MARYJUNE.
AND...
OH!
VIOLETTE!
GOOD MORNING!

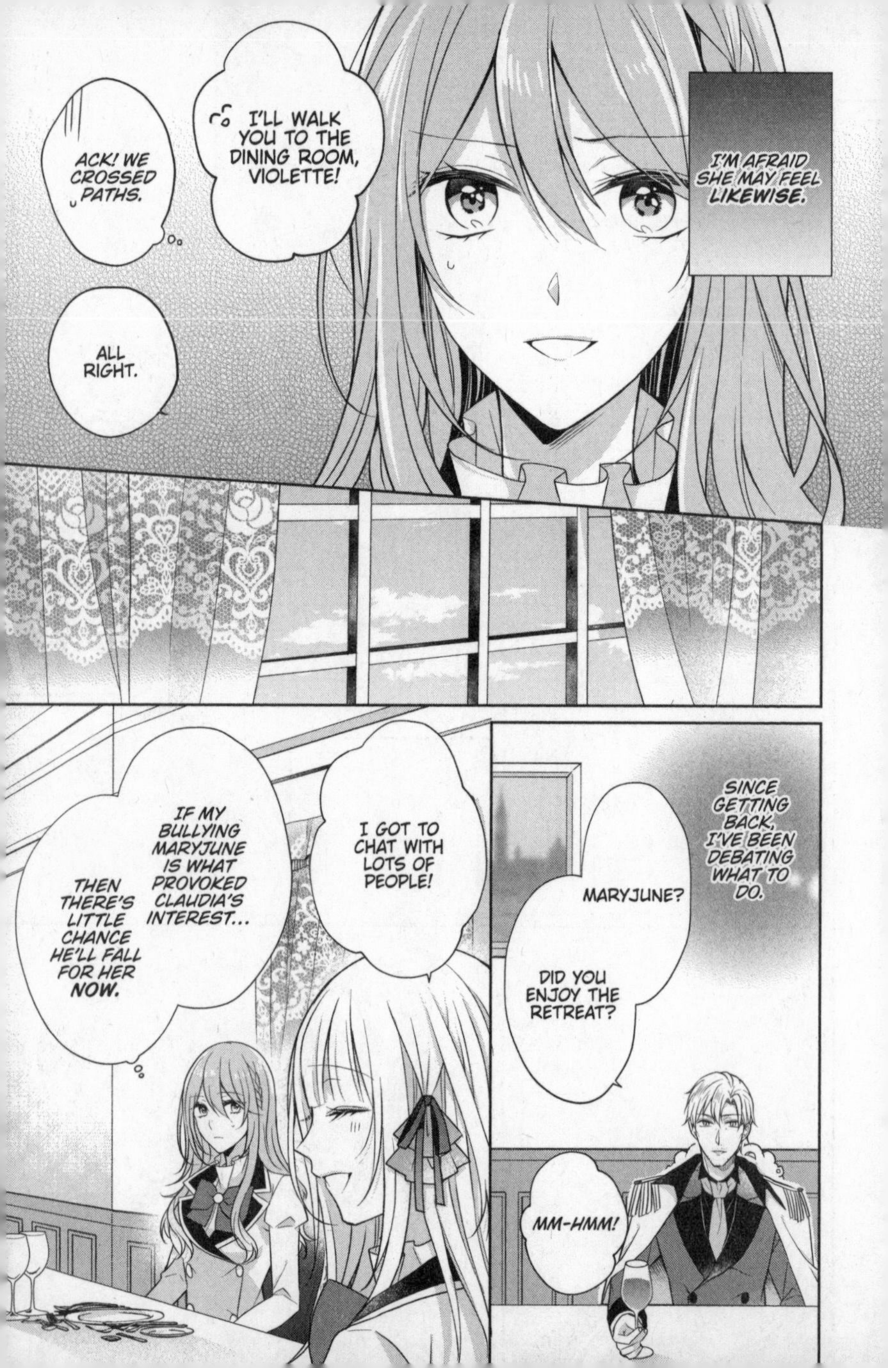
I'M AFRAID SHE MAY FEEL LIKEWISE.
I'LL WALK YOU TO THE DINING ROOM, VIOLETTE!
ACK! WE CROSSED PATHS.
ALL RIGHT.
SINCE GETTING BACK, I'VE BEEN DEBATING WHAT TO DO.
MARYJUNE?
DID YOU ENJOY THE RETREAT?
MM-HMM!
I GOT TO CHAT WITH LOTS OF PEOPLE!
IF MY BULLYING MARYJUNE IS WHAT PROVOKED CLAUDIA'S INTEREST...
THEN THERE'S LITTLE CHANCE HE'LL FALL FOR HER NOW.

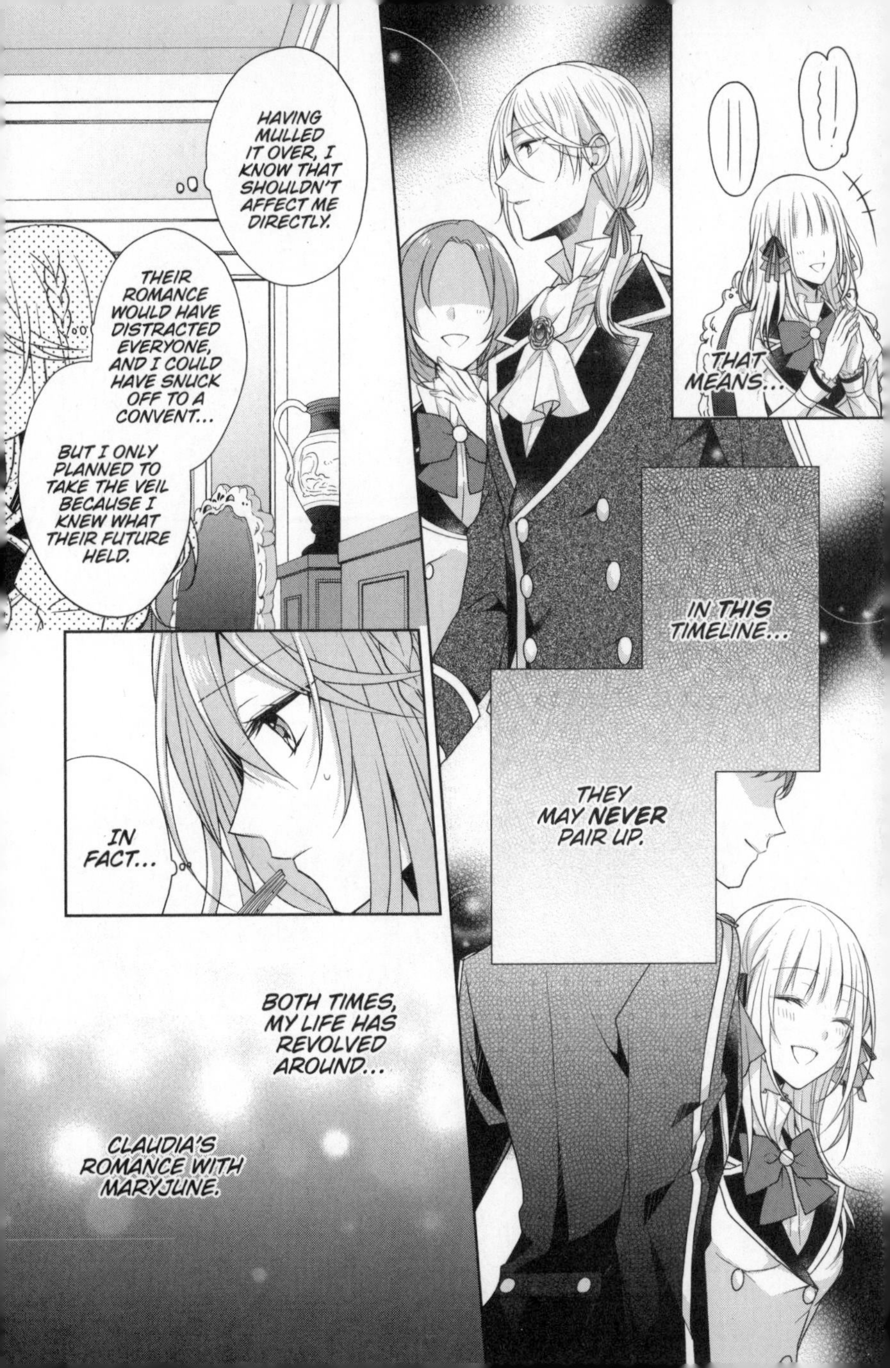
!
!
THAT MEANS...
IN THIS TIMELINE...
THEY MAY NEVER PAIR UP.
HAVING MULLED IT OVER, I KNOW THAT SHOULDN'T AFFECT ME DIRECTLY.
THEIR ROMANCE WOULD HAVE DISTRACTED EVERYONE, AND I COULD HAVE SNUCK OFF TO A CONVENT...
BUT I ONLY PLANNED TO TAKE THE VEIL BECAUSE I KNEW WHAT THEIR FUTURE HELD.
IN FACT...
BOTH TIMES, MY LIFE HAS REVOLVED AROUND...
CLAUDIA'S ROMANCE WITH MARYJUNE.

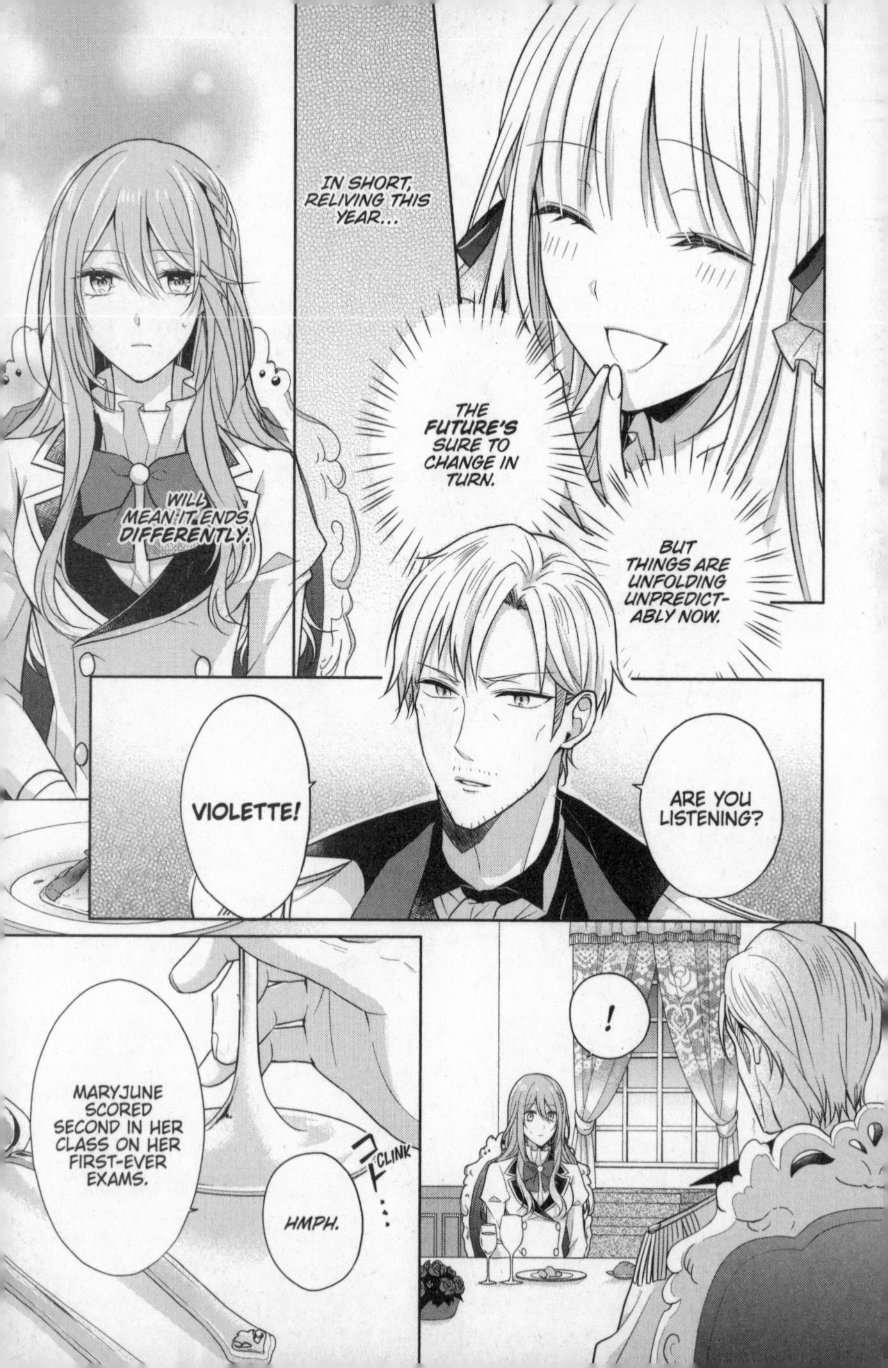
IN SHORT, RELIVING THIS YEAR...
WILL MEAN IT ENDS DIFFERENTLY.
THE FUTURE'S SURE TO CHANGE IN TURN.
BUT THINGS ARE UNFOLDING UNPREDICT-ABLY NOW.
ARE YOU LISTENING?
VIOLETTE!
!
MARYJUNE SCORED SECOND IN HER CLASS ON HER FIRST-EVER EXAMS.
コト CLINK
HMPH.

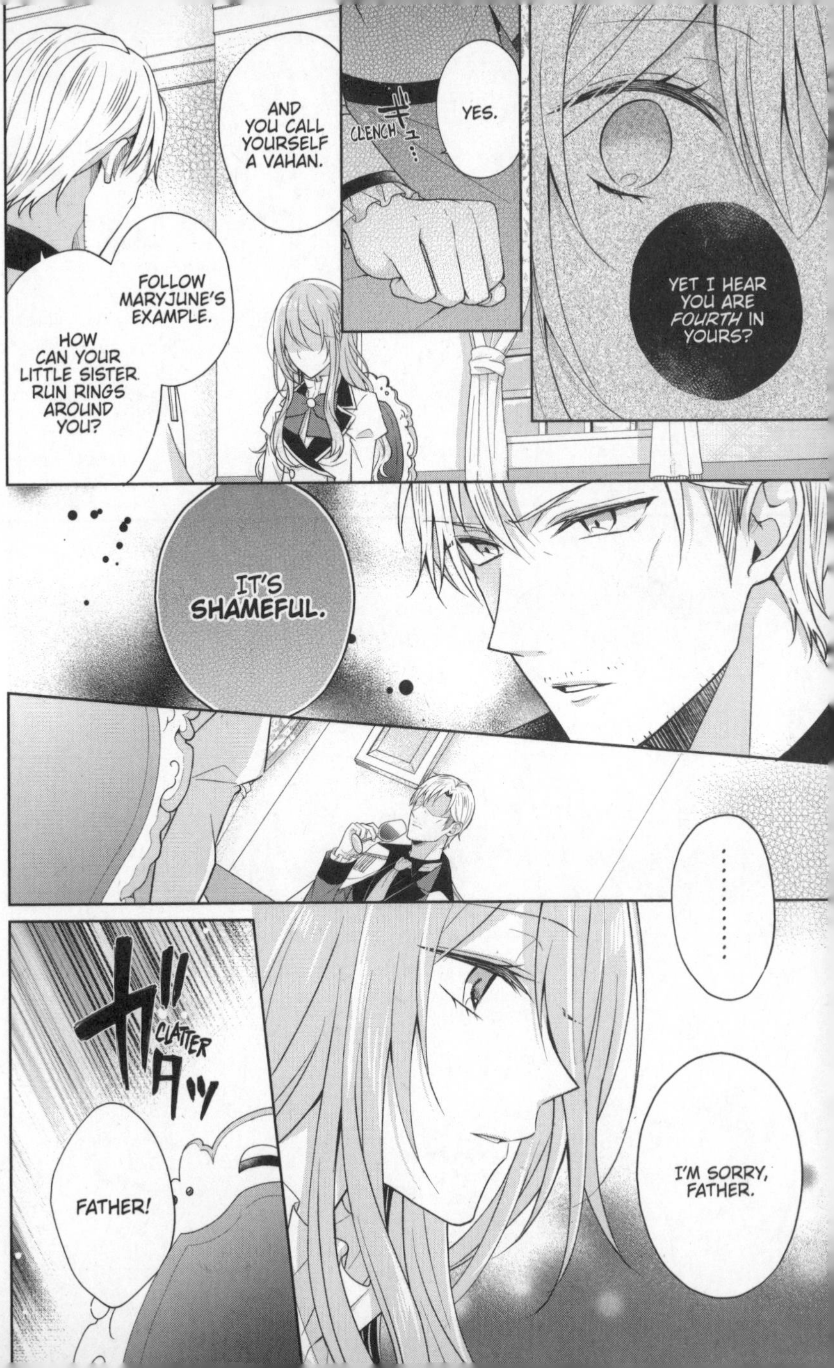
YET I HEAR YOU ARE *FOURTH* IN YOURS?
YES.
CLENCH
ギュ…
AND YOU CALL YOURSELF A VAHAN.
FOLLOW MARYJUNE'S EXAMPLE.
HOW CAN YOUR LITTLE SISTER RUN RINGS AROUND YOU?
IT'S SHAMEFUL.
......
I'M SORRY, FATHER.
CLATTER
ガタッ
FATHER!

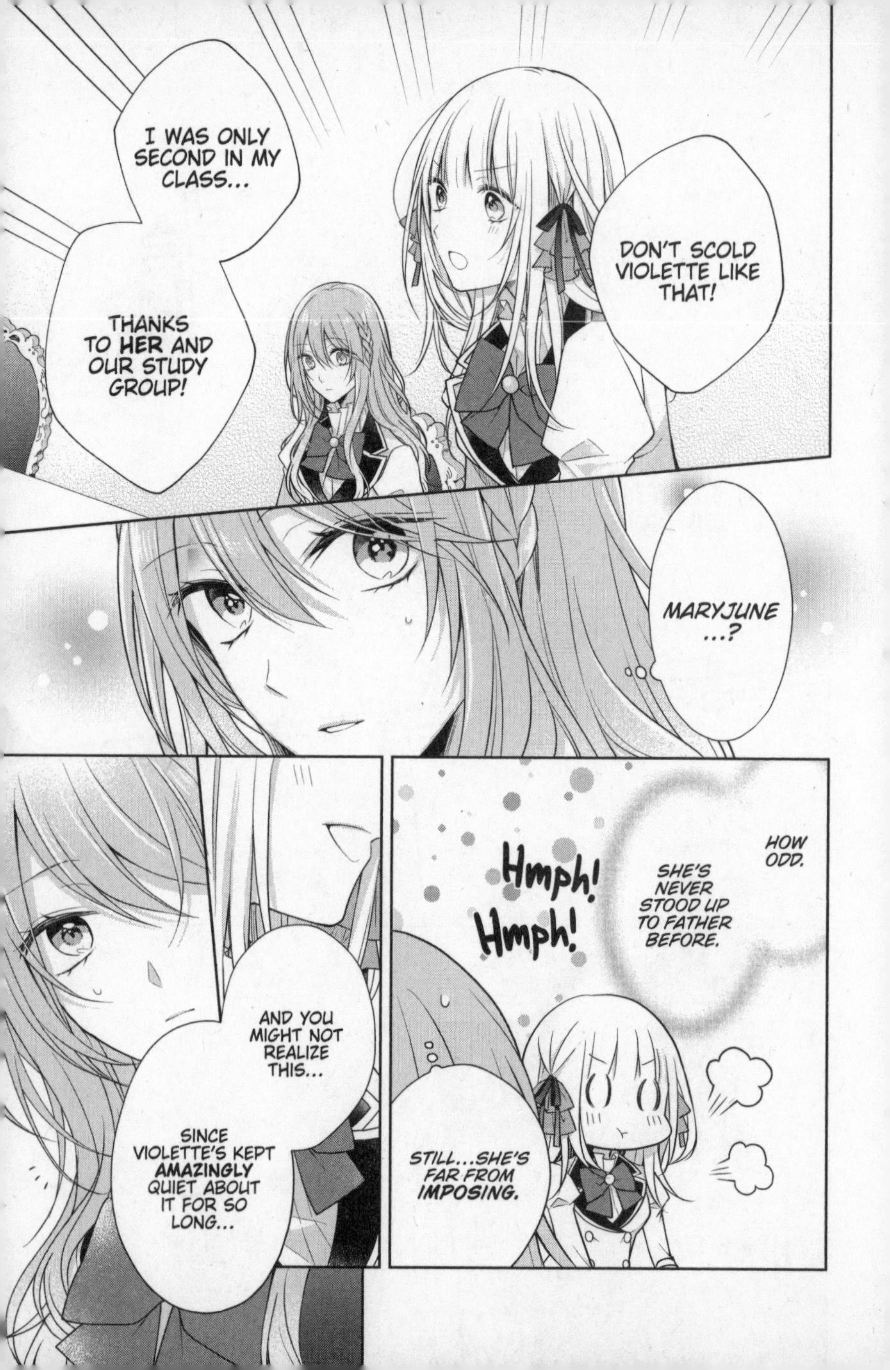
DON'T SCOLD VIOLETTE LIKE THAT!
I WAS ONLY SECOND IN MY CLASS...
THANKS TO HER AND OUR STUDY GROUP!
MARYJUNE...?
HOW ODD.
SHE'S NEVER STOOD UP TO FATHER BEFORE.
Hmph! Hmph!
STILL...SHE'S FAR FROM IMPOSING.
AND YOU MIGHT NOT REALIZE THIS...
SINCE VIOLETTE'S KEPT AMAZINGLY QUIET ABOUT IT FOR SO LONG...

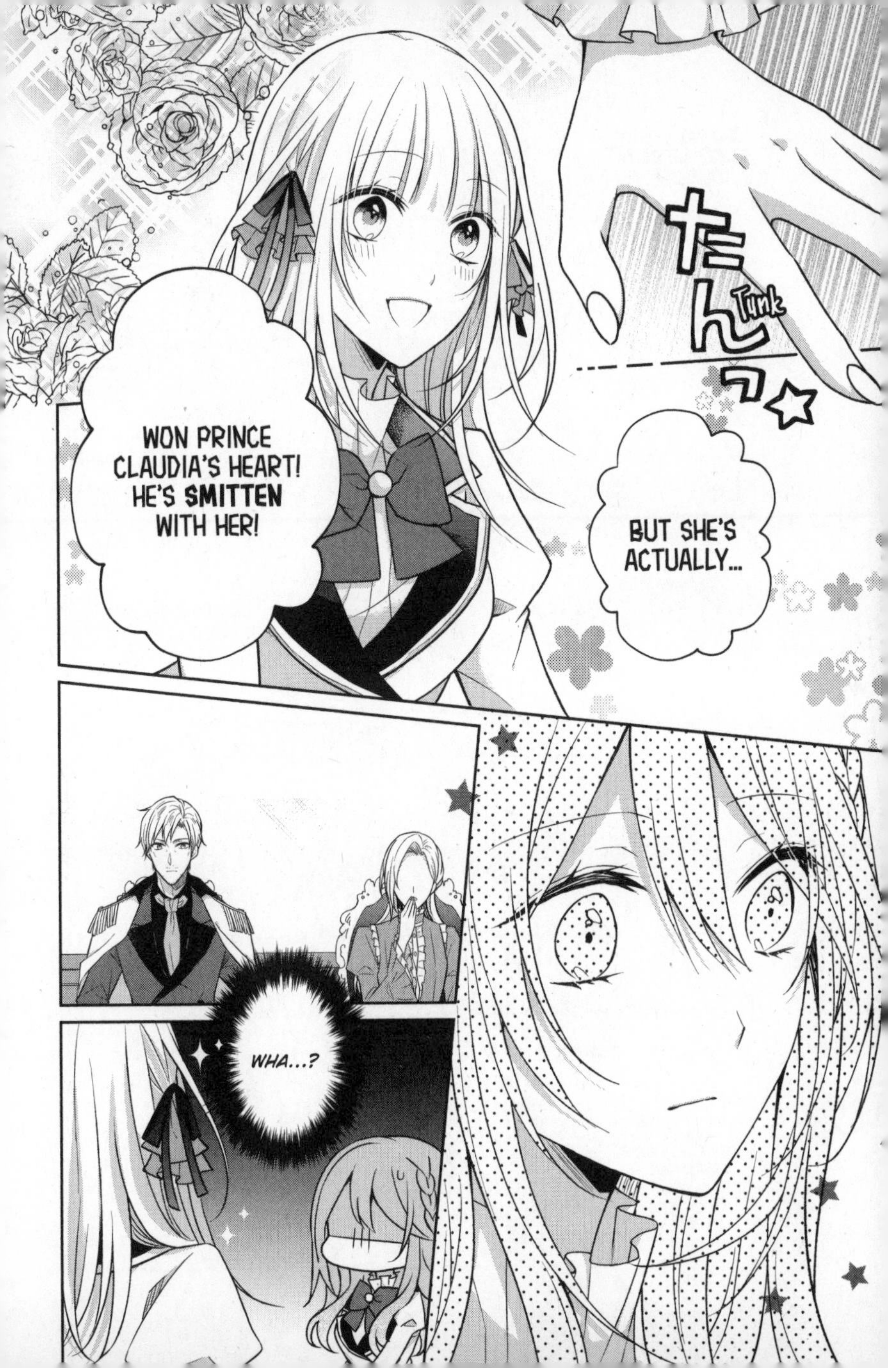
たんっ☆
Tunk
WON PRINCE CLAUDIA'S HEART! HE'S SMITTEN WITH HER!
BUT SHE'S ACTUALLY...
WHA...?

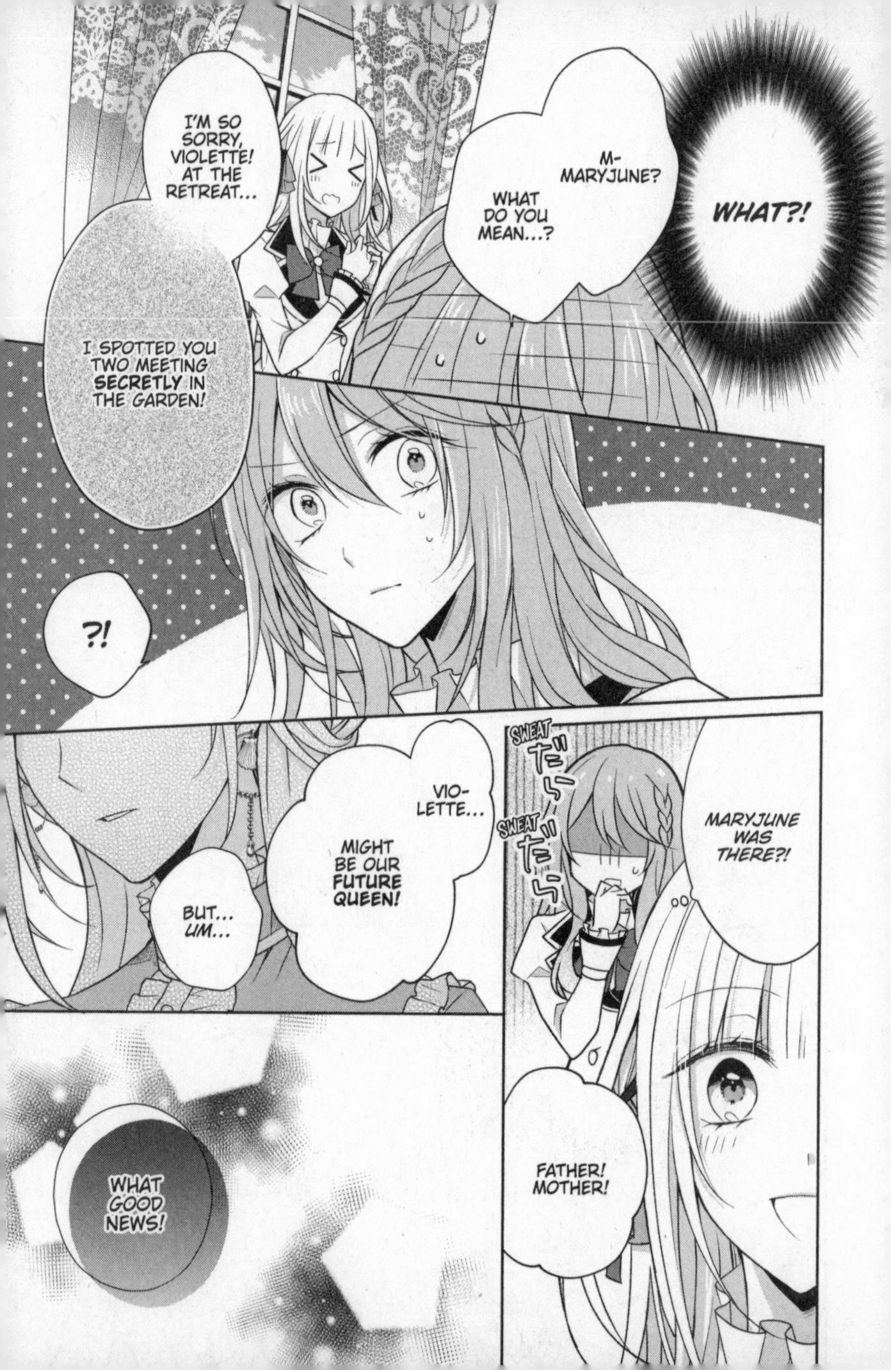
WHAT?!
M-MARYJUNE?
WHAT DO YOU MEAN...?
I'M SO SORRY, VIOLETTE! AT THE RETREAT...
I SPOTTED YOU TWO MEETING SECRETLY IN THE GARDEN!
?!
MARYJUNE WAS THERE?!
SWEAT
SWEAT
FATHER! MOTHER!
VIO-LETTE...
MIGHT BE OUR FUTURE QUEEN!
BUT... UM...
WHAT GOOD NEWS!

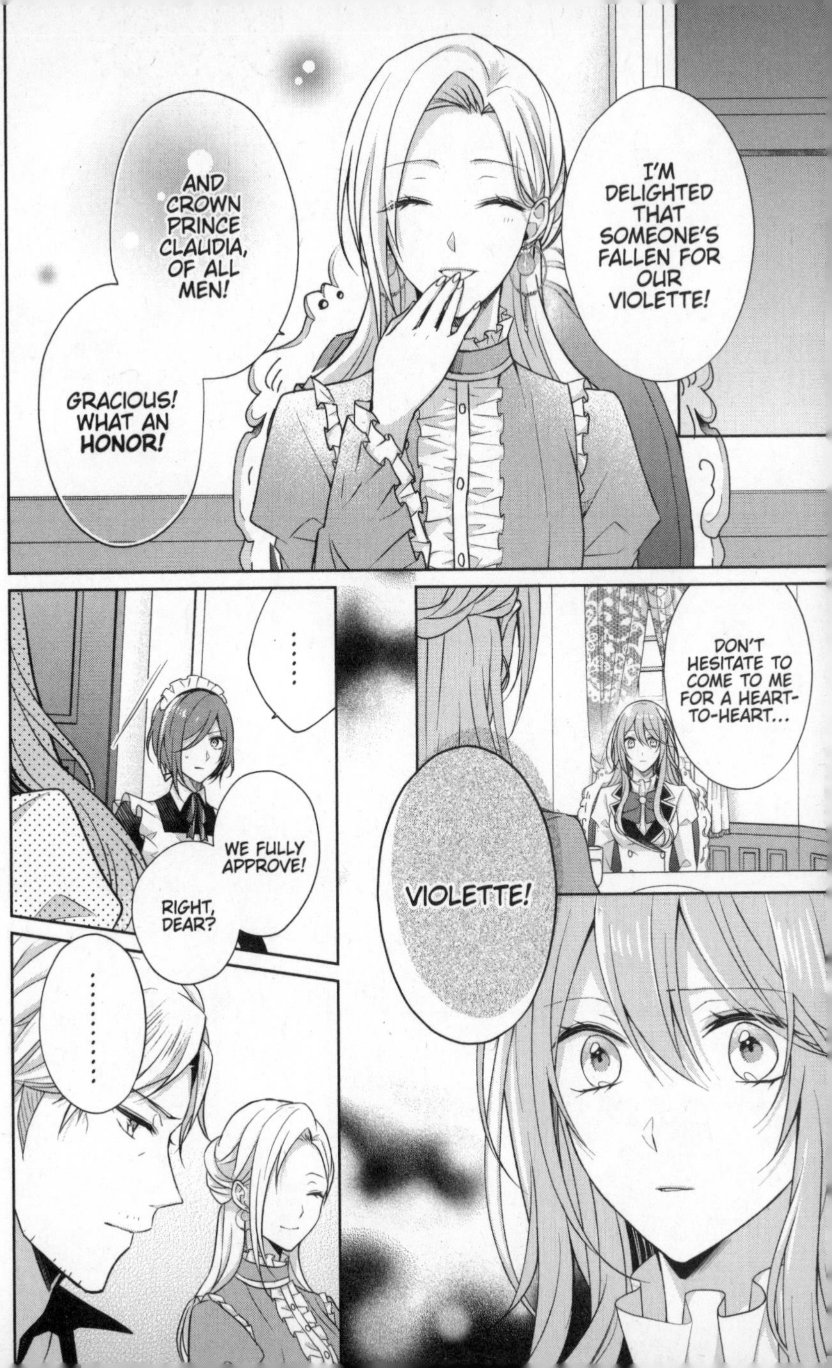
I'M DELIGHTED THAT SOMEONE'S FALLEN FOR OUR VIOLETTE!
AND CROWN PRINCE CLAUDIA, OF ALL MEN!
GRACIOUS! WHAT AN HONOR!
DON'T HESITATE TO COME TO ME FOR A HEART-TO-HEART...
VIOLETTE!
......
WE FULLY APPROVE!
RIGHT, DEAR?
......

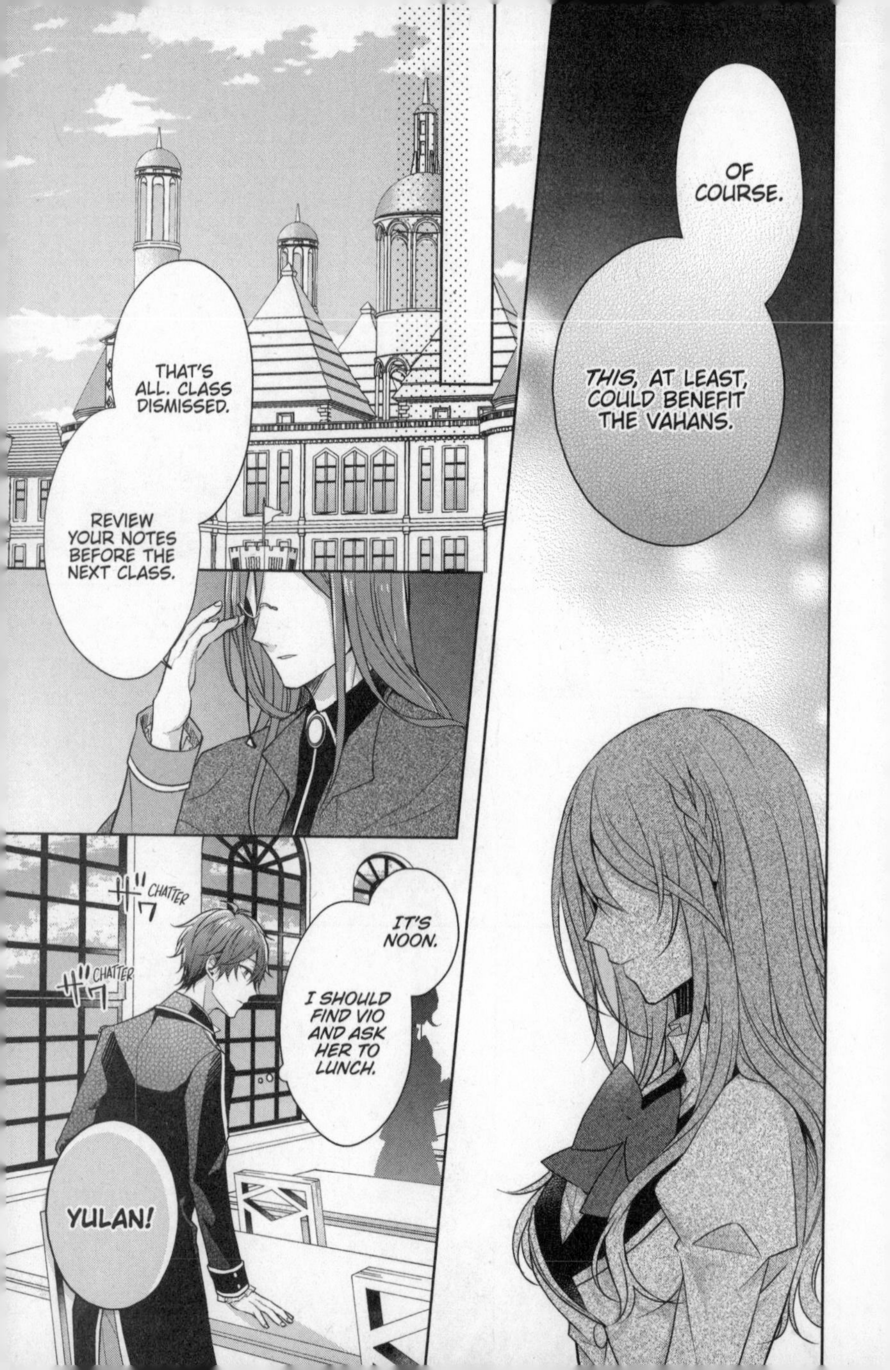
OF COURSE.
THIS, AT LEAST, COULD BENEFIT THE VAHANS.
THAT'S ALL. CLASS DISMISSED.
REVIEW YOUR NOTES BEFORE THE NEXT CLASS.
IT'S NOON.
I SHOULD FIND VIO AND ASK HER TO LUNCH.
ザワ CHATTER
ザワ CHATTER
YULAN!

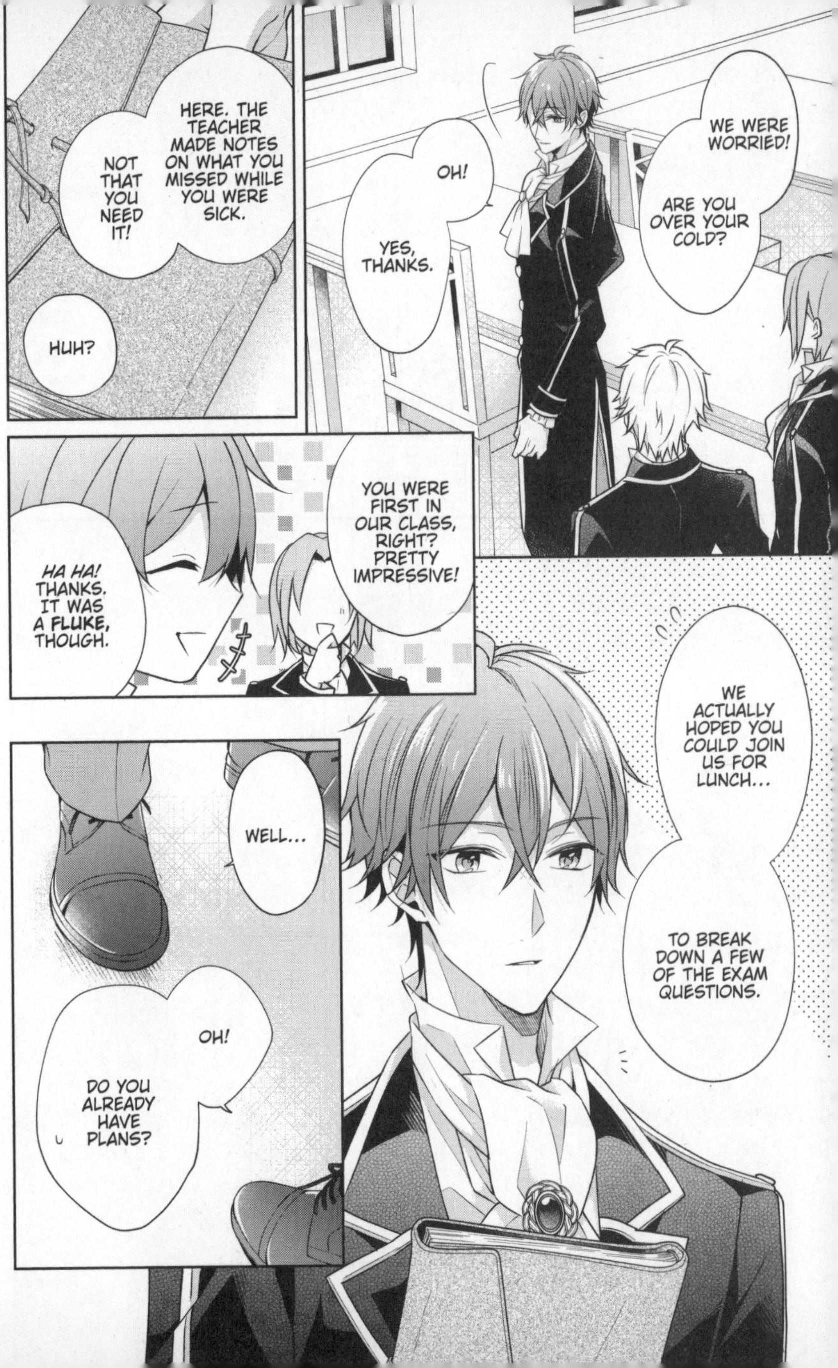
WE WERE WORRIED!
ARE YOU OVER YOUR COLD?
OH!
YES, THANKS.
HERE. THE TEACHER MADE NOTES ON WHAT YOU MISSED WHILE YOU WERE SICK.
NOT THAT YOU NEED IT!
HUH?
YOU WERE FIRST IN OUR CLASS, RIGHT? PRETTY IMPRESSIVE!
*HA HA!* THANKS. IT WAS A **FLUKE**, THOUGH.
WE ACTUALLY HOPED YOU COULD JOIN US FOR LUNCH...
TO BREAK DOWN A FEW OF THE EXAM QUESTIONS.
WELL...
OH!
DO YOU ALREADY HAVE PLANS?

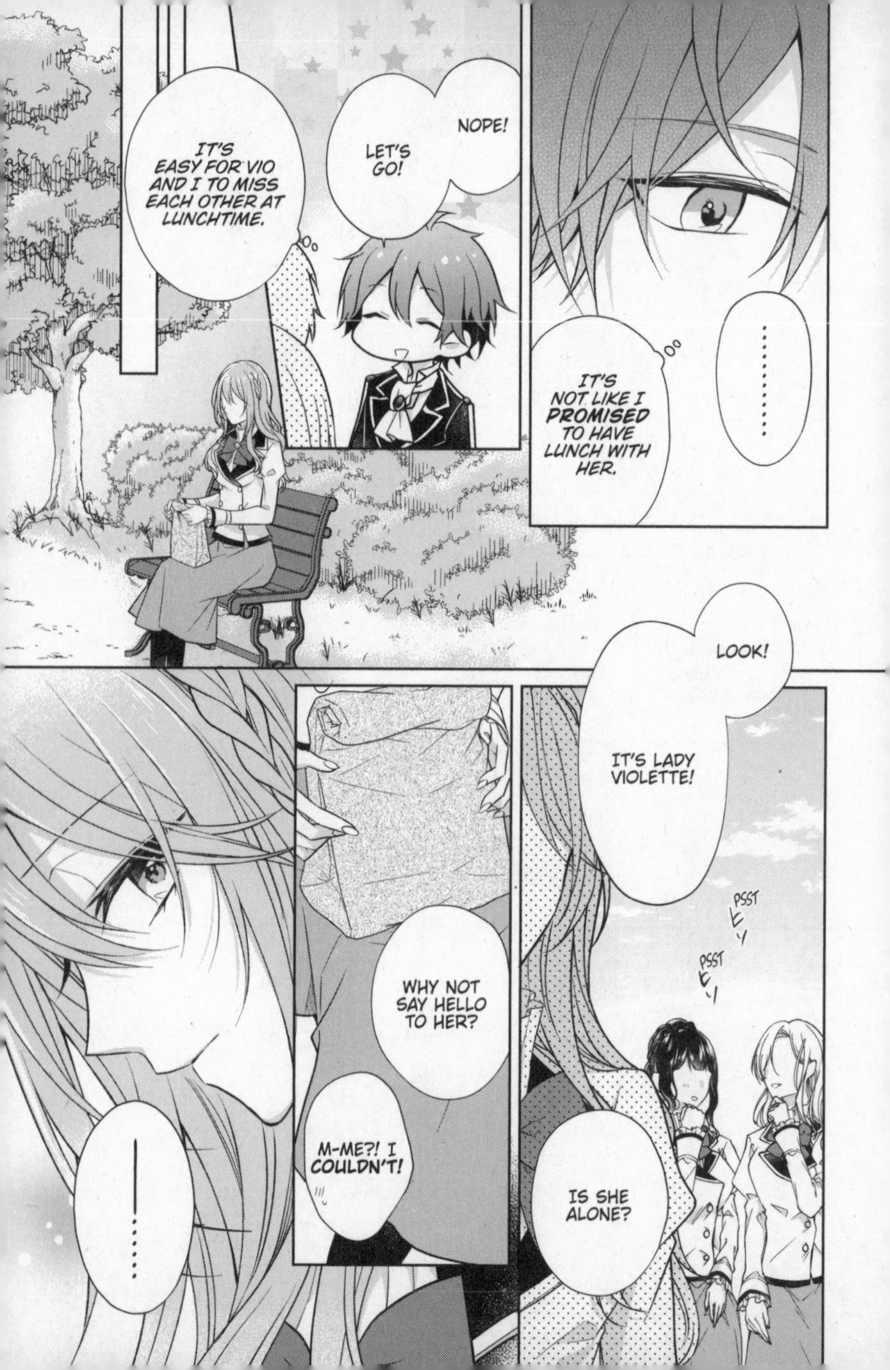
……
IT'S NOT LIKE I PROMISED TO HAVE LUNCH WITH HER.
NOPE!
LET'S GO!
IT'S EASY FOR VIO AND I TO MISS EACH OTHER AT LUNCHTIME.
LOOK!
IT'S LADY VIOLETTE!
PSST
PSST
IS SHE ALONE?
WHY NOT SAY HELLO TO HER?
M-ME?! I COULDN'T!
……

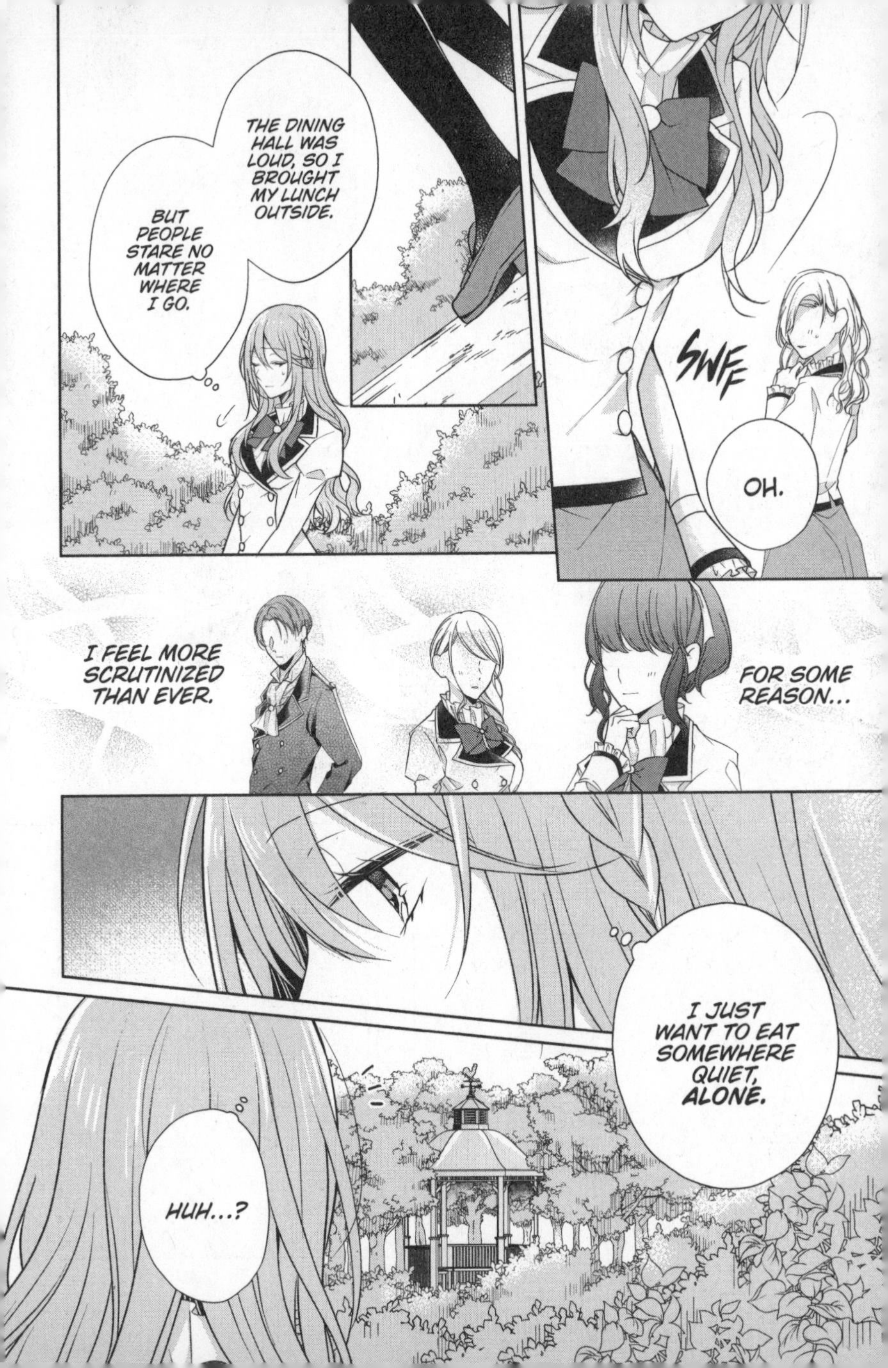

SWFF
OH.
THE DINING HALL WAS LOUD, SO I BROUGHT MY LUNCH OUTSIDE.
BUT PEOPLE STARE NO MATTER WHERE I GO.
FOR SOME REASON...
I FEEL MORE SCRUTINIZED THAN EVER.
I JUST WANT TO EAT SOMEWHERE QUIET, ALONE.
HUH...?

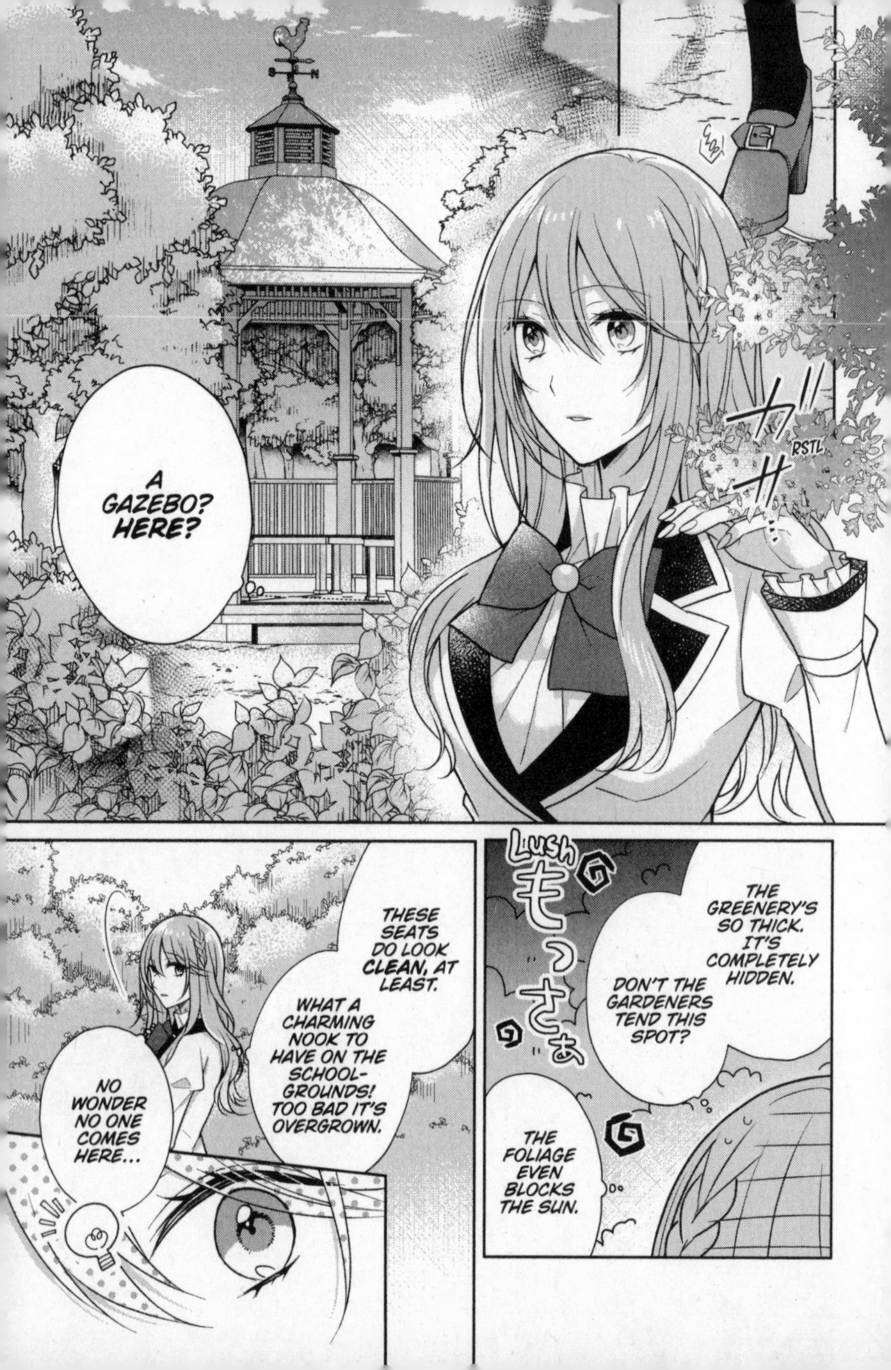

RSTL
A GAZEBO? HERE?
Lush
もっさぁ
THE GREENERY'S SO THICK. IT'S COMPLETELY HIDDEN.
DON'T THE GARDENERS TEND THIS SPOT?
THE FOLIAGE EVEN BLOCKS THE SUN.
THESE SEATS DO LOOK CLEAN, AT LEAST.
WHAT A CHARMING NOOK TO HAVE ON THE SCHOOL-GROUNDS! TOO BAD IT'S OVERGROWN.
NO WONDER NO ONE COMES HERE...

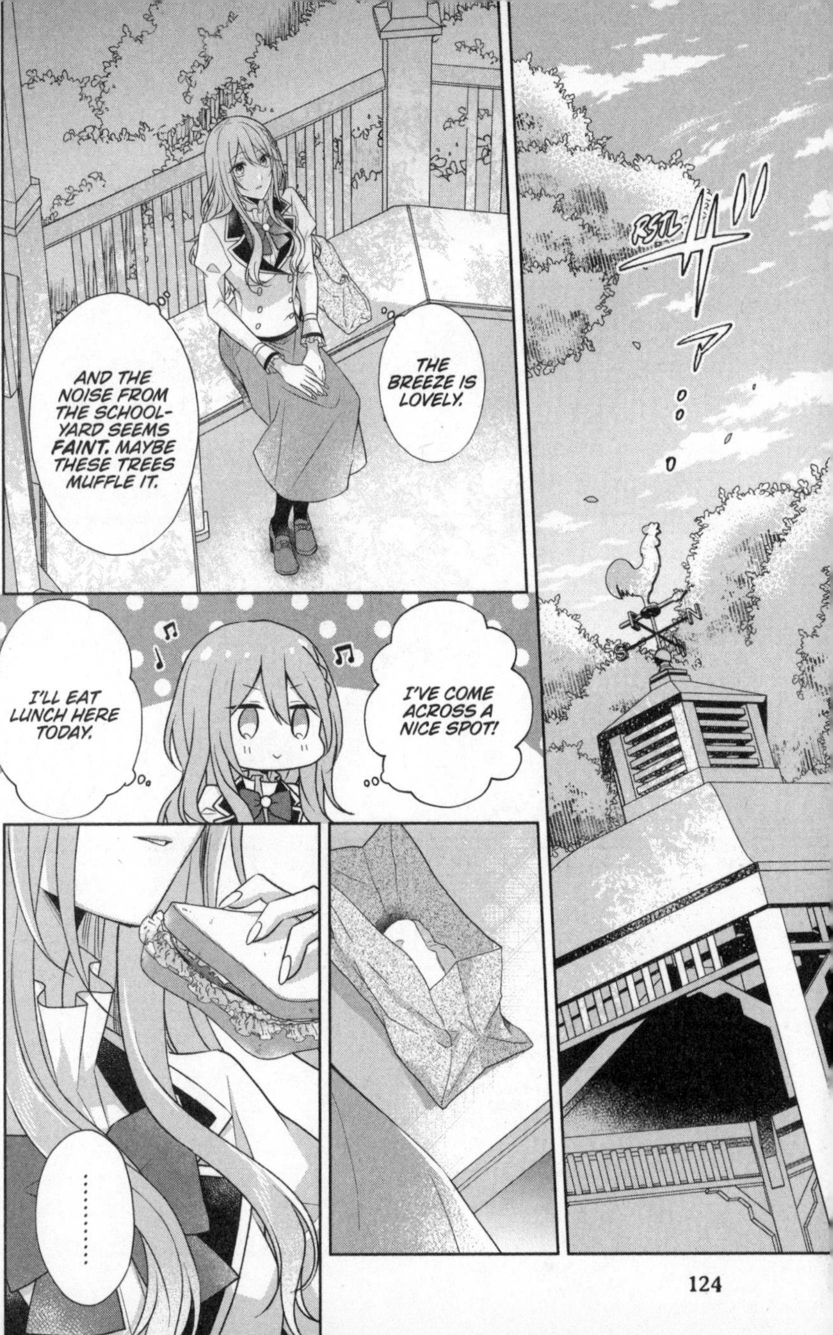
RSTL
THE BREEZE IS LOVELY.
AND THE NOISE FROM THE SCHOOL-YARD SEEMS FAINT. MAYBE THESE TREES MUFFLE IT.
I'VE COME ACROSS A NICE SPOT!
I'LL EAT LUNCH HERE TODAY.
......

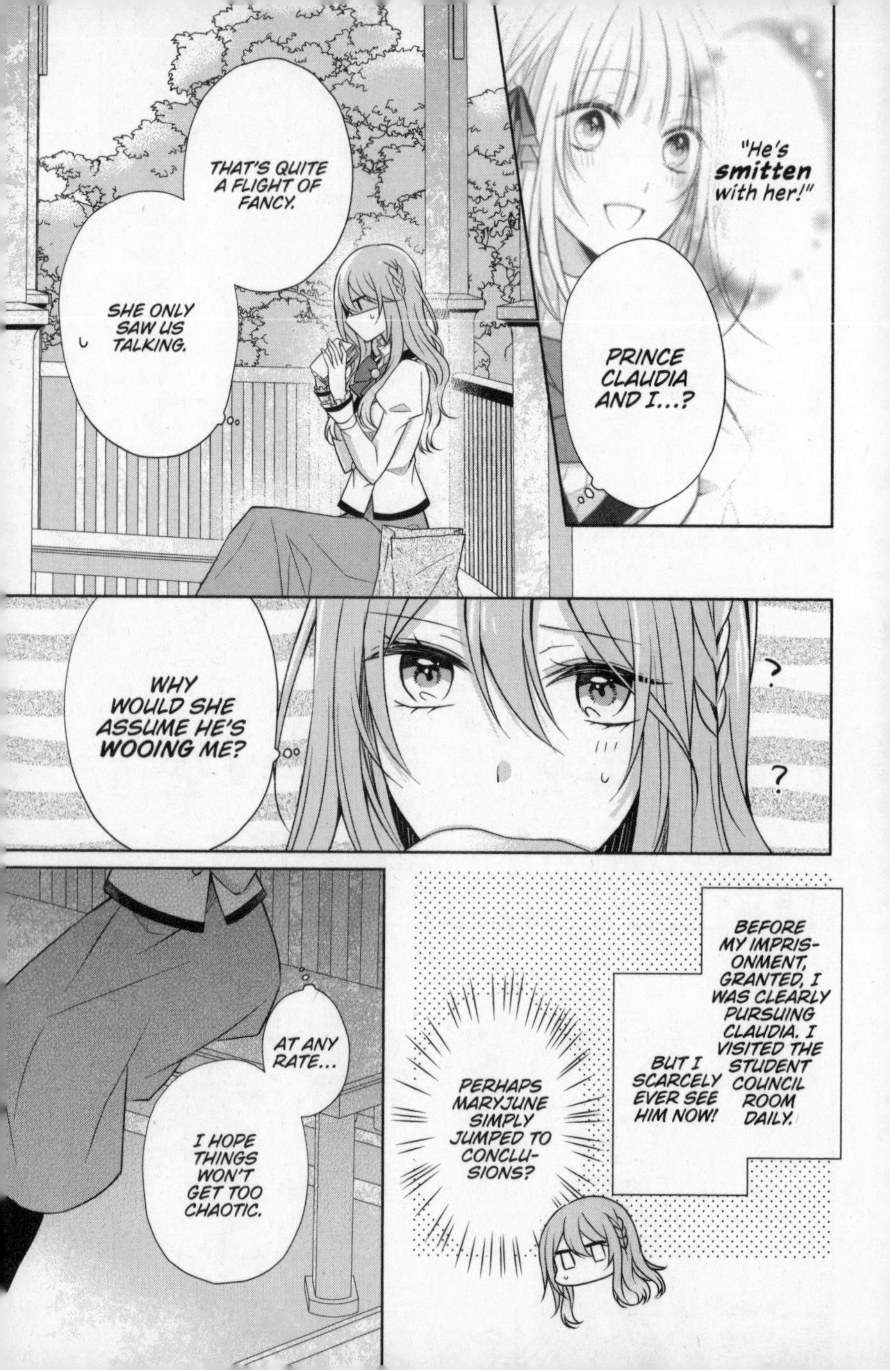
"He's **smitten** with her!"
PRINCE CLAUDIA AND I...?
THAT'S QUITE A FLIGHT OF FANCY.
SHE ONLY SAW US TALKING.
WHY WOULD SHE ASSUME HE'S **WOOING** ME?
BEFORE MY IMPRISONMENT, GRANTED, I WAS CLEARLY PURSUING CLAUDIA. I VISITED THE STUDENT COUNCIL ROOM DAILY.
BUT I SCARCELY EVER SEE HIM NOW!
PERHAPS MARYJUNE SIMPLY JUMPED TO CONCLUSIONS?
AT ANY RATE...
I HOPE THINGS WON'T GET TOO CHAOTIC.

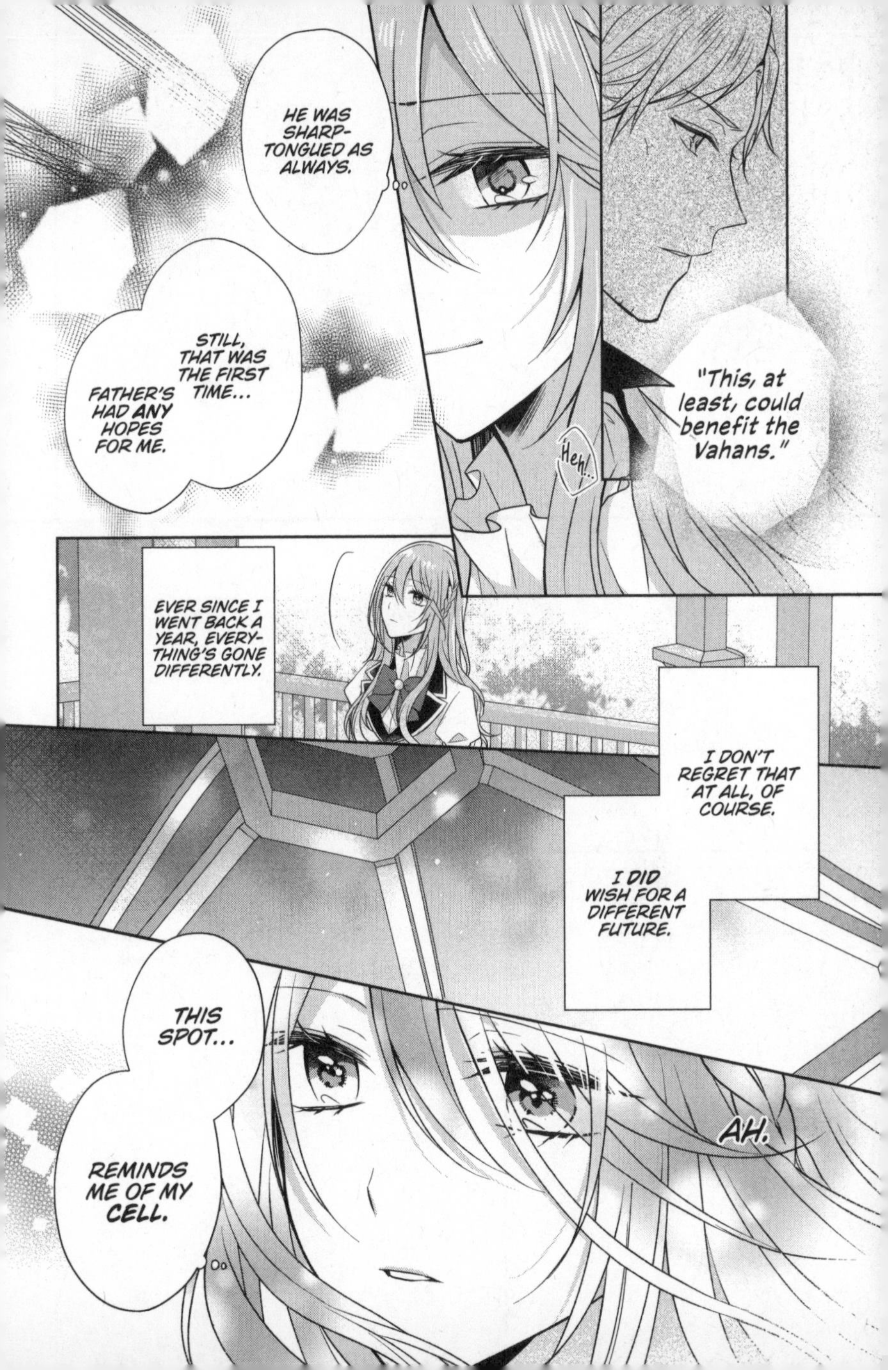

"This, at least, could benefit the Vahans."
Heh!...
HE WAS SHARP-TONGUED AS ALWAYS.
STILL, THAT WAS THE FIRST TIME... FATHER'S HAD ANY HOPES FOR ME.
EVER SINCE I WENT BACK A YEAR, EVERYTHING'S GONE DIFFERENTLY.
I DON'T REGRET THAT AT ALL, OF COURSE.
I DID WISH FOR A DIFFERENT FUTURE.
AH.
THIS SPOT... REMINDS ME OF MY CELL.

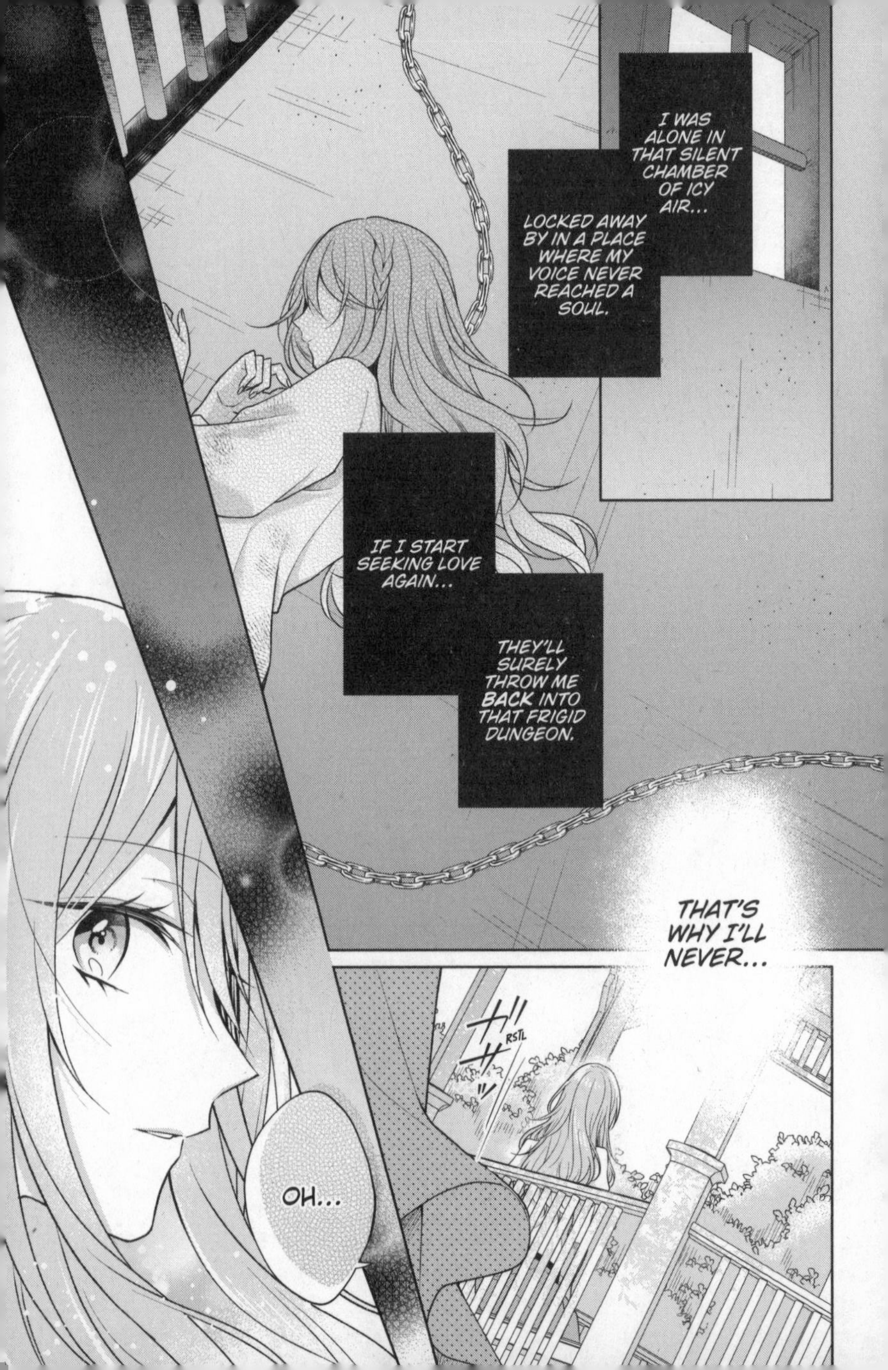

I WAS ALONE IN THAT SILENT CHAMBER OF ICY AIR...
LOCKED AWAY BY IN A PLACE WHERE MY VOICE NEVER REACHED A SOUL.
IF I START SEEKING LOVE AGAIN...
THEY'LL SURELY THROW ME BACK INTO THAT FRIGID DUNGEON.
THAT'S WHY I'LL NEVER...
RSTL
OH...

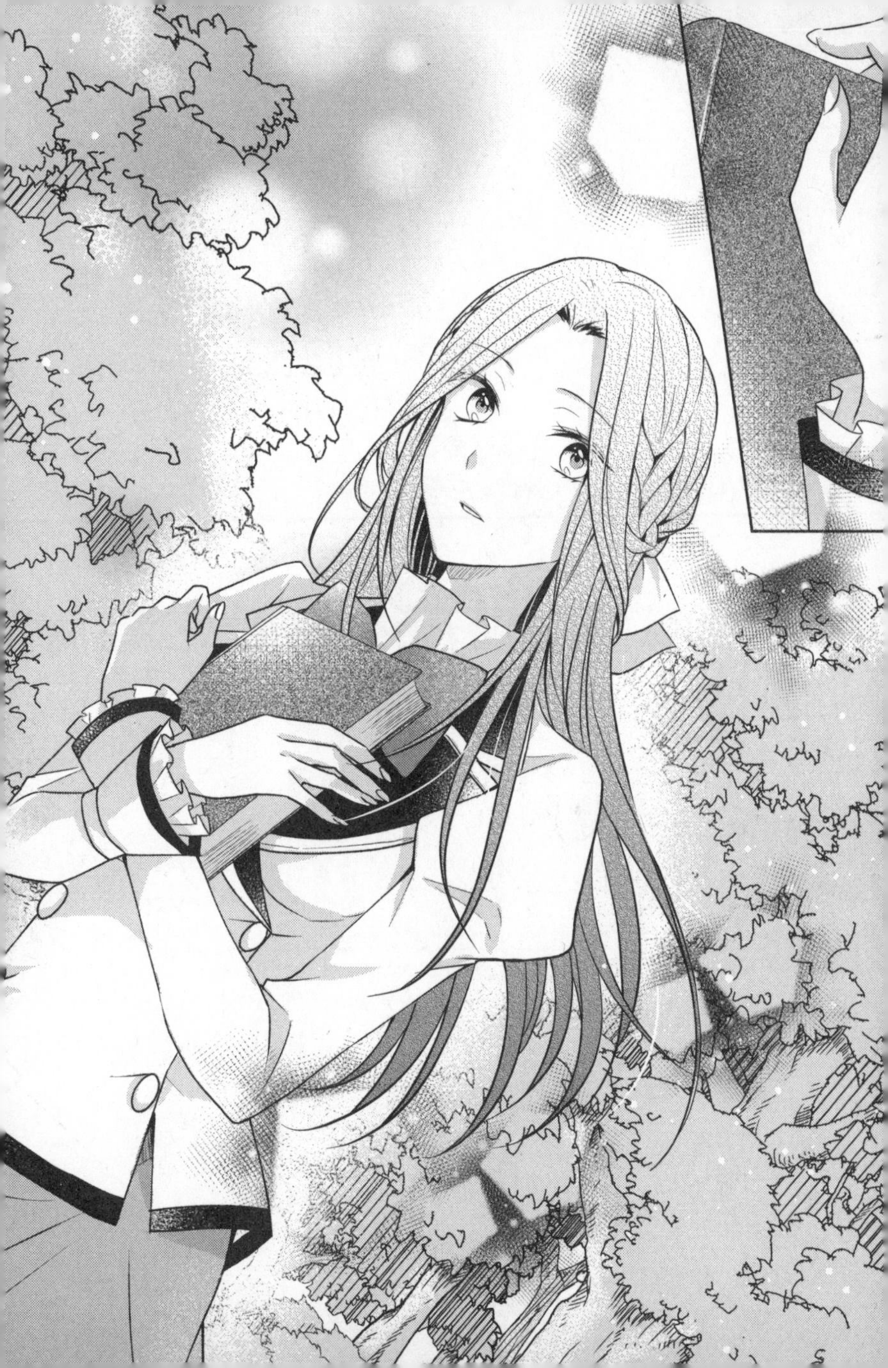

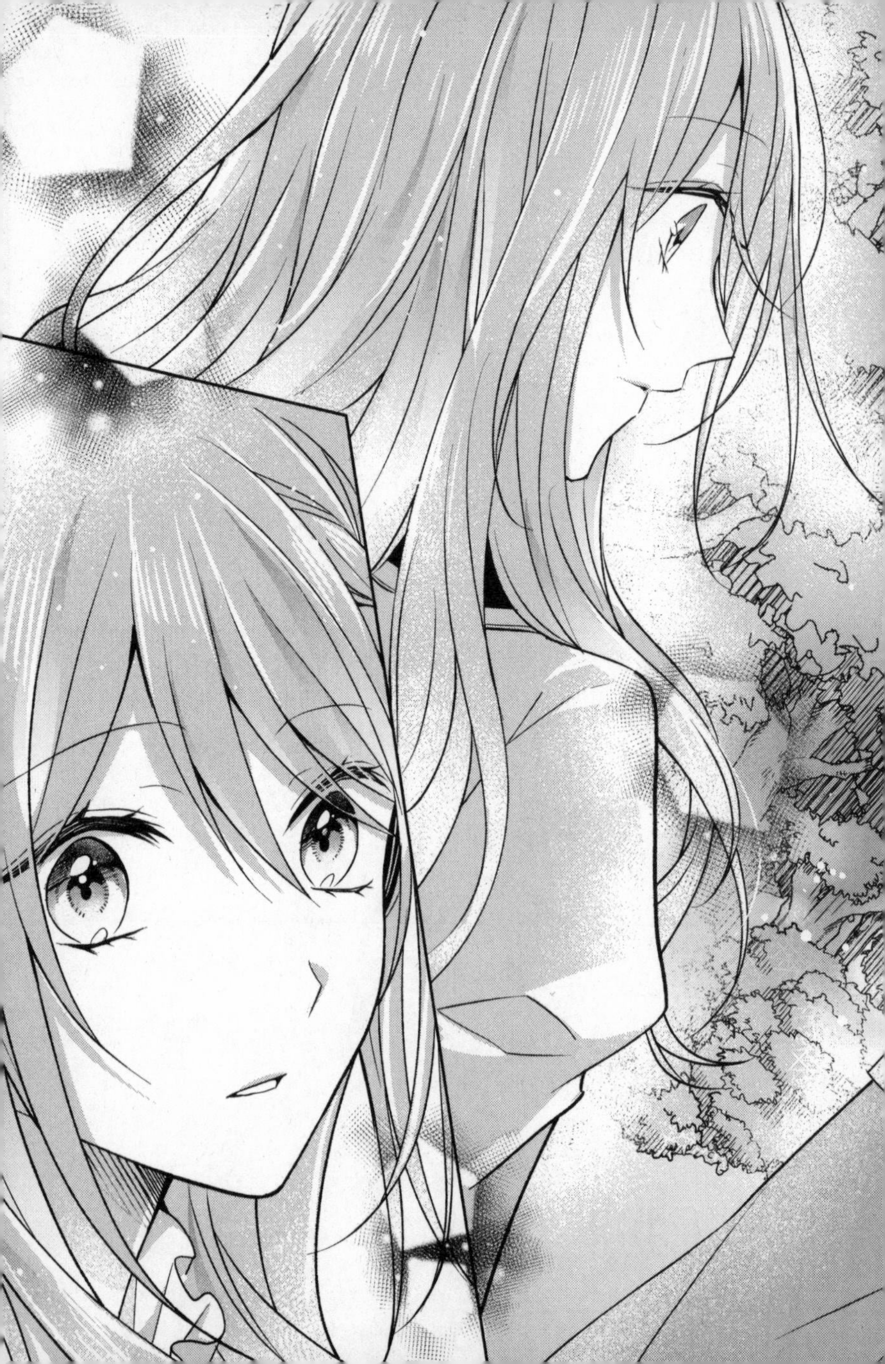

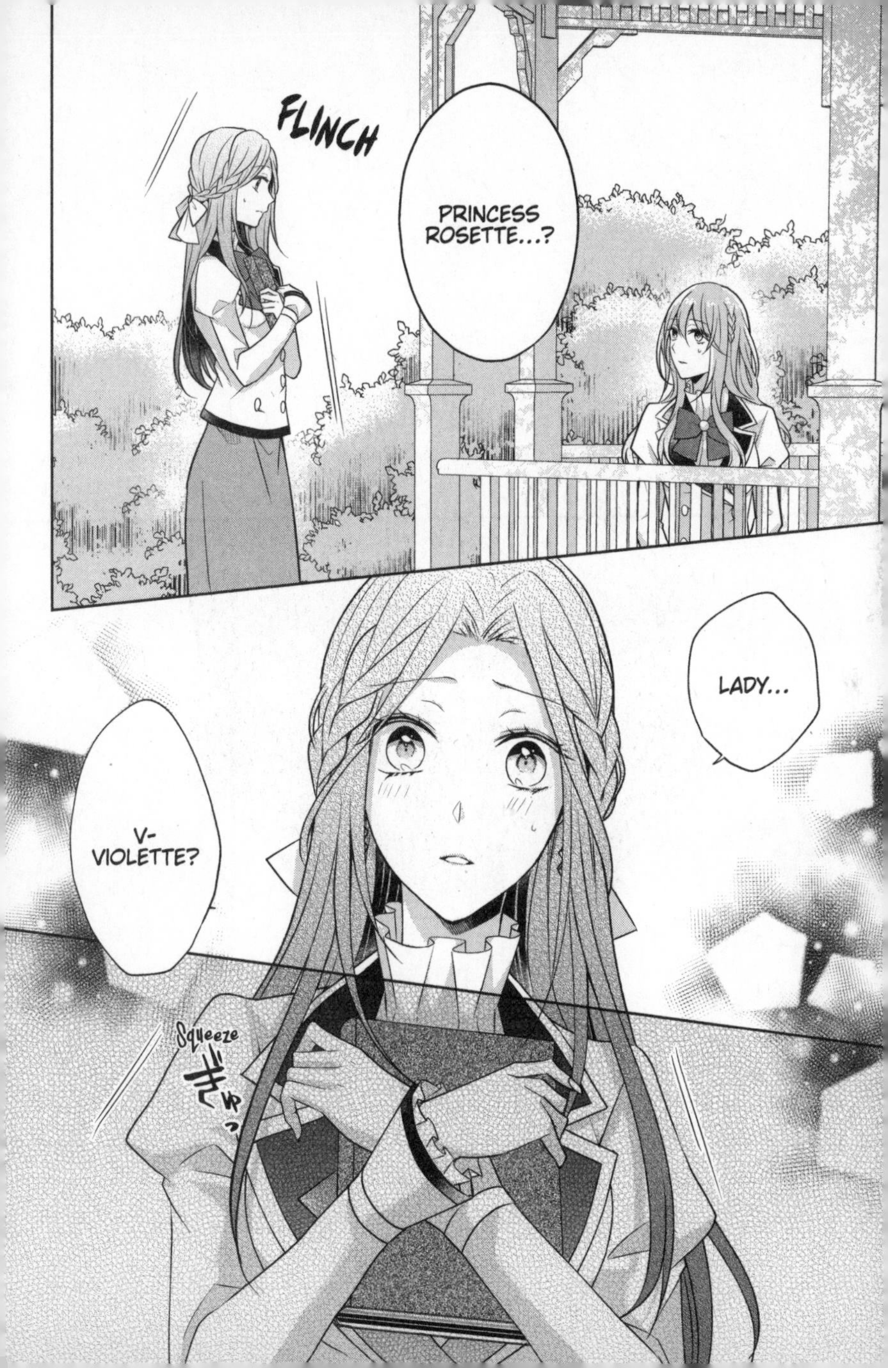
PRINCESS ROSETTE...?
FLINCH
LADY...
V-
VIOLETTE?
Squeeze
ぎゅっ

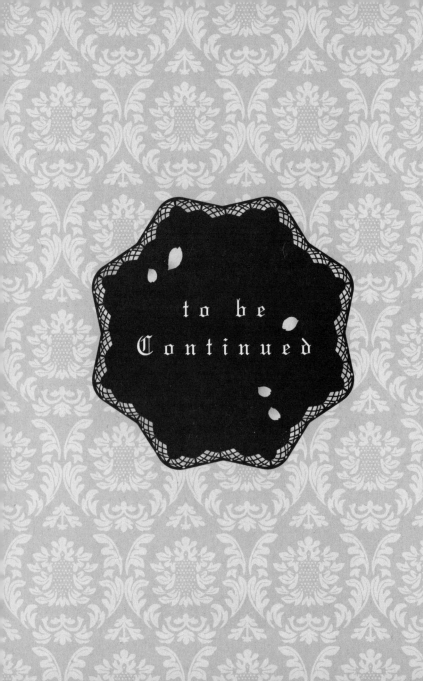

to be
Continued

## CLASS GAP

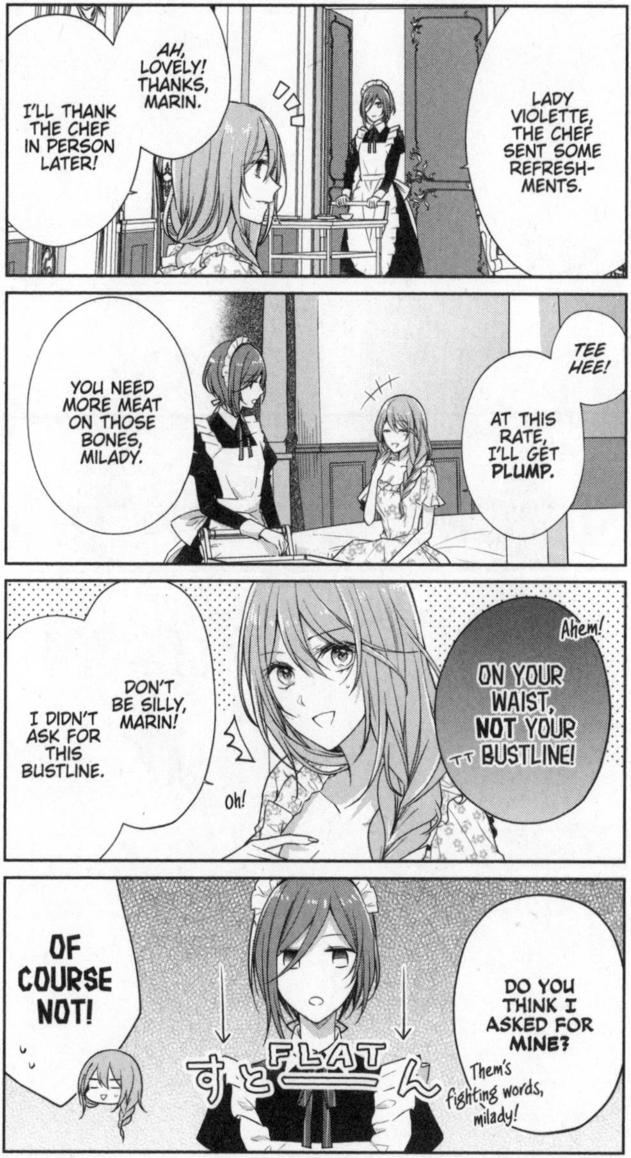
LADY VIOLETTE, THE CHEF SENT SOME REFRESHMENTS.
AH, LOVELY! THANKS, MARIN.
I'LL THANK THE CHEF IN PERSON LATER!
TEE HEE!
AT THIS RATE, I'LL GET PLUMP.
YOU NEED MORE MEAT ON THOSE BONES, MILADY.
Ahem!
ON YOUR WAIST, NOT YOUR BUSTLINE!
Oh!
DON'T BE SILLY, MARIN!
I DIDN'T ASK FOR THIS BUSTLINE.
DO YOU THINK I ASKED FOR MINE?
Them's fighting words, milady!
すとーーん
FLAT
OF COURSE NOT!

# A LIFE OF GLUTTONY

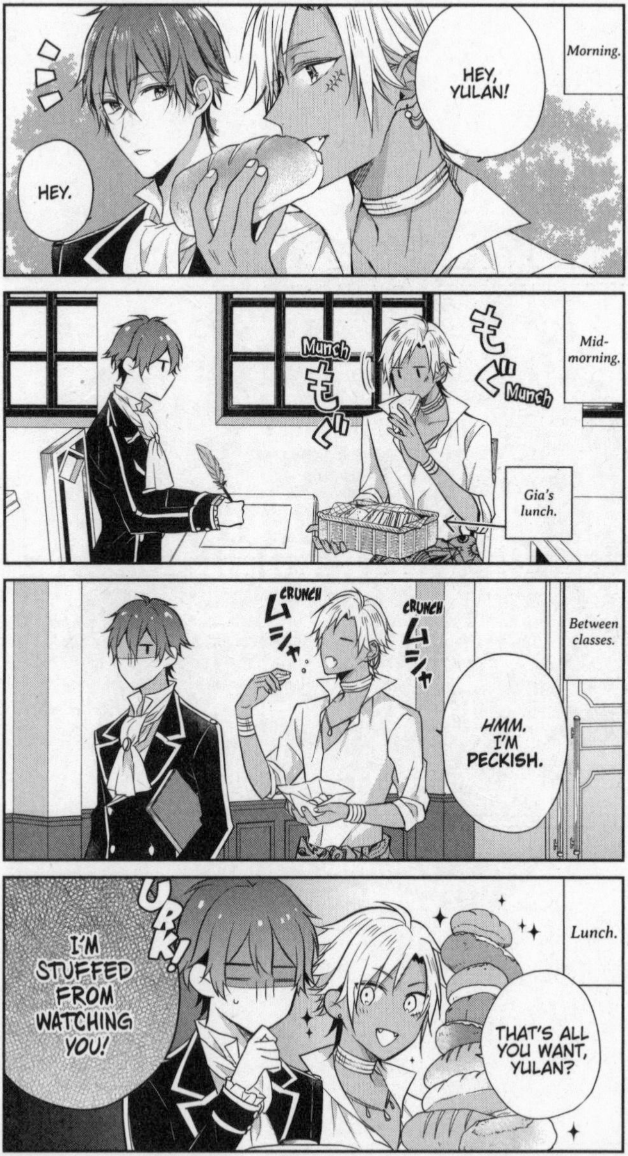
Morning.
HEY, YULAN!
HEY.
Mid-morning.
もぐ Munch
もぐ Munch
Gia's lunch.
Between classes.
CRUNCH ムシャ
HMM. I'M PECKISH.
CRUNCH ムシャ
Lunch.
THAT'S ALL YOU WANT, YULAN?
URK!
I'M STUFFED FROM WATCHING YOU!

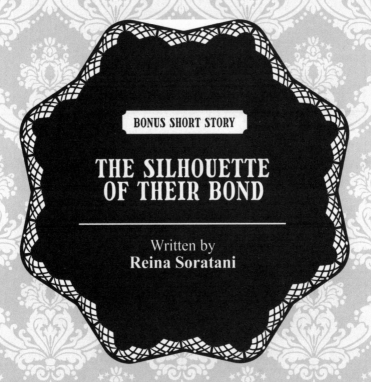

BONUS SHORT STORY

# THE SILHOUETTE OF THEIR BOND

Written by
**Reina Soratani**

If the atmosphere became any heavier, Claudia was sure he'd collapse from the pressure. Just moments earlier, the room had been filled with cheer and excitement, but once the crowd thinned, any light-heartedness was gone. But, well, the problem wasn't who left, but *who* had stayed behind.

Two of the five students left. That was bad enough, but when one more exited the room, Claudia was left alone with Yulan.

"............"

"............"

Claudia looked up, his eyes trailing towards Yulan, who was sitting diagonal to him. Just moments earlier, Violette had been seated right beside Yulan before she left. Just as he expected, Yulan's eyes were downcast, avoiding any sort of eye contact with Claudia, as if he was trying to ignore Claudia's very existence. His pen raced across the paper, answering the questions before him without even so much as a peep from Yulan. It was obvious that Yulan didn't actually *need* the help of a study group.

*I wonder...does he really **not** need the help...?*

Claudia knew better than anyone how talented Yulan was. It wasn't the first time Claudia had thought about how Yulan fit the royal mold far more than he did. Though Claudia wished that wasn't the case, he still couldn't change reality. All he could do was put in the effort to make it *appear* as though he was no less inferior to Yulan. He worked to match his grades, and was lucky enough to be born somewhat athletic, so he was able to keep up with Yulan in that area as well. The problem was that Claudia could never match Yulan's friendly and open personality.

Claudia knew that comparing their personalities, which can't be defined with numbers, didn't prove anything. But when it came to winning people over, Claudia believed that he was no match for the far more approachable Yulan. Perhaps it was like the saying goes, "the grass is greener on the other side." But this seemed to go beyond mere envy: reality seemed to bore it out. The truth remained that there were many who adored the younger man.

*Even though he used to hate dealing with other people when he was younger...*

They'd known each other for a very long time. Yulan, of course, was not introduced as Claudia's own half brother, but he had used the name, "Cugurs" when they first met. When Yulan first came, accompanying his father, Lord Cugurs, Claudia had no idea about their connection. When he saw that Yulan shared the same eye color as him and his

father, it shocked the young prince, but he concluded that it was just a happy coincidence.

It didn't take long for Claudia to realize the truth. Their shared eyes were the ultimate proof of their shared parentage. What's more, no one could stop the rumors that spread far and wide throughout high society, and eventually, to Claudia's own ears.

But just knowing the truth doesn't change anything in reality. Even when it was public knowledge that his father had a child with another woman, in the young Claudia's eyes, that truth didn't actually affect Claudia nor did it touch Yulan. There was no need for the king's children to carry the stain of the sins that their father had committed.

Reflecting on it now, Claudia realized how irresponsible that way of thinking was. Although Claudia's feelings never changed throughout the years, it's still not something he should ignore just because it didn't matter to him. That was especially true for the *royal family*, where power and attention were heavily concentrated. In that environment, standing out was not always a good thing.

Yulan was the child of a mistress, born with the royal golden eyes passed down in their lineage.

His golden eyes were the sole reason why his fate had drastically changed. All because of a single *color.*

"If there's something you'd like to say, why don't you just say it?"

"...?!"

"Your staring is very distracting."

"Oh, I see... My apologies. How rude of me."

"If you need something, then ask. Staring at me isn't going to accomplish anything but annoy me."

As he spoke, Yulan never once looked up at Claudia. It's not that Yulan didn't understand basic manners; he was telling Claudia, loud and clear, that he was not worthy of Yulan's respect.

Claudia didn't remember when Yulan started treating him this way so openly. Rather, Claudia couldn't remember a time when Yulan *ever* looked at him with any hint of adoration.

From his looks alone, Yulan's beauty could compete against the fairest of ladies. Yet, his head remained down, his eyebrows wrinkled. If only he smiled, he would look like the cutest child. But unfortunately, Yulan had never once directed a smile at Claudia.

He used to be such a small, reckless child...yet...

"You're so much bigger now..."

"What?

For the first time that day Yulan's gaze lifted to meet Claudia's. But even so, his eyes were narrowed into an angry glare as he scowled at the older boy. Claudia could tell that Yulan was on guard, picking through every syllable to find the true meaning behind Claudia's words.

Claudia also thought his comment felt sudden and uncalled for, but he never expected Yulan to give him such a dirty look. Or, perhaps it wasn't so surprising. He knew that every word that came out of his mouth would

only anger Yulan. Claudia had always been careful not to step on any landmines when they spoke, but it seemed to be a regular occurrence for Claudia to plunge straight into spikes whenever they crossed paths.

"Have you finally lost your mind? Or is it that you have always seen me as *someone smaller and more defenseless* than yourself?"

"I'm sorry. That's not what I meant... I was just commenting on how much you've grown."

"Oh, so you *did* lose your mind? Of course I grew. Everyone does, as long as they're alive."

*As long as they're alive...* Many years had passed since they first met. Though they did not see each other frequently, Claudia did remember meeting with Yulan regularly before he entered high school. Compared to back then, Yulan has grown out of his childish, girlish features. He was now a strapping young man who was even taller than Claudia himself.

Although they shared a father, their appearance wasn't all that similar. They both resembled their mothers, both in appearance and in height. If not for their eyes, no one would be able to tell that they were connected by blood.

"You're a lot more mature now than when you were in middle school."

"That was before you were even in your second year here. How many years do you even think have passed?"

"Two years...or, rather, two and a half?"

"Sure, whatever."

Yulan's gaze was cast back down to the page of problems sitting in front of him. Although Yulan sounded annoyed, he'd at least answered Claudia when he'd spoken to him. Although their talk, if it could even be considered one, was brief, it was actually quite a rare occasion for the two. Claudia thought Yulan was in a bad mood, but maybe that wasn't actually the case?

*Probably because...she was with him...*

Claudia was well aware of just how important Violette was to his younger half brother. Regardless whether if it was because they were childhood friends, or if Yulan felt something more for her, Claudia knew that Yulan was even now deeply connected to Violette thanks to the times and feelings they shared. Claudia also knew he had no way of competing against their bond.

Although she was gone for now, Violette would return before long. Without Violette, Yulan wouldn't even be here today. Yulan would even go so far as to ask Claudia for a favor if it was for her sake.

Claudia still didn't know what to think about Violette.

In the past, he would never have trusted her and he would constantly be on his guard around her. He rejected her every advance and as far as he was concerned, she was bad news. Now, Claudia couldn't bring himself to avoid her all the time, but that didn't mean he'd dropped his guard completely. Despite how much she had changed, it didn't mean that everything she had done was forgiven. Just because he learned something new about her didn't mean

he'd change his views of her so easily.

But lately there had been multiple events that had led Claudia and Violette to become closer as friends. Still, it was going to take time to unravel every last lingering problem between them.

But as the old grudges slowly unwound, Yulan and Violette were getting ever closer each second.

Yulan always called out Violette's name with a beaming smile. He'd rush up towards her and stand next to her, as if to ward off anyone else who dared to get close. Violette always allowed him into her space and gave him a warm embrace. With a bright smile that Claudia had never seen before, she'd greet him cheerfully.

The image that flashed through Claudia's mind sent a shiver down his spine. His eyes darted over to Yulan, who either didn't notice Claudia's shocked glance or chose to ignore him. Regardless, all Claudia could see was Yulan's usual cold, uncaring face as he stared down at the study questions laid out before him.

Claudia sighed in relief, the tension in his body dissipating almost instantaneously...but then, Claudia paused. What was he so relieved about?

*What's with me today?*

The scene that played out in his mind and the phantom voices that he heard in his head were like a reflection of his own desires. It was beautiful, but that's what made it impossible, both in reality...and even in fantasy.

Claudia would *never* yearn for such a beautiful, kind, and loving interaction with her. *Never,* would he ever desire to see Violette smiling lovingly at him as she calls out his name—"Claudia!"

-END-

# I Swear I Won't Bother You AGAIN!

# SEVEN SEAS ENTERTAINMENT PRESENTS

# I Swear I Won't Bother You AGAIN! 3

### story by REINA SORATANI    art by HARU HARUKAWA

TRANSLATION
Jacqueline Fung

ADAPTATION
Rebecca Schneidereit

LETTERING
Aidan Clarke

COVER DESIGN
H. Qi

LOGO DESIGN
George Panella

PROOFREADER
Kurestin Armada

COPY EDITOR
Leighanna DeRouen

SENIOR EDITOR
Shannon Fay

PREPRESS TECHNICIAN
Melanie Ujimori
Jules Valera

PRODUCTION DESIGNER
Christa Miesner

PRODUCTION MANAGER
Lissa Pattillo

EDITOR-IN-CHIEF
Julie Davis

ASSOCIATE PUBLISHER
Adam Arnold

PUBLISHER
Jason DeAngelis

Kondo wa zettai ni jama shimasen! Volume 3
by Soratani Reina, Harukawa Haru
© 2021 SORATANI REINA, HARUKAWA HARU/GENTOSHA COMICS INC.
All rights reserved.
Original Japanese edition published in 2020 by
GENTOSHA COMICS Inc.
English translation rights arranged worldwide with
GENTOSHA COMICS Inc. through Digital Catapult Inc., Tokyo.

Seven Seas press and purchase enquiries can be sent to Marketing Manager Lianne
Sentar at press@gomanga.com. Information regarding the distribution and purchase of
digital editions is available from Digital Manager CK Russell at digital@gomanga.com.

Seven Seas and the Seven Seas logo are trademarks of
Seven Seas Entertainment. All rights reserved.

ISBN: 978-1-64827-373-5
Printed in Canada
First Printing: January 2023
10 9 8 7 6 5 4 3 2 1

## ///// READING DIRE~~CT~~

This book reads fr~~om~~
Japanese style. If th~~~~
reading manga, you ~~~~
the top right panel on ~~~~
take it from there. If yo~~~~
follow the numbered dia~~~~
It may seem backwards at first,
but you'll get the hang of it! Have fun!!

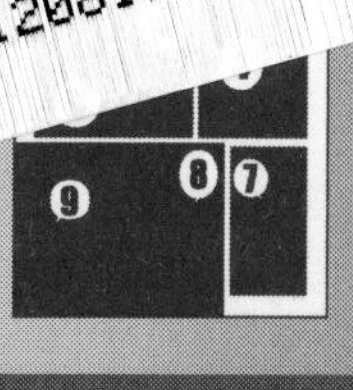

D1208105

9 8 7